Figures in a Spare Landscape

Serving in the Twilight of Empire,
Bornu Province, Nigeria, 1959–60

Peter Haring Judd

Ma'arri
New York City

© 2018 by Peter Haring Judd

ISBN 978-1-947980-57-0 pbk.   978-1-947980-58-7 hdc.

ISBN 978-1-947980-86-0 b&w pbk.

Library of Congress Cataloging-in-Publication Data

Names: Judd, Peter H., author.
Title: Figures in a spare landscape : serving in the twilight of empire,
   Bornu province, Nigeria, 1959-60 / Peter Haring Judd.
Description: New York City : Ma'arri, an imprint of Spuyten Duyvil
   Publishing, 2018. | Includes bibliographical references.
Identifiers: LCCN 2018018937| ISBN 9781947980570 (pbk.) | ISBN 9781947980587
   (hardcover)
Subjects: LCSH: Judd, Peter H.--Travel--Nigeria--Maiduguri. |
   Nigeria--History--1900-1960. | Maiduguri (Nigeria)--Social life and
   customs. | Teachers--Nigeria--Maiduguri--Biography. |
   Americans--Nigeria--Maiduguri--Biography.
Classification: LCC DT515.77.J83 A3 2018 | DDC 966.903--dc23
LC record available at https://lccn.loc.gov/2018018937

Contents

Preface

One
Getting There 1

Two
To the bush; the Northern Cameroons Plebiscite of 1959 19

Three
Interludes: a visit to Lake Chad,
perceptions of past and future in Bama 123

Four
From the savanna to the hills,
preparing the vote, the Nigerian Federal Election of 1959 138

Five
Creating a Map in the Mind
Lake Chad, "French," the ruins of Ngazergamo 177

Epilogue 240

References 244

Acknowledgements
About the Author

Nigeria on the eve of independence in 1960 showing its three administrative regions and the UN Northern and Southern Cameroons Trusteeship territories. I was assigned to the government secondary school in Maiduguri, the capital of Bornu Province.

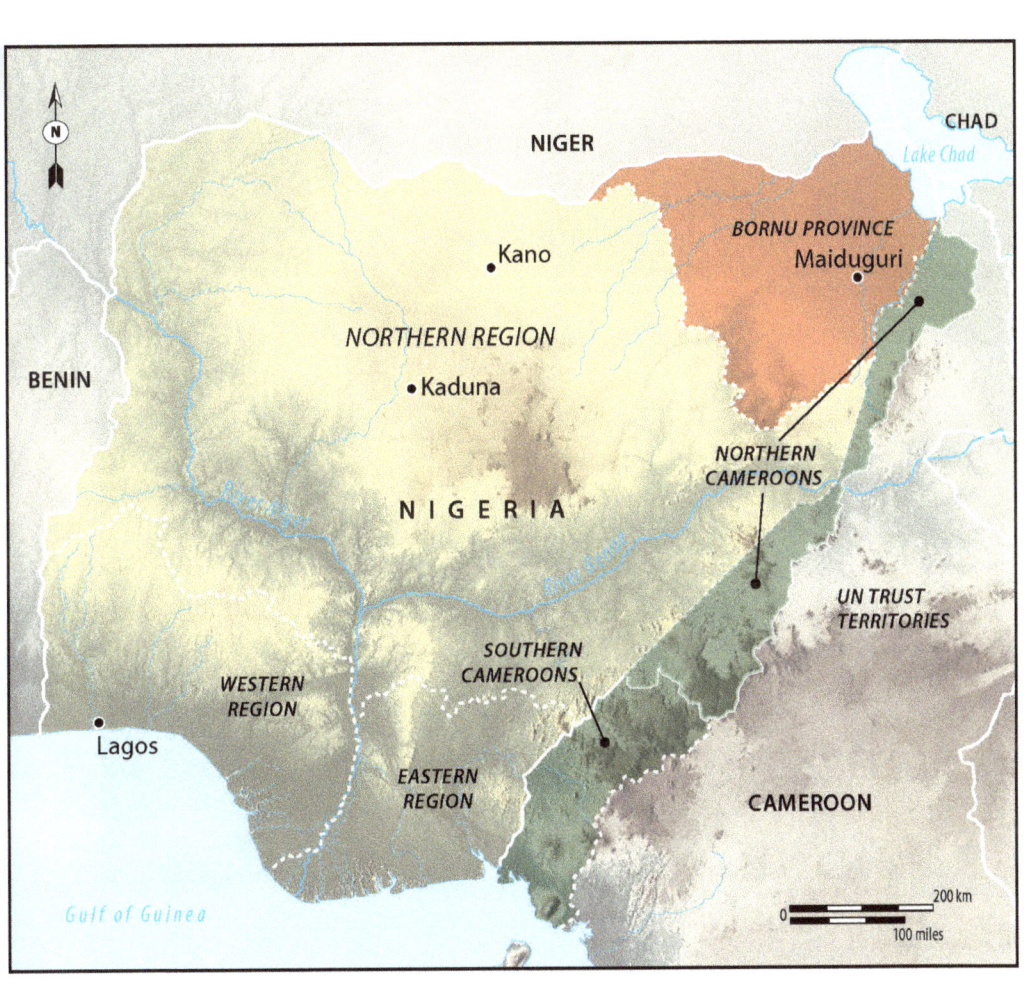

Preface

What follows is a memoir of a land that half a century later lies devastated, villages burned, fields abandoned, hundreds of thousands of its inhabitants living in temporary shelters and refugee camps. This was Bornu Province, now Borno and Fune States in northeastern Nigeria where I spent nine months shortly before the country's independence in October 1960. I was in my 20s, a university graduate with two year's military service, an American who had an appointment as a history teacher in the government secondary school in Maiduguri, the provincial capital. It was a small city in the large and remote province of Bornu with a name I heard for the first time when I was assigned to the school.

By the second decade of the 21st century the world has become familiar with the name Maiduguri from media reports of the activities of the Boko Haram Islamists who pillage the population to purge it of the Western values of secular education and science. The towns and villages I knew are now desolate. The terrorists use late model wireless communications and automatic weapons to enslave, murder, and hold territory. Refugee camps replace villages, fields are untended. One million people are now sheltered in Maiduguri compared to the 60,000 residents in 1960. Malaria, measles, and other infectious diseases are widespread; farming and herding have been disrupted leading to malnutrition and starvation. Northeastern Nigeria has joined South Sudan and Syria as humanitarian disasters.

I kept a journal in ledger-sized notebooks that I opened 50 years later, prompted by the continuing stream of reports, most notably the abductions of the Chibok school girls in 2014. Along with the notebooks were slides that, after being restored, reveal faces, dress, habitations, and landscape that tell a story in and of themselves. They witness a time when the people—the settled, dark-skinned, dignified Kanuri with centuries of tradition, the nomads and their herds continuing their own centuries-old tradition of seasonal migrations between Lake Chad and the Niger River, and tribes in the hills, some untouched by modernity, were no longer in danger from slaving raids. The journals and the images celebrate my students and African and expatriate officials on their jobs, and describe a settled people in a changing world. Nowadays a military escort is essential for any travel outside of the city, but back then, on roads hardened by the sun, I could tour freely throughout the province. On extended weekends, I ventured into Chad and Cameroon. In some villages where I went for election duty, mine was the first white face to be seen in years, a ghostly sight for small children.

I was a rare bird, an American working within the colonial systems. As an election supervisor, I had a first-hand experience of the soon-to-end colonial system. Appointed to teach at a government school I unexpectedly found myself transferred to the field—bush—duty in two elections, unique experiences for a young American—I had unmatched access to remote places and peoples in traditional settlements.

I share here what I saw and did, who I talked to. I celebrate the freedom of movement of that era, the friendliness and openness of so many I met; these are the responses of a young man fascinated by what he saw and keen to understand and sometimes to criticize.

Figures in a Spare Landscape is an adventure story, a glimpse of one place in the midst of a then worldwide process of transition from colony to self-government, and a poignant reminder of what was in this outpost in the fading light of empire.

§

Two weeks after arriving at the Provincial Secondary School in Maiduguri, the headmaster told me I was to be temporarily assigned to election duty in the Northern Cameroons Plebiscite. This made me realize that the inclusion of "officer" in my title meant I could be loaned to another department on secondment. On this assignment, I would be three weeks away; two of them spent camping out in the bush. I'd be getting a closer look at people in their fields and villages.

Just how close this would be I found when I woke up the first morning in the village where I was to be based for two weeks, comfortable in a grass hut with table and cot set up by Sarke, my esperienced cook-steward.

On the first morning I was awakened at dawn by the call of the

Imam and the braying of donkeys. The *rumfa* was a spot of quiet amid the sounds of people who are born, work, age and die within sight and hearing of one another. In this moment I lived in public; I stepped out of the hut in a blue bathrobe to look at the dawn. Women from the strangers' quarter and the pilgrims' camp were already at the well to draw water. One jackass chased a female with brays sounding like creaking gates and with pathetic little leaps constrained by his hobbles. Servants in their sleeping robes like shrouded corpses prodded these animals, moving them to their masters' houses. Women were starting the days' fires. An unhappy dog scurried from the kitchen where Sarke had left an opened tin for him. Men stretched by the doors of the huts across the border. The sun rose from beside a large bump to the east in French territory, northernmost of the mountain chain that extends from the Southern Cameroons. Framing it were swatches of yellowed grasses on the far bank of the dried-up riverbed.

The morning was comparatively cool—a welcome contrast to the searing heat of the middle of the day. The custom of the country is to travel in this coolness, leaving the hot time of day to rest. I wanted to use these early hours for writing and told the *lawan* to bring the horses after 9 a.m. He had received this with a critical look so he was teaching me a lesson when the horse arrived at seven, and I heard the horse boy greeting Sarke and Yusufu and the animal leaping about, whinnying and snorting as though preparing for a great occasion. Could I take him on? I had not ridden for over two years.

Banki was a village in the British Northern Cameroons, a strip of territory bordered by Bornu Province in northeastern Nigeria and the French Cameroons to the west. The vast, ever-changing Lake Chad was about 50 miles north. The villagers were Kanuri, the dominant ethnic group of Bornu, converted to Islam centuries before, descendants of a once powerful land empire. The rumfa consisted of circular grass huts, one for my bed, another for a table, two small ones for Sarke's kitchen and a sleeping place for him and Yusufu, my interpreter. The temporary encampment, erected a day before, was set in the middle of a field that only a few months before had been the village market and remained a public space used by women fetching water from the well, men and boys driving animals, and children rolling hoops. A clump of trees at one end provided shade for men to gather and observe. At the eastern edge of the field was the border with "French," as Yusufu referred to the international neighbor. There were no signs, no control posts. Beyond this invisible line were huts—gambling and drinking dens. Across the border, the Iman had greeted the dawn at a camp for pilgrims en route to far-off Mecca.

Sarke was my newly hired cook-steward who the night before had set up the folding table with a tablecloth and cutlery to serve a hot dinner by the light of a pressure lamp; earlier, in the second hut, he had unfolded a cot, laid out sheets and pajamas and hung mosquito netting. Yusufu was fluent in the Hausa lingua franca, with enough Kanuri to get by and sufficient imagination to make up the rest.

The *lawan* was the village head, directed by his superiors in the Native Authority (NA) to erect the huts, and provide guards—at dawn I discovered two figures rolled in blankets asleep on the ground. The transportation he laid on was the snorting black stallion that called me from the table/desk that morning, a "horse boy" with him and our guide, an elderly fellow in bare feet with a long spear. This was to be my transport and support team on my rounds to the polling stations in four other villages.

I was on duty with the colonial administration to supervise both the construction of polling stations and the voting in this and four other villages that were part of the UN-supervised Northern Cameroons plebiscite.

The Northern Cameroons—until World War I part of German Kamerun—was a trust territory established by the League of Nations with the UK as trustee. In practice it was administered as part of Bornu Province. With independence for Nigeria to come within months, the UN required a vote by the inhabitants as to their preference for their future political affiliation. They could choose to affiliate with Nigeria, or to defer the decision. We administrators were there to ensure that ballots would be cast in private, that they would be secure and would be counted accurately.

What was an American doing in an official role in this operation? I had begun teaching history only weeks before at the Provincial Secondary School in Maiduguri, the capital of Bornu Province about 70 miles east of Banki. The headmaster treated the assignment as unwelcome news for me: "You'll be three weeks in the bush." I responded noncommittally when colleagues commiserated about the discomforts I would face, but I knew this would give me an experience of the land and people beyond the school and the expatriate community, and I had enjoyed camping since Boy Scout days. This vast land was quite unknown to me, surely an adventure was in prospect. Ahead was voting by illiterate farmers who would make an unexpected choice through the ballot box.

I had a second experience of election duty in the bush a few weeks later in the Nigerian Federal Election of December 1959. No black stallion this time, Land Rover support to cover a constituency stretching from near the Sahara, south through the savanna to hill country.

Each tour of duty provided a view from within of colonial ministration in its closing days while introducing me to encounters with a dramatic landscape and diverse peoples. I knew these elections were part of a key historical moment, the withdrawal of European powers from overseas colonies. I had studied the expansion of European empires and followed the independence movements that were forcing the Europeans to leave, but my studies paled in comparison with what I was about to experience in these elections, at the school, and in trips I made in Bornu and across the borders into French territory. I observed with wonder.

In ample British 11"x17" notebooks I kept a journal and with a single lens reflex, I photographed my experiences. Fifty years later, my chief obstacle in decoding the faded notebooks was my scrawling hand; slides needed to be digitized and then worked on with Photoshop.

Chapter One
Getting There

To go back a bit.

I was 27. I had first became aware of the outside world during the Great Depression in Waterbury, Connecticut, just old enough to see the shantytowns and understand a bit of what the adults were saying. By the 1940s and the war I was a keen reader of *Life* and the *Herald Tribune* which came to the house along with maps and radio broadcasts. I followed the progress of the war, well aware of the British Empire's involvement, that seemingly most powerful nation on earth, judging by the red areas on the world map. At the end of the war my father became the sole owner of one of the smaller metalworking factories in the city, then employing between 200 and 300 people. The factory became part of my life—my father's accounts at the dinner table, regular visits as a oy to the idle premises on Sundays, and where I had my first job at age 16. I early visited war-ravaged Europe as a Boy Scout in the *Jamboree de la Paix* on the banks of the Seine in 1947. After boarding school I chose Harvard which would lead me further into the literature and history interests that I favored. As an undergraduate I visited the inexpensive Europe of the 1950s, spending a year at Oxford. I knew my father wanted me to join him in the factory and eventually take it on, but his wishes were implicit, intuited by me. I had two years in the US Army once student deferments were done.

During basic training which I could not leave, the factory was subjected to a bitter strike that prompted a number of major customers to take their business elsewhere. Concurrently, in the aftermath of the Korean War, the industrial economy of Waterbury began to decline. Losses in the family firm accumulated. I listened and watched but had no solutions to offer. The firm was in trouble and had a fraught future. I mention this here not only as a preoccupation that shows up in these notes, but because it heightened my sensitivity to the situation in the school where I was to be placed, which also seemed to be drifting.

Thus, by my late 20s I was educated in the liberal arts and by travel, and contantly aware of the declining fortunes of my father and the factory.

My service in the US Army had begun after college. I spent most of the two years as a typist in the Pentagon. It was a peacetime duty after the Korean War in a gracious city, but without challenge. I found no career path for myself. Some months after discharge and with the impatience of youth I sought a jolt, a challenge in new direction. Africa appealed because of interest generated in my university courses—change was in the air with the independence for Ghana, Nigeria to follow. I was searching, for adventure, yes, but there was something more. I remembered what the writer, Joyce Cary, had told me at an Oxford lawn party a couple of years before, that a determining challenge for a young man in his 20s was to be given responsibility. I knew that he had been in the colonial service in Nigeria in his 20s. Responsibility and challenge go hand-in-hand; could I find them?

Beyond the Pentagon message center there was a transforming world. The phrase "developing country" was becoming commonplace, and there were contradictory approaches in Cold War terms, state-sponsored versus the market, alignment with the West or the USSR, or non-aligned., and there were multiple views of what "developed" meant and how such development could be achieved. A worldwide process was underway, and I wanted first-hand experience, I wanted to find adventure when my military service was completed.

How could I participate in this transformation with a degree in English history and literature? I learned of a call for teachers in soon-to-be independent British West Africa. The African-American Institute, a private agency, was processing applications—this was two years before the Peace Corps was formed. My degree, it seemed, would qualify me as a history teacher. I applied, was interviewed, vetted by a psychiatrist and accepted. They gave me an air ticket to Accra, Ghana, where the field office would direct me to a school. (It was the Cold War and there was competition for the allegiance of the newly-minted nations. I couldn't confirm a rumor that the agency was financed in part by the CIA to enhance American interests. In Bornu later I heard that there were whispers I was with the CIA. I was not.)

In those pre-jet days a long distance air ticket could be written to provide layover days at little or no extra cost. I used mine to make a first stop in London to see friends, one of whom put me in touch with the veteran journalist, Basil Davidson, then working on a book about the medieval kingdoms at the edge of the Sahara. At lunch at his club he advised me to "choose a school in the North of Nigeria," adding that "it is the least westernized part of the country. Its traditional Muslim society has been preserved by the British, its colorful festivals and hierarchies remind of India, once the jewel of Empire."

CELEBRATING THE YEAR OF AFRICA IN TRAFALGAR SQUARE, SUMMER 1959.

He referred me to David Williams, editor of *West Africa,* a weekly publication of commercial and political news. Yes, the Northern Region of Nigeria would be "a fresh field for work" as government-sponsored secondary education was just beginning. Thanks to him I called in on the Permanent Secretary for education for Northern Nigeria at an Oxford conference. I introduced myself between sessions, and he sent my name via TWX to the Ministry. Basil Davidson gave me a heartening farewell when I reported this: "You'll have an experience to carry with you for all your life, fascinating and deeply attractive people at a critical turning point in their history." Right.

En route to Accra, Ghana I stopped in Morocco, Cote d'Ivoire and Guinea, using my magic carpet ticket for a glimpse of changing Africa. In Accra I surprised the placement agency by asking for a school in Northern Nigeria, a region new to them. Wouldn't I want to be in a more developed area such as Ghana or southern Nigeria? I persisted, and

UNIVERSITY OF IBADAN

they TWXed my application to the Education Ministry in Kaduna, capital of Nigeria's Northern Region. The ministry replied that I must come to Kaduna, using the final lap on the air ticket. From there I headed north to Kaduna by bus and train.

On my way north I stopped overnight in Ibadan to see the handsome new university, a jewel bestowed to Nigeria by the departing Raj. From there I took the overnight train to Kaduna. The compartments were packed; there was a market at each stop as passengers rushed out to buy food and drink. In my compartment a mother cooked for her family on a portable stove; the cooking smells mingling with the rich odor from the locomotive's coal smoke. This brief immersion was what I needed to understand fully that I was in Africa.

IBADAN MARKET SCENES

IBADAN TRAIN STATION

"You came by train? We've never heard of that," was a comment when I arrived at the Education Ministry. The officials were quizzical about the American, an oddball who took an overnight journey on an African train, but they were welcoming and the North needed teachers.

They told me of an opening in the provincial secondary school in Maiduguri, the capital of Bornu Province, 500 miles from Kaduna in the northeastern corner of the country, bordering Chad and Cameroon. The remote location and the international borders attracted me, and in May the first VI Form class would take the General Certificate Examination (GCE), a challenge for any teacher. The final step was approval by a committee of senior civil servants. They asked the expected about education and interests. Then came a penetrating question from the one African in the group, a man in a handsome blue robe, wearing a braid-decorated cap. Why did I want to teach in Nigeria, in Africa? Remembering a conversation with a scholarly friend before I left, I spoke of the need to transmit Western values on the eve of independence and mentioned the rule of law and the achievement of representative government. It didn't take me long after the interview to be ashamed of my "civilizing" viewpoint. I was responding to a man doubtless learned in Islamic law and culture and skeptical of Enlightenment secularism. He may have attributed my opinions to naïveté rather than arrogance, as the panel approved me. I wonder now at my lack of understanding. Like others at the time, I assumed it was my role to convey skills and outlook comparable to those in the "developed" world with which the students would have to cope as their country developed. And it is true enough that teaching of English equips students to deal with a modernizing world then dominated by Western Europe and North America. Of course in the 21st century there came a violent reaction to this approach and its local epicenter was Maiduguri.

My appointment was as an education officer in the civil service of the Northern Region. I was surprised to shortly receive an official letter of appointment from Sir Alan Lennox-Boyd, the Colonial Secretary at Westminster; could I be the first American to have such an appointment? (In fact, the Northern Region was then self-governing; someone from Westminster made a mistake.) I thought the title of "officer" was peculiar for a teacher but paid no attention.

One of the first lessons in social nomenclature I learned from people in Kaduna was that in the Northern Region there were two categories of persons, African and European. I would always be considered the latter, as were the English, Scots, Irish, Canadians, Poles and others in the civil service, in "trade," and the military. An African-American with the UN I later met was a European because of his speech and dress. All were expatriates living away from their countries, visiting "home" periodically on "leave," the military term used for vacation. Syrians and Lebanese who had businesses in most of the commercial areas of the North continued to be referred to by their national identities.

Once approved, I shopped for a car and settled on an Opel with a fold-down seat in the back making room for baggage and sleeping. There was only one paved route for the 500 miles from Kaduna to Maiduguri, the first 420 of which were on a conventional two lane road, not difficult to navigate in my limber and comfortable vehicle. I enjoyed the "mammy wagons" with jaunty slogans painted above the windshield, toys bouncing on springy wire inside the window, and benches in the back with a tarpaulin to shield passengers from the sun. The last 80 miles were on a single paved lane with wide earth shoulders. That meant regular games of chicken, calculating whether an oncoming driver would give way and move to the shoulder or persist on the tarmac. The tar had been rippled by heavy lorries, resulting in little hills and valleys and bumps at a machine-gun pace. (This road from Potiskum to Maiduguri I was to know well over the next months, and later I tried to follow the advice of an old hand by driving 60 mph in order to fly over the depressions between the peaks. The official speed limit was 45 mph, so a smoother high-speed ride was more dangerous than chicken.) I survived this first harrowing ride by opting out of chicken, moving to the shoulder before oncoming vehicles. I soon found that road conditions and driving techniques were among the best conversational topics among Europeans and Africans.

After a large roundabout reminding of England, I found myself in Maiduguri's commercial district, a hodgepodge of low rise cement block structures roofed with corrugated iron: petrol stations, auto repair, tables with richly-colored and patterned fabrics and pots and pans and other useful items for sale, all set up on the hard-baked clay edge of a road animated by pedestrians.

The local term for this part of the city was *sabon gari*, or strangers' quarter, populated mostly with enterprising southerners, Yorubas and Ibos, and by Syrians and Lebanese. A unique reminder of the UK "home" was the demure blue sign of Barclays Bank.

I soon arrived at the school buildings where I was expecting to spend most of my time over the next two years. Within a park-like setting were rectangular concrete block structures, painted white, corrugated iron roofs, buildings and grounds deeply shaded by canopies of green leaves, the soil beneath hard- baked clay.

THE SCHOOL COMPOUND IN MAIDUGURI INCLUDED BUILDINGS FOR THE PROVINCIAL SECONDARY SCHOOL AND A SENIOR PRIMARY SCHOOL. THE STAFF ROOM FOR THE PROVINCIAL SECONDARY SCHOOL WAS IN THE LONG, LOW BUILDING WITH A PORCH RUNNING THE LENGTH OF IT.

FIGURES IN A SPARE LANDSCAPE

The mud and brick walls of the native town were a few steps from the school grounds. There I found deeply shaded wide dirt avenues lined with the mud brick walls of residential compounds. I did not expect the elegant, deeply shaded town, a sharp contrast to the commercial area and teaming concentrations of Lagos and Ibadan. The odd auto or lorry shared the avenues with tall, dignified men on foot in long robes and brocaded caps, women in long dresses with hair sculpted into a helmet shape unruffled by a load on the head. Boys drove goats and cattle. Occasional camels come from the north.

SHORTLY AFTER I ARRIVED THERE WAS A DURBAR IN HONOR OF THE SHEHU'S BIRTHDAY. HERE WAS THE COLOR AND PAGEANTRY I'D BEEN TOLD ABOUT. THE SHEHU'S PALACE WAS THE MOST SUBSTANTIAL BUILDING IN MAIDUGURI.

THE WHITE AND RED UNIFORMS ARE THOSE OF THE SHEHU'S RETAINER ASSEMBLED IN THIS BIRTHDAY DURBAR.

Sarke leaving the Opel to pick up something at the "cold store" in Maiduguri that carried imported frozen food.

Beyond the *sabon gari* and the native town was a garden suburb created for civil servants termed the Government Residential Area, always referred to as the GRA. On one of its curving roadways was the house allocated to me, a single-story brick with a living room, bedroom, guestroom, kitchen, sheltered by a peaked metal roof. Two huts in the back were for servants. There was electricity, running water and a septic system, but no telephone. I soon found that the light breeze that occasionally crossed the front porch was preferable to the overhead fan in the bedroom and moved my bed and mosquito netting outside. Similar houses were nearby, shielded by the green of trees and shrubs.

It was customary for a civil servant to hire someone for housekeeping and meals. A colleague at the school told me his servant knew an experienced cook-steward looking for a place. Through the oral telegraph and within hours, Sarke Gombe arrived to meet me, a man I took to be in his 40s. He was a Hausa, as he told me in his easy Pidgin English, a member of the largest language group in the North. He opened a folder with letters from officers he had served over the years. I hired him on the spot, not realizing until our first bush tour what an able and devoted fellow he was. An officer "going home" sold me household items, crockery, flatware, pots and pans.

*Bukar by the porch of my house in the GRA.
I moved the bed out to catch the occasional breeze.*

Sarke bought chicken and meat, vegetables and fruit from the local markets; he planned and prepared meals, made the bed, did the laundry, cleaned house. He told me I should have a "boy" to tend the vegetable garden and trim the shrubs and the grass. He brought in Bukar Gwoza, a young lad from an animist tribe in the hills to the east. When he left his tribe and came to the city he had converted to Islam and learned Hausa. Within days my household was a going concern, a great change from bachelor digs and college and Army living. It took me a while to understand that Sarke and Bukar used the names of their home villages as surnames—as many of the students also did. Some students alternately used a patronymic which confounded my class list until I got used to the alternatives.

The most prominent building in the GRA was the Residency where the senior colonial officer lived with a large enough interior for receptions. Amidst the green shade of the GRA there was a clubhouse with bar, pool tables, and tennis. A Catering Rest House had rooms and meals, in effect a small hotel, mostly used by civil servants. I was a guest until my house was ready. It was a short drive from the GRA to the school: leave at 7, return for mid-morning breakfast, and back after a workday ending at about 2:30, return to the GRA for a nap, then tennis or field sports and drinks at the club.

I was one of seven teachers at the school, six Europeans including the headmaster and one African. From the staff room we went to and from classes over the hard clay, no need for raingear in the dry season. The school day also reflected the colonial schedule, beginning at 7:30 with an hour and a half break for breakfast; at 10:00; classes resumed finishing at about 2:30, earlier on Saturday. All of us commuted from the GRA by car. In the late afternoon some returned to coach sports or preside over "prep," supervised study. I taught history to boys ranging in age from 11 or 12 to 18 and 19, Sections I-VI. The latter was the first class in the province to take the General Certificate Examination (GCE). The history curriculum began with the cave dwellers, ancient Egypt, Greece and Rome and on through the Industrial Revolution and into recent times; Section VI studied the origin and functioning of British parliamentary government. The core purpose of the instruction was always to develop spoken and written English whatever the subject. As was British practice, examinations required written essays.

Students came from primary and senior primary schools throughout the province, all with some English. The school uniform was white, short sleeved shirts, shorts, and caftans for special occasions. My largest class numbered about 20 of the younger boys; there were just six in the class that would take the GCEs at the end of term.

Within weeks of my arrival came the assignment to the Northern Cameroons plebiscite.

AT THE EDGE OF THE GRA WERE FIELDS FOR FOOTBALL AND POLO. HERE MAIDUGURI POLO CLUB AT PLAY.

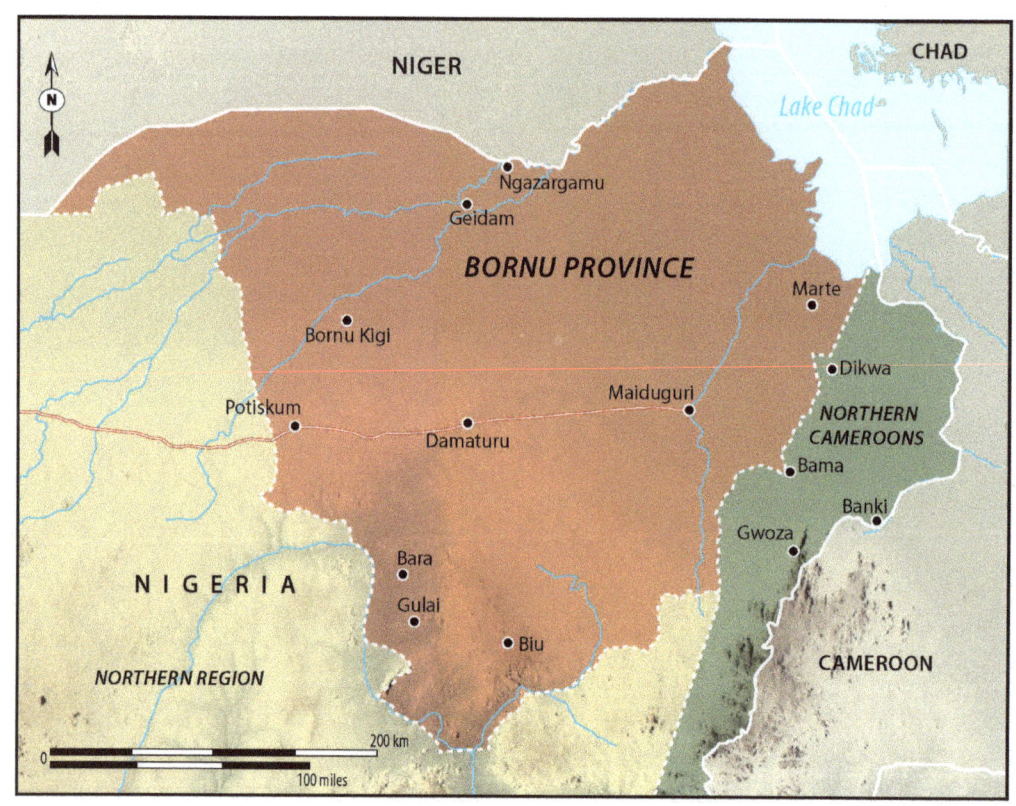

Bornu's principal road extended from Potiskum in the west to the capital at Maiduguri; its single tarmac-surfaced lane the only such in the province. In 1959-60 an Italian contractor was constructing a paved extension from Maiduguri to Bama in the Northern Cameroons UN Trust Territory. Established north-south intersecting "trunk" roads had scraped surfaces of the local soil, hard as concrete in the dry season, muddy in the rains. From Potiskum a tarmac road connected to Kano and connections throughout Nigeria.

The Northern Region and Bornu Province

In the early 1900s the British negotiated treaties with the emirates in the vast territory that became Northern Nigeria. These guaranteed maintenance of traditional authority, and the British governed in that framework, termed "indirect rule" in 1923 by Sir Frederick Lugard, the first Governor of the Protectorate of Nigeria. The largely Muslim northern territories including Bornu were then joined with the coastal colonies. In the North the emirs were at the apex of traditional religious, administrative, and legal authority in each jurisdiction. In Bornu Province the Shehu (as the Emir was termed) was a descendant of a line of Kanuri tribal chiefs. The senior British official in Bornu was the Resident, signifying an advisory role. Over the decades the "indirect rule" under pressure from the "advising" Residents had successfully eliminated slave raiding in the territory and maintained peace between emirates and the "pagan" tribes in the hills. Bornu, like other provinces in the North, was divided into Native Authority (NA) districts each with a District Head (DH) and villages with a designated head or *lawan*. The NA was responsible for tax collection, police, markets, courts, and public works. The colonial advisory framework intersected with the NA structure through District Officers (DOs) and specialist officers in medicine, agriculture, forestry, public works, and education. As a prelude to expected independence, the Federation of Nigeria was established by the British in 1954 combining the Northern, Eastern, and Western Regions with an elected federal parliament. In 1958 the British agreed that the Federation would become independent on October 1, 1960.

Bornu Province was at the far northeastern corner of the Northern Region, bordering Chad, Cameroon, and Niger on the north and east. Sixteen years after Nigerian independence Bornu was divided into two states: Borno, which included Maiduguri as its capital, and Yobe to the west with Potiskum its capital. In this account Bornu refers to the province as it was before this 1976 division.

The Nigerian independence movements originated in the south where there had been western education for decades via mission schools. Missions were permitted only in restricted areas in the Muslim North, and it was in the 1950s that the government in the North established schools beginning at the primary level. In the Nigeria Federation the Northern Region was by far the largest in area and population, and it differed markedly from the southern areas in terms of education and westernization. Most of the north was dominated by Muslims, most in societies structured by a traditional Islamic political hierarchy and law. The southerners had been exposed far longer to western eduation and Christian missions and lived in a largely secular polity though tribal identifications remained strong.

Chapter Two:
In the Bush

NORTHERN CAMEROONS PLEBISCITE

NOVEMBER 7, 1959

Administrative Instructions to Presiding/Polling Officers

YOU have been appointed as a Polling Officer in the Northern Cameroons Plebiscite, for which the polling day is Saturday, November 7, 1959. On this day the people of the Northern Cameroons Trust Territory will come to your polling station to vote on these two questions:

(a) "Do you wish the Northern Cameroons to be part of the Northern Region of Nigeria when the Federation of Nigeria becomes independent on October 1, 1960?"

OFF TO THE PLEBISCITE

I was to report to Bama, 46 west of Maiduguri, where the administrators were organizing the plebiscite voting procedures. A pocket-sized brochure gave me basic information about the procedures. My job title was Assistant Returning Officer (ARO).

First a bit of history. In the late 19th century Germany as part of the European "scramble for Africa" seized a section of West Africa extending from the Atlantic coast to Lake Chad between French and British colonies. Early in the 1914-18 war British forces from Nigeria invaded *Kamerun* and the French did the same from Equatorial Africa. The German resistance was stiff in many places particularly at Mora Mountain, not far over the border from Bama where I was to report, but the Allies took full possession of the territory by 1917. While the war was on, the diplomats apportioned the territory, the larger share to France and a strip bordering Nigeria to the British, the latter divided for adminstration into southern and northern sections. After 1919 these were made trusteeships under the League of Nations, denoting a provisional legal status rather than colonial ownership. The United Nations Trusteeship Council assumed oversight after World War II. The French administered their territory as a single entity with independence scheduled in 1960. The British administered their smaller portion of the old German colony as part of Nigeria, the northern Cameroons seemingly an integral part of Bornu Province. My assignment was in the northernmost section, a narrow strip which included the eastern edge of the Bornu plain and the northern end of a mountain chain. Banki, where I was assigned, was at the far edge of the plain, long settled by the Kanuri in fealty to the Dikwa Emirate within the trust territory. To the south was the mountainous area densely populated by indigenous tribes sheltered from the Muslim majority by the rugged terrain. The hill people were termed "pagans" by both Muslims and Europeans. There were Christian missions near the mountains, but most tribes kept isolated in the mountains. As I was soon to find out, they survived by subsistence farming on terraces with soil scraped from among the rocks. Except for ornaments they went naked and used prevailing stone for their dwellings. I would visit that part of the trust territory, but my responsibilities were in the savanna land with the Muslim Kanuri.

The structure of government in the Northern Cameroons was identical to that in Bornu, and there was free interchange of goods and travel. To its residents the Northern Cameroons had been little more than a geographic expression until the UN Trusteeship Council decreed that the inhabitants must have the opportunity to vote on the future of the territory before Nigeria's independence. People I talked to in Maiduguri expected that there would be little controversy because the traditional leaders of the Kanuri majority supported union with Nigeria. In keeping with the democratic premise of its charter, the UN required a vote, set for November 7, 1959. Only males could vote, and few were literate so the choices were identified by color. Ballots placed in a white box were to be counted in favor of incorporating the trust territory into the Northern Region of Nigeria; ballots in favor of deferring the decision to an (unspecified) later date were to be put into an orange-red box. As it turned out, in the privacy of the voting booth voters made an unexpected choice that neither the UN overseers nor the veteran colonial officers in the field expected.

Packing

What equipment did I have for what was described as a "bush tour?" In London en route to West Africa I had visited the gigantic Army and Navy Store near Victoria Station. In the vast rooms of this palace I was served by a dignified older man. I felt proud when, with a twinkle in his eye, he asked me if I was "going out" to the colonies. My head was turned by the camping equipment and khaki outfits, but I purchased little because, after all, a teacher wouldn't be doing much camping. Now, in my GRA bungalow I laid out what I had brought. A zinc-lined steel trunk with purchases from Army-Navy had arrived the week before. The Safari camp-bed looked splendid, but I found I had neglected to order the attachment for the mosquito net. The tropical suit was good-looking, but not suitable for the bush. What was I to do with the tins of saddle soap and jars of leather conditioners brought in preparation for the dry wind of the *Harmattan*, the hot wind that blows over West Arica in the dry season, full of dust and sand from the Sahara. I was consoled by the station doctor and his wife who sympathetically told me they had brought out a similar variety of stuff that they didn't need.

I had an Italian knapsack, suitable for the Alps but not for the bush, and a splendid down sleeping bag, useless in this heat. On a hike before I left for Africa I spent a week living on what I carried in this knapsack. But now I had lumps of bedding and cardboard boxes for dishes and pots and pans, an amateurish looking assemblage compared to the neat loads of the old timers' tableware and kitchen sets, drink cabinets, portable desks, and folding easy chairs. (Nomenclature note: baggage was always referred to as loads, the term originating in the days when boxes and bags were divided by size and weight to be carried on the heads of bearers.)

I was somewhat a loss, but I reckoned without the resourcefulness of Sarke. On the morning we were to leave I heard him giving lengthy and stern instructions to Bukar, and, between my breakfast and a trip to the post office, the two of them packed food, cutlery, plates, and kitchen equipment into three wooden tea crates, along with tightly rolled up bedding and mosquito nets. They fitted all this neatly into the car, slowly subsiding under the weight. I thought of the trim 40 pounds I took on backpack trips; here there is no pretense about using lightweight equipment; the packing depends on the steward. I put myself into Sarke's hands. He assured me, "master, it is all here—all closed quite," this with a ring of finality, an air of authority.

The interpreter I engaged arrived just as Sarke and Bukar finished loading the car. A colleague's cook who had heard I was looking for an interpreter had brought Yusufu to me. In halting English he told me that in addition to the lingua franca Hausa he spoke Kanuri, the difficult language of the dominant tribe of Bornu and the section of the Cameroons where we were headed. In manner he was casual, as his just-in-time-arrival showed, but available men with some English and the two local languages were hard to find, and I was glad to have him. He was in his late 20s, from one of the "pagan" tribes in the hills to the south of the province. By adopting Islam he had entered the wider society of the North and picked up enough of the languages to make himself useful. He proved to be a willing and cheerful informant, my "eyes and ears" as well as voice. It was once again magical how from a mention to a colleague and from him to his steward I found within a day or two a person who had time available and some skills. All this without telephone or note paper.

We set off, Sarke in the front by me, Yusufu cross-legged in a space on the floor in the back, sliding and bouncing with the car, grasping his bedroll.

En route to Bama

We left Maiduguri heading east over a punishing road surface of furrowed sand, bouncing us up and dropping us down to gain another couple of yards. A truck ahead, raising billows of dust, was a local version of public transport, packed with people holding on to wooden 2x4s above their heads, straphangers on a routine journey. When the car window was closed it was a furnace inside; open the window and there was dust, and so it went in traffic. The billowing sand and dust obscured the road as the car banged over unseen ridges and fell into hollows. After a few miles there was relief, a stretch of single lane tarmac just completed by Italian contractors, a section of a 46-mile paved road between Maiduguri and Bama. Only about six miles of tarmac were completed, but the project was meant to assure people soon to vote in the plebiscite that there will be an up-to-date transport link to the capital of Bornu and thereby to the rest of the Northern Region.

On the smooth surface the pots and pans in the back stopped chattering and we were able to enjoy views of the savanna on either side, tawny grasses spotted with green shrubs and small trees. As the temperature rose the horizon formed an iridescent line between the land and the pale blue sky. The apt textbook term for this landscape is "orchard savanna:" trees with tough gnarled trunks and dark green foliage spotted irregularly in a sea of tawny grasses. The pools of shade beneath the larger trees contrast with the prevailing brightness. Scattered in the grass are thorn bushes and shrubs beginning to lose their leaves in the heat of the advancing dry season.

The tarmac ended and a sandy road continued along a ridge a dozen or so feet above the plain. It is the highest elevation around, and the views compensated a bit for the roller coaster ride on the slippery sand. In the remote past the ridge had likely been an edge of Lake Chad, now 50 miles to the north.

I was elated, unsure as to what I was going to, but full of anticipation. Burly, suntanned workers from the Italian construction company waved greetings from the new road being built alongside the dirt track.

We were in the midst of the easternmost section of the Bornu plain, grasslands dominated by the Kanuri for centuries. I had earlier been told the tribal legend that forebears in about the 11th century A.D. left Yemen and passed through what is now the Sudan to conquer and occupy the area extending south and west of Lake Chad. These people brought Islam with them and named this region around the mysterious lake, "Bornu" or "Noah's flood," appropriate for territory where much land can be underwater during the four-month rainy season. Through the centuries there were cycles of anarchy followed by order during which strong emirs built feudal loyalties. The British military conquest of what is now Nigeria did not touch Bornu which by treaty accepted British authority. In the 1890s the land had been ravaged, however, by a warlord named Rabeh, a Shuwa Arab from a nomadic tribe still present. With two cannons he routed the Kanuri warriors. I had learned about Rabeh a few days after my arrival when the school made a field trip to the ruins of his fort. During the "scramble" for this part of Africa in the 1890s French troops killed Rabeh, and the Bornu emirate was revived under British rule and centered in the newly established capital of Maiduguri.

The 60 plus years of British administrative oversight brought stability to Bornu. Its agricultural economy prospered with the cultivation of groundnuts, an export crop used for industrial oils.

The well-kept villages we passed were laid out to include a square with the largest street leading to the village head's compound, surfaces of packed earth. Large and thickly matted round grass huts are set in compounds fenced by woven grass matting. Roofs and fences were now covered with nut-bearing vines set out to dry at this harvest time. Outside the villages were large plots of cultivated land for millet and guinea corn.

Most of the villages had a few large trees with canopies of green leaves casting extensive shadows. In one village I watched women in ankle-length gowns draw up water from a well, pour it into earthenware pots that they hoisted onto a shoulder as though it was empty and return to the family compound. The hair of the Kanuri women is tightly packed into a helmet-like shape; a braid hangs over the center of the forehead often as far as the nose. Their faces are heavily scarred by lateral cuts on the upper cheeks made at puberty. They appear solid and dour, but one of my students told me that "the difficulty with our women is, sir, that they are too much rascal."

While the women fetched water, men sat cross-legged in the shade, their long flowing robes forming pools of blue or green or white, the dark brown of their faces almost lost in the shade. The car as it moved slowly through the village momentarily stopped the buzz of their conversation.

This far along the route there were almost no vehicles and few pedestrians. We passed a lone man driving a donkey followed by his wife bearing a load on her head. He leapt unnecessarily far to the side at the sound of my horn and beat his animal out of the way with a stout staff. I asked Sarke about another man on foot with a sack in one hand and a goatskin bag over his shoulder. He was a Koranic malam, a teacher, moving from one village to the next to earn fees by presiding at wedding and burials and instructing the young.

Men on horseback herding young cattle had lighter complexions and narrower facial features than the Kanuri. "They be Shuwa," Sarke offered, "peoples who do travel all the time and never rest." This was my first sight of the Shuwa Arabs who frequent this region, the ethnic group from which the warlord Rabeh had come. They have aquiline features and light brown skin, their language a variant of Arabic. Their relationship with the settled Kanuri is uneasy because of the damage by the herds to crops and grasslands during their annual migrations between Lake Chad and the Niger River, hundreds of miles south. I had been told of a project or a "scheme," as the British put it, to drill deep artesian wells to bring a steady supply of water to the surface so the herds have a regular supply of water during the dry season, thus encouraging the Shuwa to settle.

Midway to Bama we stopped at Konduga, an exceptionally shady village, and, judging by the number of mud walls, prosperous. How did it come to be that in Maiduguri and in these villages there are magnificent shade trees? I had asked that question soon after I arrived, and was told that a British officer serving in India had observed trees there that could tolerate months without water, growing large canopies of branches with leaves that remain green all year. Serving in Bornu later he imported seedlings of these neem trees; they require watering for only a year and mature without further care. Over the decades these trees were planted throughout the region, even in the smallest villages.

It was in the glare of high noon that we stopped in Konduga and found a shady spot to park. I restrained from drinking in one gulp the the sweet liquid Sarke had prepared for me and took it slowly. The dry heat pulls moisture from the body leaving no trace of sweat. Refreshed, I visited the primary school. The malams—"Learned Masters," as teachers are called—greeted me from the porch. In Western dress, the principal smilingly welcomed me and introduced me in the classrooms. In one the children sat cross-legged on the floor listening to a talk from a teacher who illustrated his points on the blackboard. On the room's crumbling mud walls I saw color photographs of the Queen and the Duke of Edinburgh and posters depicting the visits of members of the royal family to Nigeria. In another classroom the malam called on the children to rise; they bowed low in unison, and in high pitched and delighted tones, said "good morning, sir," with the accent strongly on the last word and laughed exuberantly at the achievement. After a reproving glance from the malam, they gazed at me with intense curiosity as I said a few words of greeting.

After the tour of the classrooms the malams assembled to bid farewell. Two of them told me they hoped to be off soon on scholarships to an advanced teacher training course; many Nigerians I met have something of the sort in the wind, the ultimate being a year in the UK.

We pushed on, mindful of the bumps and the occasional lorry or Land Rover heading in the opposite direction. At one point there was a standard English road sign to inform the drivers on this sandy track that there was a curve ahead. Another sign from the home country read, "Animals must be kept off the roadway," an injunction that neither animals nor their masters could read and none obeyed.

Finally a large placard announced "This is the Northern Cameroons under United Nations Trusteeship." A concrete bridge spanned a dwindling stream. We had arrived in Bama, the headquarters of the plebiscite administration and the capital of the Dikwa Emirate. I guided the car around a deserted roundabout, another home country export intended to control a larger amount of traffic than we had seen all day. I asked directions of a policeman in a handsome blue and red uniform. He saluted smartly and pointed to a sign that read "New Bama." We drove along a broad avenue shaded by neem trees and lined by small shops (canteens in the local usage); dignified men in long robes stopped conversation to to take note of the car, another sign of the activity the plebiscite was bringing to the town. After another roundabout, there was a Union Jack on a flagpole to mark the District Office. Under the eyes of a warder, prisoners in what looked like numbered potato sacks were hauling water and cutting grass. As I pulled up, the warder, his baton tucked beneath his left arm, braced into a splendid salute. I replied with the understated American army salute. Yes, he said, the District Officer was in, "come this way."

At the door the warder turned me over to a towering man in a turban, a badge of office pinned to a long white robe. This nobleman, I shortly learned, was the DO's messenger, a Shuwa Arab. The DO himself came out of his office and introduced himself as "Lawrence" with a handshake, adding that he could only say hello as "I am meeting with the federal Minister of Trade." I glimpsed a dignified figure within which explained the late-model Ford Fairlane in the shade at the entrance. Mr. Lawrence looked worn—his arms were covered with painful-looking tropical boils, his face was drawn. "We put you over at the Ali Roz house," he told me as though I knew where it was. "I think they've hauled water there today, and I told them to start the fridge again, but first you must check in at plebiscite headquarters. I'll be around to see you later."

I negotiated the car through another traffic circle to find the plebiscite office housed in a small concrete structure next to a shed where there were half a dozen new Land Rovers, marked "Cameroons Plebiscite Administration." A clerk within motioned me to the Assistant Plebiscite Administrator's office. I introduced myself to a tall African who wore impenetrably thick dark glasses. He rose, and in an exceptionally polished tone said, "Oh, yes, you are ARO under Pembleton, aren't you?" I guessed quickly that the initials stood for Assistant Returning Officer, but when I hesitated, he doffed his glasses and said coolly, "yes, that is what you are" and told me to wait.

Shortly Pembleton's Land Rover drove up. A man in his late 30s, he came in wearing the classic colonial dress of brown suede shoes, long khaki socks, knee length shorts, and an open necked short sleeved khaki shirt. He pulled on a pipe but looked harassed—a look I was to associate with him throughout the plebiscite. He was my immediate superior, in charge of the living arrangements. I followed his Land Rover to the Ali Roz house, a large mud and concrete structure in the canteen area near the United Africa Company and John Holt, Ltd. Stores and a Mobil petrol pump, the businesses comprising the commercial area of "new Bama." The greater part of Bama is the native town of mud walled compounds and grass huts with only a few concrete block structures. One of the latter was the Ali Roz house, let by a Syrian of that name to the administration during the plebiscite. Maiduguri had traders and business people from the Levant, but Roz was the only one in Bama.

I was the first of the AROs to arrive. Pembleton went off, saying he would be back in the late afternoon. I looked about the empty house while Sarke and Yusufu briskly unloaded the car and put the bundles—the loads—on the porch. The interior was not inviting, a barren living room and a bedroom filled by an enormous double bed. Better to camp out on the porch. Though Sarke seemed to think this peculiar, in no time he and Yusufu set up my chair, table, and camp bed with its netting frame. They established a kitchen in the yard using an old kerosene stove and bricks. This was the first of many times that I would observe Sarke setting up a field kitchen in a few minutes. An hour and a half later he served a three-course meal on the porch.

Meanwhile, the two other AROs who were to share the house arrived. The first was a burly lowland Scot named Williamson who drove up in an Opel sedan followed by a small truck with his gear. He complained loudly about tubeless tires, terming them a fraud after two blowouts that day. His cook steward was a tall, reserved Nigerian from the south who wore a mustache with artfully twisted strands of hair hanging down on each side. His manner was military; he came to attention when spoken to and did a parade ground half turn when he walked away from Williamson. He was Jamie, Williamson's "boy," or, as his "master" explained to me, he left his experienced boy with his wife and had to make do with Jamie. "He's a good enough lad, but you know, like all of them, he needs a bit of prompting." Such prompting went on noisily over the next half hour as Jamie sorted out Williamson's loads, a contrast to the self-reliance and quiet of my capable crew. Williamson chose a spot at the other end of the porch, saw to it that tall bottles of Heineken were put in the fridge, and, after a bitter monologue on the trials and expenses of traveling in this country, left to see a friend, the station doctor.

Mr. Powell was the third in the house, a government auditor. He was mild mannered, accompanied by his cook, Samuel. Powell pronounced the name in high pitched tones to emphasize each syllable, "Sam U EL." The lad was from southern Nigeria, unsettled by being in the North; his frightened expression was only aggravated by unpacking his master's loads and preparing a meal in the kitchen space already crowded by the other "boys." He almost lost his nerve when he attempted to inflate a new mattress. Mr. Powell called him a clod and blew it up himself, releasing Samuel to sort himself out in the kitchen. Powell and I soon settled down sufficiently to share a bottle of beer and discuss the road conditions *en route*. Pembleton stopped by to tell us that nothing would be going on until the morning when we would start by learning the voting procedures prior to training the men who would officiate at the polling stations.

We had the evening free, a "break" which Williamson scornfully met with the observation that he would have preferred to spend the time back with his wife. He settled on his cot to read a mystery novel as we all waited for the heat to break. At five he offered me tea. I was thirsty from a walk by the river and welcomed the hot liquid fortified with condensed milk. Tea prompted Williamson to reminisce. In the War he had been an engineer with the 8th Army in the desert. "We used to drink masses of tea in the Army. You know, although I remember how much we used to complain, the great thing about the Army was the companionship. I expect you felt that way too; there will be nothing like that again." I drank more and more tea until Jamie had to be summoned from where he was struggling with a portable gas stove to refill the teapot. It was only after several shouts from Williamson, each more confusing to Jamie than the last, that we managed to have more water heated. Williamson railed against plebiscite duty, "wasting my time with this stuff. They have no right to take us from our proper jobs. Because I am here there are a couple of houses that will go unbuilt. Same with you, your kids will be untaught. This is a job for the administration, not for us. My Boy Scout days are over." When I commented that I was looking forward to the experience, he gave me a benevolent look and assumed the role of the old timer. "Oh yes, young and enthusiastic. I was like you once. Why I knew every bush rest house in the whole territory of Sierra Leone. I used to love to bush tour in those days. But not now, no sir. No more Boy Scout stuff for me. Ha, ha." He said this as if he were living his life over again. Mr. Powell and I sat silent, listening to endless ensuing criticisms of the coming operation and continuing to drink vast amounts of a good, strong tea. The hot dry air leads to a powerful thirst.

Before the light failed I went for another walk along the edge of the river that borders the town. I walked through the fast-gathering darkness, responding to the soft greetings of passersby, listening to the sounds of dinner in the compounds and conversations beneath the trees. The sun vanished quickly and the light of the clear sky was unsteadily reflected in the water threading through the vast sand bed of the river. I had arrived in the Africa of my imaginings.

Back at the Ali Roz house the pressure lamps were sending their sharp, blinding radiance from the porch. Accompanied by their hiss Mr. Powell and I joined for dinner; Williamson had gone elsewhere leaving Jamie to sort out the complexities of his master's kitchen equipment.

After reading for a time in the delicious, dry cool of the evening I crawled inside the mosquito net and was soon asleep on the concave surface of my camp bed.

Learning the Procedures

Before six and with the dawn Sarke woke me bringing a pot of tea on a tray just as he did in Maiduguri. The custom of the country is to have this early morning tea and a biscuit at six and go to work at seven, but I took a full breakfast early, and this earned Mr. Williamson's favor. As Sarke carried my plate of fried eggs and ham onto the porch, he boomed out, "that's what I like to see, a man who starts his day right."

The three of us in separate cars motored the short distance to the *dendal*, the main avenue of a Kanuri town or village, in this case leading to the NA district office. This was a brick building next to the primary school; within I joined AROs at a table in the NA meeting room, about ten of us. For the next six hours Pembleton went through the logistics of the plebiscite and the detailed procedures to ensure a fair and valid vote. It soon was evident that some of the group shared Williamson's resentment at being pulled from their regular jobs. Pembleton's explanations were often interrupted by arguments critical of the procedures, others dealing with practical matters of transportation and supplies. Pembleton at last had to resort to an epithet heard often in the colonies for troublesome people, evoking the Russian Revolution: "I'm just as Bolshie about this as you are, but the job must be done." On went the complaining which made the task of mastering the procedures unnecessarily tedious. With the expansion of technical services in Northern Nigeria in the previous decade, interdepartmental rivalry had become a fact of life, and the district officers in the administration like Pembleton, once ascendant, had had their scope reduced. I was quick to understand the departments of my fellows. In the colonies everyone is known by last name followed by department, "Judd, Education; Williamson, PWD [Public Works Department]." Pembleton belonged to Administration, a latter-day descendent of the colonial civil servants who had "advised" the emirs and the NAs since early in the century. These colleagues represented a cross-section of the colonial service. Loudest and roughest were Williamson and his friend, Jim Rogers, a mechanical engineer who maintained a fleet of Caterpillar tractors at one station, and Dixie Deans who supervised another big equipment depot. These PWD men were civil engineers, road and bridge builders, designers and builders of water supplies. Many of them worked in remote bush stations supervising construction with African labor. They were often Scots or Irish, bluff characters with a large capacity for drink, and, in my experience, goodhearted and able. The isolated conditions of work, the remoteness of the bridges and roads they worked on often induced an almost shattering melancholy and depression which led to the idiosyncrasies and roughness for which the department was known. I heard references to "PWD types" as a kind of breed.

Keith Jones was a young geologist with a black beard and a rich Welsh accent. Most of his time was spent in the bush with his car, a battered Peugeot pickup ("kit car" in local parlance), and on horseback, and, occasionally in the north of Bornu, on camelback. "Water!" he said and rolled his eyes, "that is what we're looking for. Beneath the sand there is often pure water, water that fell on the earth during the time of Christ." He was working on the scheme to bring to the surface water to settle the Shuwa. But plebiscite duty interrupted Keith's work. As a touring officer he had months before helped to register voters for the plebiscite. Some weeks later I saw him during the federal election, he had by then spent four or five months on election duties and shook his head sadly over a pile of paper, saying that this sort of thing was not his field.

Deep artesian wells for water to settle the nomads.
Peter Crews, Senior District Officer with a field worker.

A senior member of my own Education Department, a quiet, intense man, conscientiously took notes during the preliminary sessions. A few days later, however, he was seized with a typhoid-type of infection and returned to recuperate in Maiduguri.

Dixie Deans was the improbable name of a PWD man in the group with whom I would become friendly. I first noticed his trim and athletic appearance with no trace of a belly and wiry, strong legs. He was in charge of a depot that maintained the vehicles used to build a new highway along the eastern edge of the Northern Cameroons. Work on this highway had stopped some months before, but Dixie stayed on to mind the depot, a role that clearly pleased him. In a thick upland Scots accent, Dixie spoke of India and "Eyerak," of gifts he had received from the president of Lebanon, the skills needed to bring whiskey in the necessary quantities into Pakistan. He swaggered and blustered and steadily worked every common obscenity into noun, verb, and adjective. But "he will do anything for you," Mr. Lawrence commented to me, and I found Dixie to be a warm-hearted companion. His trim figure belied his intake of beer and whiskey. He claimed to be 49.

Stanley Litowski was a Cooperative Officer whose job it was to encourage the farmers to form cooperatives and to oversee them, often a discouraging task. At 58 he was the eldest of the group, an age which is vulnerable to the vicissitudes of the fierce climate. He was a small, powerfully built man, with a double-handled mustache. He followed every detail of the training sessions with interest and conveyed them to his African clerks with painstaking and enviable care. He had been an officer in the Polish Army in 1939, was captured by the Soviets, and later released to join the Polish Brigade that fought with the 8th Army in Italy. He became a British citizen after the war and was passionately devoted to that country's monarchy. Like other Poles I met in Nigeria whose lives were displaced by war, he found opportunity in the colonies and had been serving in Nigeria since the end of the war.

The group was completed by Mr. Powell and Abubakar Kano, one of the few Northern Nigerians in a "senior service" post. He sat with quiet dignity at the table, and I often wondered what he thought of the wrangling going on around him. His politeness would not let him voice an opinion.

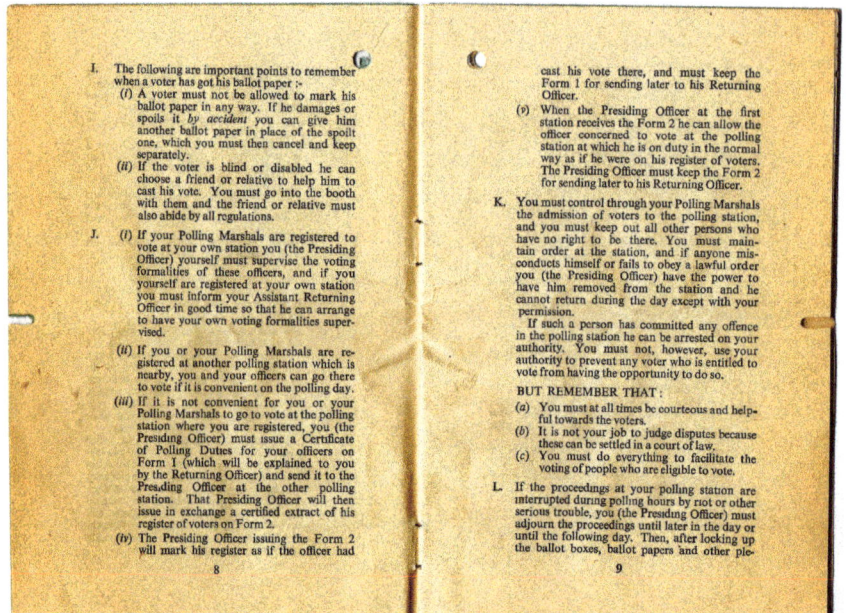

Polling and administrative procedures for the plebiscite.

Pembleton passed out a folder containing densely printed sheets of electoral instructions, booklets of regulations in English and a portion of a map showing our respective polling areas. The first paper I glanced at was a sheet giving the official rates for horses and bearers. A porter was to be paid 2/8 shillings a day, about $.35, a horse for a day was 3/6 or $.51. We were to be allowed a maximum of twelve porters each, a horse for oneself and one for the interpreter. Some of the areas would not require trekking and could be covered by Land Rover. The village assigned to me, Banki, on the border between British and French Cameroons, could be reached by a maintained track. I was to be driven there and left to supervise four other village polling stations to be reached by horse. Pembleton warned me that I must not let bearers carry the ballot boxes at night as this was an area notorious for bandits.

Some of my colleagues could go to their villages using their own cars. Malam Abubakar, however, would have to trek about 13 miles, and Rogers had to provide himself with a punt to get across a stretch where the land was still flooded from the rains. There was a persistent buzz as these assignments were given out, questions having to do with the transport of loads, and, repeatedly, how to get back to Maiduguri during the two weekends between now and the voting. There were arguments about the placing of various polling stations by men who had worked in those areas. It all went over my head, so I devoted my time to pouring over the map and imagining what I would find.

Next followed an explanation of the voting procedure. Each polling station was to serve about 500 people; Northern Nigeria allowed only male suffrage so these would be men over 21 from as large an area as possible around the polling station. The voters had already been registered, their names inscribed on an electoral roll, and they had been issued with cards bearing an assigned number. The polling stations are to be manned by a presiding officer and a polling officer. The latter will write with blue ink the name of the voter on his hand and issue a ballot stamped with a "secret seal." If the presiding officer had cause to believe that the voter was hiding ballots to stuff the boxes, he could take him to a grass hut "searching booth" to inspect clothing. If all was in order, the voter would proceed to the voting booth, a larger grass hut where he would choose in privacy between the two metal ballot boxes. Each of these boxes had a sign in English and Hausa noting the alternative for which the ballots would be cast. As over 95% of the population in this area was illiterate, the boxes were colored, white, for uniting with Nigeria and orange-red for delaying the decision. We understood that announcements had been made in every village tying the colors to the two choices.

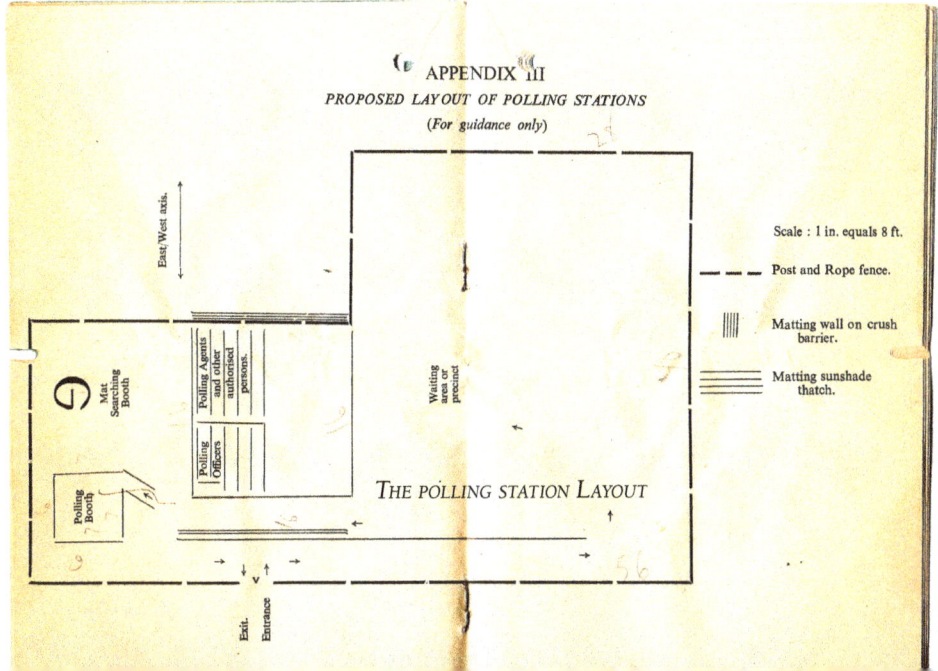

The procedures provided for special circumstances. What if a voter had lost his registration card? We expected this to happen as the cards had been issued several months ago and before the rains; also, it was rumored that many of the villagers had deposited their cards with leading men of the village for safekeeping; and as they would not remember or could not read their numbers there could be confusion at the polls when voters came with the wrong cards. In such cases, these voters were to wait until those with cards voted and then be interrogated and the matter sorted out by the presiding officer. There were also forms to deal with ballots that had been torn in the process and for ballots dropped on the ground of the voting booth by someone who panicked. Poll watchers from political parties could observe the process. If they challenged a voter there would be an elaborate form to be completed. There were also detailed instructions for opening the sealed envelopes containing the election materials before the vote, sealing of the boxes at the close of the day, and accounting the day's work before the ballot boxes were delivered to the counting station. It was to be an honest election conducted according to practices developed in the home country, applied in a very different society.

As the details of the procedures accumulated, it was hard to keep them all in mind and I knew it would require further study. On the morrow we were to have the first session to instruct the presiding and polling officers. Several of today's colleagues vehemently contended that the procedures were too complex, but Pembleton plugged along. Once learned, the procedure would be straightforward, but like a complicated filing system, it was almost baffling at first and provoked contentious comments. These were put aside after we broke up at about 2:00 pm. Williamson left to have beers with the doctor, and Mr. Powell and I had a quiet luncheon on the porch and speculated on how it would all turn out.

Mr. Lawrence invites us to a gathering

That evening Mr. Lawrence invited all of us to his residence for drinks. Powell and I shared a ride with Williamson. As the car entered the drive marked "District Officer," its lights picked out a smartly dressed NA policeman who in a kind of ceremony clicked his heels and braced to a salute as we parked.

Mr. Lawrence's cook led us through the house, dimly lit by a pressure lamp in the kitchen and another on the porch. In the garden, guests were seated on folding armchairs in a circle around a pressure lamp atop a stand about six feet high. The brilliant light illuminated only people and objects in the circle; beyond was impenetrable darkness. The chiaroscuro was sharp; light and shadow reversed on faces when people turned to speak to someone on the other side. The hiss of the lamp underscored conversation. The center light was blinding, making invisible a person across the circle. With the hiss, the sharp chiaroscuro, and impenetrable African dark beyond, the scene was highly atmospheric, redolent of similar scenes reaching decades in to the past. The temperature was in the 90s, skin temperature and the dry air in balance.

All the men were in shirtsleeves, colleagues from the training session and a few others, though I could not make them out in the sharp contrast between light and shadow. It was an all-European gathering. In the darkness outside the circle, Kachalia, Mr. Lawrence's "small boy," passed about to ask what we wished to drink, and, since the usual request was beer, returned with Imperial half-pint mugs and the tall bottles that are standard in West Africa. This evening we had Heineken, the strong, tasty Dutch brew, a specialty elsewhere, but ordinary here. (There was also Star, a beer brewed in Lagos with a broader bitter taste that I eventually preferred.) With the tall bottle came a small bowl of groundnuts, a tougher, smaller version of the American peanut, whose taste, particularly with salt, I already associated with evenings in Bornu. The dry heat keeps thirst active, slaked by all the water and squash during the day. Beer was irresistible, the tall bottle equally so.

My housemates had told me to wear a tie because there would be two "mission ladies" at the gathering. This was surprising because we were in a Muslim area and one of the terms of the agreements made with the emirs of the North at the beginning of British domination was that there would be no Christian missions in the territories without permission of the Muslim rulers. There were missions in the hills in Bornu and just to the south in Northern Cameroons, but in the heart of a Muslim emirate I never expected to meet missionaries. I chose a chair next to one of the women who was eager to chat; the other was reserved until she saw Dixie Deans and promptly asked him what she should do to salvage her venerable Morris Minor that was in such bad shape she could not drive it back to the nearby mission. She spoke rapidly in perfect English but with enough of an accent for me to ask her colleague where they came from. Denmark was their native place, and the mission was a Baptist maternity clinic just outside Bama. By giving attentive care they hoped to allay suspicion. She admitted that attendance was slight in their small chapel, but "hope sustains us." Their previous assignment had been in Agades, the plateau town in the Sahara, where the mission was to the nomadic Tuareg, some of whom did become Baptists. I felt a twinge of envy when she told me of the French schoolmasters who were sent out to live with the Tuaregs on their wanderings, the only way to provide the sustained instruction that would lead to literacy. That would be a rare adventure in constant movement.

Mr. Lawrence encouraged Kamallia to ply us with groundnuts and beer, as, looking weary, he moved around the circle to speak to each of us, asking where we came from, what we did, and our departments. He did this with great courtesy, but I sensed he barely listened, preoccupied with his own concerns.

The party seemed over and time to break up, but in my weeks out here I had learned that the protocol held in the colonies that at a social event no one could leave until the senior officer had left. In an out-station such as Bama such protocol was not strictly observed, but tonight I had been told by Mr. Powell that we must wait for the mission ladies to leave. It happened suddenly—one woman turned to the other to say she was ready to go, and the assembled company rose as one to bid them good night. As soon as they left the circle each of the men took his leave of the DO. Our cars pulled slowly out of the driveway, the headlights fleetingly illuminating tree trunks, mud walls, sometimes people walking in the pervasive dark. There were no streetlights, no traffic lights and no light spill from houses. There were only flickering candles on tables by the small African shops.

At Ali Roz the three cooks were waiting in the back and brought our meals within minutes, my first experience of the African cooks' ability to have a hot meal ready at any moment between 7:30 and 11 p.m. We had not told them when we would be back.

At dinner Mr. Williamson's indignation at being seconded to the plebiscite seemed tempered by the party. He retired early and read his mystery novel under the net before extinguishing his kerosene lamp. I turned in before 11, pleased with the little bout of sociability.

Training our Election Officers

"Did you do your homework?" Williamson boomed out across the porch in the dawn. He jovially announced that he had not, and that he would learn it as he went along. After breakfast we were to face the young men who would run the polling stations to teach them procedures we dimly grasped.

When we assembled, Pembleton went over unclear or contentious issues, although most of the men seemed keen to get on with the instruction. Outside the shade filled with seated figures, the presiding and polling officers who had come in from their villages days before. Most of them were primary school teachers and had some English. One told me later that they were pleased to have several days to visit the largest town of the emirate and receive good pay at 10 shillings/day ($1.40).

Pembleton was accompanied this morning by a burly man wearing khaki with a Rolleflex on a strap around his neck. He was introduced as Marshall Williams, the UN observer for our area. He spoke to us briefly, his rich measured tones and American southern accent giving me a whiff of homesickness. Williams was careful in his remarks, presumably aware that many of those present resented being pulled from their normal jobs. An African-American who I later realized was considered by the young Africans I was training to be a European because of his dress and manner.

So that teachers (malams) could serve in the polling booths, the primary schools in the emirate had been closed until after the voting. We AROs met the future election officers in the compound of the junior primary school next door. Each of us was assigned twelve, a presiding and polling officer for each of our five stations and two alternates. Once I had gathered my group we took over an empty classroom; others were teaching in the shade of the trees. It seemed to me that a school room with a blackboard would be a more effective training place, though as the sun's power increased, the galvanized iron roof—also the ceiling—focused the heat within the room; by afternoon it was close to intolerable, and I doubted my choice. These malams were literate, but their English was slight, in some cases nonexistent. My first task was to choose an interpreter. I had brought along Yusufu so that he might learn the procedure, but his English was not sufficient to grasp the technicalities, and his Kanuri was not fluent enough to translate what he did understand to the students. However, he dutifully sat through the lecture and demonstrations and treated the experience as though he was to be one of the presiding officers. When I asked for a volunteer interpreter several eager hands went up. I chose Malam Abu Kagu, a forthcoming young man with a ready smile. It wasn't a successful choice. His translations were often challenged by Babu Wakilbe, a slow-speaking man about the same age. He was a clerk from the NA treasury and stridently attacked mistranslations until Abu Kagu gave up and Babu took over. The pattern was set: I would hold up a sheet of paper to describe a procedure such as examining the credentials of a voter; I remained still while the interpreter poured out vigorous Kanuri, a language rich in sound, lending itself to oratory even on these mundane topics. When the tirade ended, I lowered the temperature using simple, direct English.

Those among the group who were assigned as presiding officers seemed to come from the more responsible jobs under the NA. The first eager interpreter, Abu Kagu, was a cotton examiner in the Agricultural Service who had learned his passable English at a technical school in another province where he had been trained as an electrician. As there was no electricity in this, his native emirate, he was assigned to inspect cotton, a crop that was just being introduced in the area. Malam Sabra was a veterinary assistant whose regular duty it was to check cattle and help set up mass inoculations under the supervision of a senior veterinary officer. His large, sullen face was heavily scored with Kanuri tribal markings.

Abba Kyari, a tall, lean young man with refined features and a bright, attentive expression, wore a gown with small blue designs in a brilliantly white field, making him noticeable in a crowd of blue, green and off-white ankle-length robes. He was an Arabic malam who taught in a Bama school, soon to go off to Kano, the largest city in the North, on a scholarship for advanced study in Arabic under a new program initiated by the regional government. He spoke no English or Hausa, but he was one of the best of the students, quick to catch on to a point and conscientious in taking notes. How I wished I knew his language or he mine so that we could talk.

There were not enough among the NA employees to serve the entire plebiscite, so boys still in school, even in primary school, were pressed into service. Some of the presiding officers in the other groups could not have been over twelve years old. Malam Gimba, the youngest of my group, had graduated from senior primary school a year before. He was a short, slim lad who spoke a formal English slowly and carefully, and during these classes he was almost painfully attentive in an effort to understand. He was in the NA Forestry department, working in newly designated areas in the savanna to promote an economic use of the scrubby trees. He spoke of his work with pride, and when I responded, his eyes lit up in evidence of his enthusiasm for English and what he expects in life from fluency in speaking and reading. We became friends, and after the plebiscite he frequently came to "greet" me at the school in Maiduguri and stay to exchange courtesies and news—and to speak English.

Many primary school teachers learn English in their teacher training, though they don't teach it. Malam Abba Kyari was literate only in Kanuri. He was tall, stolid, and handsomely dressed in a light blue robe, on his head, a high black cap with a tassel giving him a somewhat august appearance. He proved to be the slowest and least attentive of the group and caused me worry as polling day approached.

The polling officers (assistants to the presiding officers) were all literate in Kanuri but few of them knew Hausa, the language of the vernacular instruction pamphlet. These men and boys had rarely been away from their villages and were delighted to have several days of employment in Bama. Several were village scribes, the literate village official who assists the village head by keeping records, the most important of which pertain to the annual tax. One of my group was a village carpenter, another a farmer.

In this first session I outlined the procedure and distributed the instruction booklet in Hausa. After each item I asked if all understood and was greeted by enthusiastic assent that I assumed was largely a response to please the instructor. Comprehension was another matter as soon became clear. The difficulty was not the intelligence of these fellows, but their slight command of English and the foreignness of the voting procedures.

A PLAYFUL APPROACH

After a break, I decided it was time for play. Over the next three days we engaged in a continuous dramatization of polling day. Each of the presiding and polling officers had to sit and accept the votes of the others who presented them with every conceivable complication. We drew an outline of a polling station on the floor of the classroom. Taking turns, two officers in each simulation appointed a polling marshal to keep order and to guide voters into the waiting area. Before the polls opened the presiding officer showed the empty ballot boxes to the marshals and sealed them in their presence as two others acted as political party poll watchers. The boxes locked permanently when the lid was closed, but to make certain there was no tampering, a string was passed where the lid clamped down to be sealed with wax. The slot for the ballot had its own lid, opened by a bicycle spoke. This slot was sealed open so that no voter could close it on voting day. Everyone in class by turns opened a polling station, displayed the empty boxes, prepared them for voting and closed and sealed them.

The class then tested a range of difficulties. In a much-enjoyed skit, the waiting voters began shoving and quarreling and the presiding officer summoned the polling marshal and the village head to quiet them. In another, a journalist, played by Aba Kagu, shoved his way into the polling station claiming he was a correspondent for *The Times*; there were cheers all around when the polling officers ejected him. Malam Aba Kyari attempted to enter the station wearing a party button, that of the Northern People's Congress (NPC), the dominant party of the Muslim North. He was ejected under the provision that no party emblems and uniforms be displayed within 50 yards of the poll. We paused for a discussion of what to do if all the voter owned was a green gown (*riga* in Hausa). We decided that it would be sensible to let him vote.

In another simulation the marshall brought certain voters to the presiding officer's desk. One had the correct card; as its number was checked against the registration list, he was permitted to vote. Then came a man whose name was not the same as that beside his number on the registration list; the polling officer searched the register to find the correct number. Another voter had a registration card indicating he should vote in another area. The officers energetically dismissed him and told him to go to the proper polling station. One of the class portrayed a nervous old man who accidentally ripped the ballot; he was given a replacement and the officer filled out the necessary tally form. One of the village scribes portrayed a blind man, shutting his eyes for many minutes while the presiding officer, accompanied by a party poll watcher, took him into the booth and cast the ballot for him according to his verbal instructions. Malam Abba Kyari convincingly portrayed a man who became terrified in the booth at the moment of decision and threw his ballot on the ground. Such a compromised ballot had to be recorded on yet another form. Aba Kagu stayed too long in the polling booth, was apprehended and the presiding officer then inspected him in the searching booth where he found a score of ballots in his clothes, presumably bought from voters who had kept them instead of depositing them. To laughter from all, he was handed over to the polling marshall who took him to jail.

None of us liked the accounting drill after such vivid scenes. The number of ballots issued, ballots torn, ballots found on the ground, all had to be accounted for to prevent fraud, but I feared for the day of the real vote when I saw the glazed eyes as we went through the topic.

Friday mosque interrupted training. By then I was jaded by the repetitiveness, though the trainees were confident of their grasp of the procedures and keen to move on. We were kept at it until the last minute by Pembleton, responsible to assure a fair and honest vote.

Evening walks

After 2 p.m., the end of the workday, I settled into a routine. On the porch I had a bowl of Sarke's thick soup made from a pot of perpetually renewed stock—he always kept one on the fire—followed by a hearty stew. I was ready for the siesta that most of the Europeans took in the afternoon. Waking from his nap at four Williamson bellowed for Jamie, and in a few minutes the boy came running with a pot of tea for us both. The hot liquid, taken in quantities, brings on a hot sweat, not uncomfortable in the prevailing dryness. When I wearied of Williamson's recitals of the flaws in the operation of the plebiscite, I stole away to the back of the house to find Yusufu for a walk through the town. I wasn't sure if he enjoyed these walks and my repeated "What are they saying?" "Who are they?" "Where do those people come from?" At his request, I would correct the English of his replies. I thought he must dread the walks, but one evening when I did not go out he came around to fetch me. He was diffident at first and insisted on keeping a step or two behind, but after an evening or two I convinced him that he should walk beside me.

We began the walk by the river, not far from Ali Roz. The riverbed was sunk below the level of the plain, a sandy strip, created by a broad, flowing river during the rains, now with a narrow stream. The sky was crisscrossed with enormous swatches of pink and red over massive white clouds, contributing to the evening's splendor after a cloudless day. A thin band of water flowed slowly through the sand by the far bank. Men on horses splashed through the stream, women, with long dresses pulled up, walked through it, calabashes balanced on their heads. I walked upstream and found a rig with a line extending from poles at either side of the stream holding the lines of a dozen or so hooks into the stream. A fish swimming in the murky water could mistake the hook for bait. As the fisherman checked the lines, I watched him repeatedly pull up tiny wiggling fish and remove them from the hooks.

The riverbed attracted activity. When the naked boys in the water saw me they leapt about and screamed with delight that an "Ebaturi" (European white man) had visited them. A boy wearing a simple white gown briskly walked along the sand with a strikingly erect posture. He had a slingshot in his hand, and when I asked him what he was doing, he replied, "At one in the afternoon I killed a blackbird."

Darkness comes suddenly so close to the equator, and we headed back through the town where there were small lights and indistinct figures on the sandy streets. Opposite the Ali Roz house a hospital was under construction, framed with concrete blocks and roofed with asbestos, simple architecture using ordinary materials, a present of the departing Raj to the Northern Cameroons. Walking nearby was a young European with a military haircut in tomato-colored short shorts, as different from my English colleagues as Yusufu. He was only 24, from a town north of Turin and was supervising the construction of the hospital, one of many Italian engineers and mechanics who were building public works in the new Africa. He told me he had signed on for a few years in order to save up money to start a business in Italy. He slept in an improvised shack nearby, a dazzling box made of aluminum roofing materials. He used a cane because of a boil on his leg, and he had a touch of malaria. Like many ex-pats he regarded a stay in Nigeria as something to be endured, not even thought about. "Let the time pass as quickly as it can, and may I feel and experience as little of it as possible." His mind was elsewhere, and he had apparently given up hope that any human contact here would penetrate his loneliness. There are moments with ex-pats when conventional chat fails, and the starkness of isolation in a foreign culture takes over. I felt this in him. There was nothing more to say. He called his dog and said good night. Yusufu, who had been chatting with one of the workers on the site, rejoined me, and we headed back into the center of the town through the enveloping dusk.

At the moment when the evening transforms from a soft grayness to night the twinkles from the vendors' candles—wicks set in a cup of wax—show the way. Shapes pass, faces imperceptible in the shadow but recognizably human. In an instant the gray becomes almost absolute darkness. The traders who sell cigarettes, sweets, bromides, combs, pack up their wares. Around them move the sports of the town, friends arm in arm out for an evening of talk, prostitutes looking for trade ("harlots" as per Yusufu), but mostly men out visiting. There is a rustling, unseen animation that denotes the transition to the profound dark. I loved to walk through Bama then, to hear the exchange of greetings—a Kanuri can spend several minutes of repetitive conventional salutations with a friend—to feel the closeness, the connectedness of the community.

The next evening in the gray a horse and rider passed by heading out of town. The rider was heavily cloaked and perched sideways on the saddle. I peered through the dusk. Yusufu said quietly, "it is a woman." The hooded figure was escorted by a retainer with a long, unsheathed broadsword resting on his shoulder. I learned later that this medieval vision was of one of the emir's wives leaving the town to visit her native village.

Examination Day

Saturday was examination day for the presiding and polling officers. In the skits they had developed an *esprit de corps* making me confident of my team. Abba Kagu came to me several times to share his view that our group was the best of all. It was encouraging to have such spirit, and I hoped for the best in the examinations. Mr. Williamson and the others, anxious to get back to see their families and to enjoy "open night" at the club, reiterated to Pembleton that "you can talk and talk and still these people will not understand." Others noisily averred that even if the training lasted another week the young men would not understand any more than they did now. Pembleton announced that, unless the examinations were disastrous, we AROs would be released for the weekend. He gave us the transport arrangements to our stations, sorted out the few Land Rovers between the most needy (or vociferous) of the group, and we proceeded to the examination.

Mr. Powell and I agreed to examine our groups together. My first question was, "what do you do if a man comes to your polling station when he is registered elsewhere?" All too promptly came: "I will call the district head and have him put in jail," to which I had to provide the right answer. And so it went, the examinations revealed that most of the instruction hadn't stuck. Abba Kyari, dignified as ever, haltingly described how to issue a substitute ballot to a registered voter but could not deal with other contingencies. Malam Kyari did better than the rest, most were disappointing. By noon, with the heat holding our heads in its vice, we sternly told our men to read and reread the instructions. This was pitiful advice as there was nothing in Kanuri, and the dry, technical writing of the instructions would challenge anyone from a different culture. "There is a good chance that the plebiscite will collapse in confusion," I wrote in my journal that night, "we all think that the voting procedure is too complicated and are disappointed by the results of the examination."

NORTHERN CAMEROONS TRUST TERRITORY PLEBISCITE
QUESTIONS AND ANSWERS

Q. 1. Who is at present responsible for the government of the Trust Territory of the Northern Cameroons?

A. 1. The Northern Cameroons is governed under a Trusteeship Agreement drawn up in 1946 between Her Majesty's Government and the United Nations. Under this agreement the Northern Cameroons is administered as an integral part of the Northern Region because it is not large enough to be a country on its own. The Northern Regional Government therefore administers the Northern Cameroons as the agent of Her Majesty's Government and the same laws apply in the Northern Cameroons as in the Northern Region. Six Members are elected to represent the peoples of the Northern Cameroons in the House of Assembly at Kaduna. One of these has been appointed Minister for the Northern Cameroons Affairs and a Ministry for Northern Cameroons Affairs has been set up to look after the interests of the people of this area. In addition, Members are elected into the Federal House of Representatives at Lagos to represent the people of the Northern Cameroons in the Federal Government.

Q. 2. Is the Northern Cameroons therefore in exactly the same position as the rest of the Northern Region?

A. 2. Not quite. Because the Governor of the Northern Region has certain powers in respect of the Northern Cameroons since Her Majesty's Government is ultimately responsible to the United Nations Organisation for the well-being of its peoples under the Trusteeship Agreement. When the Federation of Nigeria becomes Independent in 1960 this agreement will have to be revised because Her Majesty's Government will no longer be responsible in any way for the Government of Nigeria.

SUPPER WITH MR. LAWRENCE

I had Ali Roz to myself for the rest of the weekend as my porch mates had left to be with their families. On Saturday afternoon, I caught up with correspondence and read Burke's *Reflections on the Revolution in France*; its cautions about political action seem apt in a Nigeria a year from independence.

Mr. Lawrence knew that I was staying in Bama and kindly invited me to supper. The two other guests were Dixie, who swaggered about with a proprietary air, and my departmental senior, Bill Miller, still with a typhoid-like infection. Dixie served the beer, praising Mr. Lawrence and suggesting that because of the Muslim prohibition on alcohol no African had been asked to join us. "But, you know, although these fellows don't touch the stuff themselves, they don't mind having others do it." Mr. Lawrence left to have his painful boils dressed by the doctor, telling us he would be right back. As soon as he was gone, Dixie shook his head in appreciation of the man as "a real pukka sahib. We'll never see the likes of him, made the fucking Empire, but gets no appreciation here. That man led the Gurkhas in the victory parade down Pall Mall after the war." He rambled on for my benefit about an American he had met not long ago. The story purported to show that not all Yanks were blunderers who took over situations they knew nothing about. (That Yanks were blunderers I had already encountered talking with "old hands" who considered American support for African independence premature and ill-informed.) I preferred hearing Dixie describe the intricacies of smuggling whiskey into Pakistan, but as the evening progressed his anecdotes and memories blended into mostly vigorous interjections.

We sat in the garden by the pressure lamp high on its stool. By day I had seen that the DO's garden was not far from the river; a path led to a flagpole, and from there was a view of furrowed sand hills and the tawny grass and sturdy thorn trees of the savanna. At night due to its slightly raised elevation—maybe fifteen feet above the riverbed—a slight breeze stirred the darkness.

Mr. Lawrence returned, well bandaged, and took the chair next to me. He began talking, not so much to me, although he was saying things that he knew would be of interest, but he seemed to be talking mostly to himself. He had come to Nigeria from the Sudanese civil service, which, after the Indian had been considered the cream of the overseas services. In Sudan the political parties rushed to independence; once achieved, the new government dismissed the expatriate service *en masse*—a decision they later regretted when they tried to rehire the officers. However, "the Sudan run by the Sudanese we trained is run better today than Nigeria by the British. We were not a colony—we worked in cooperation with the Sudanese, and we got things done by means of a highly trained civil service. We had a much closer relationship with the people there; we had to know the language; our practice was always to work with the African civil servants, bring them along with us—they are only beginning to do that here now."

"Nigeria is full of nasty stories," he went on, "anything they can find to say to do a man dirt they will." I thought of the nasty gossip I heard in the school staff room, but Mr. Lawrence meant intrigues within the NA. "I wonder why I keep trying to do something for them. The NAs are riddled with corruption—the system of indirect rule they have here has simply set up an opportunity for corruption to entrench itself in the administration and in the courts. I'm glad to say that I finally caught my treasurer in a £50 extortion; I've been a long time getting him. These people have no idea of service to their fellow man, no conception of duty. The crooks are nice enough people to meet, but the whole older generation will have to go. It is up to the younger generation, the ones in your school, to do something about their country. That seems to me to be the only hope."

As we moved into dinner he told me, "I wouldn't be doing this if I had not a wife and four children to support." Their pictures were on the mantle—four cheery faces, young children and a plump wife. The strain he was under showed when he fell asleep over the soup shortly after we sat down. Later a messenger arrived; he fetched a torch to talk with him outside and returned to the table, not eating at all, intermittently falling asleep and asking questions about me and the US whose answers I knew would not interest him with his unsettling preoccupations. I returned to my porch early, distressed at witnessing Mr. Lawrence's fatigue, but impressed and moved by his dedication and nobleness of purpose.

Dixie shows me Gwoza

For our Sunday off Dixie offered to show me Gwoza where his maintenance depot was located; it was the day for the hill people to come down to the weekly market. We set out early. Dixie, somewhat subdued, sat quietly on the back seat with Kyari Dikwa, a junior staff member at my school, joining us to visit his friend, Shettima, the headmaster of the Gwoza Senior Primary School.

I drove the car slowly into the morning glare. The stretch of road outside Bama was treacherous—great pits in the sand that could wreak havoc with the suspension. "There's been a lot of trouble with this road," said Dixie, "hundreds and thousands frigging pounds overspent. The fuckers pushed the thing right along a route that floods every wet season. The road is useless three months of the year, and it is so damaged after the rains it will have to be rebuilt yearly. Bloody scandal about it." Later I learned that this road was part of a key north-south link in the Cameroons; work had stopped as the construction department had heavily overspent its allotment. Dixie was stationed on his own at a depot to oversee a few maintenance vehicles.

After about four miles weaving and lurching we reached a broad dirt highway that had been graded not long before by one of Dixie's machines. Shortly I saw the sharp outlines of mountains to the south. Africa seems to provoke more of these quick, intense changes of scene—and mood—than occur in temperate places. The hills looked smoky and indistinct; outlined against the sky they looked to have been sketched by an unerring pencil making purple edges that trembled slightly. Dixie said the mistiness was from the *harmattan* wind beginning to blow particles of the Sahara into the atmosphere which from now until February would become increasingly misty with dust.

We were now on a section of the road raised up a few feet above the plain, according to Dixie a vain attempt to keep it from being flooded. The drying out of the rainy season floods made the savanna on either side look as if an army had been through it.

By the villages men with big brooms were smoothing the furrows in the roads made by heavy lorries. As we passed, the foremen doffed their caps of office and saluted smartly, the workers smiled and waved, delighted to see us—why I couldn't imagine, for after we passed they received a cloud of dust raised by the car.

After three quarters of an hour the hills to the south seemed no closer, but the road curved slightly and suddenly we were in an ancient world. It was the foot of Pukka Hill, the northernmost of the mountain chain that stretches from the active volcano Mount Cameroon in the south. Thousands of boulders littered its sides, dark black rocks, not the roughhewn, glacier-broken stone seen in North America or Western Europe; here dark brown, almost black. Some were great oblong slabs, others cube-shaped with slightly rounded corners. On the top of the next peak I saw three enormous rocks piled on each other making a tower, surely by the hand of man, but Dixie said it had been nature's work.

At the mountain's base the rocks were tumbled about; big as automobiles, some were poised on each other. A tall slab stele rested by its narrow edge on a sloping surface seemed about to slide downwards, but in fact it was fixed until the next geologic epoch. Dixie affirmed that these rocks were positioned as erosion had left them "I tried to pull that big tall stone down, but the frigging pagans wouldn't let me. They think the place is sacred. They do little plays in front of those rocks; in some of them a man puts on a white helmet and pretends he's the DO come to maintain order."

I spotted the small maintenance depot amid the boulders at the base of the mountain and near to what looked to be a frontier village, small buildings of concrete blocks, shacks made of a mix of blocks and, grass and whatever else was at hand, rippled aluminum sheeting for a roof. I pulled the car onto a parking lot for large vehicles now littered with empty petrol drums and other debris. In the comfortable shade of a large tree were several horse traders; nearby was a cluster of naked hill people, vulnerable-looking figures peering curiously at the traders from less sumptuous shade. We were in a village improvised around the construction depot, a frontier place at the boundary between the hill people and the Muslims of the plain.

The hill peoples' attention was soon riveted on our car though they were too timid to approach. Several women passed by, bowed beneath heavy baskets of corn on their heads, according to Dixie to be used to make beer. A southern Nigerian came up, apparently the foreman in charge, to tell us that there was to be a big party in the hills that evening, hence the calabashes full of corn for the brew. Judging by the effort the women were making with their heavy burdens, the pleasures of the feast required hard work. Dixie related that one night after an evening of feasting in the hills a clan of men descended with staves and proceeded to beat the parked lorries and earthmovers to make them move, "hitting a Caterpillar the wrong way with a frigging stick to make it go."

The foreman told us that there was a European in the nearby rest house. As Dixie went off to investigate, he warned me not to walk into the native area on the hillside. The Gwoza hills are classified by the administration as an "unsettled area," and strangers must be accompanied by armed police. Too bad, as I was keen for a walk, and the day was pleasant with a light breeze, so I followed Dixie.

The rest house, built for the use of touring officers, was a mud-walled structure with a corrugated iron roof. Inside we found a sickly looking young man and his wife seated at a table. Tins of food were stacked about, magazines and paperback books piled on an adjoining table. There was a small kerosene refrigerator. Mr. Small was an Agricultural Officer from another district here for plebiscite work in the constituency south of ours. He received us in a lackluster manner. He and his wife were others of the lonely ex-pats who take no interest in the surroundings, and indeed, in this case, seem to have sickened.

Dixie accepted his first beer of the day and settled in to talk to the Smalls. I excused myself and went out to look at the hills, restless for a walk, whatever the official restrictions. I found Malam Kyari and Yusufu nearby looking intently at something on the slope of the nearest hill. "Listen sir," said Yusufu, "a pagan is playing his pipe." From the hill we heard a high-pitched noise, a reed flute playing a wandering melody. I scanned the hillside with binoculars and, after prompting by Kyari and Yusufu, spotted the source, a man seated on a boulder with an instrument to his mouth, a Pan! Abba Kyari took the glasses for a moment; he laughed as he picked out another man using a primitive hoe in a plot on a terrace next to a small beehive hut. Kyari had never seen such a sight and was as delighted as a tourist spotting a distant mountain goat.

Yusufu and I walked along the slope. Since the pacification of this area a few of the hill people had dared to farm at the edge of the plain. Here we saw old women picking the corn from the dried-up stocks, isolated figures. Colonial oversight has not succeeded in assuring the hill people that the intentions of their historic Muslim oppressors are now peaceful, but these few had chosen to resettle. There was not an inch of untilled land on the slope. Corn was planted wherever there was a patch of soil. Terraces covered the slope, keeping what soil there was from eroding. With ingenuity and hard work these people had created an agronomy largely on rock and gravel to sustain a large population. As we continued along the track, women in small groups passed us caring corn for the feast. At dusk the hill would become alive with drumming and the villagers would rejoice with the brew until they fell senseless.

The designation "unsettled area" was established to protect strangers from the beer-happy tribesmen, some of whom throw spears in their excitement. According to Dixie, the ADO who regularly tours the hills with a squad of police occasionally separates drunken clans who meet in pitched battle at the height of their respective feasts. A young ADO was murdered in the hills about ten years ago.

Yusufu and I followed a path that led to a cluster of solidly made beehive huts on a ledge above us. A group of young women screamed at our approach and leapt into the tall grass by the side of the path. Their clothing was a leather cord below their bellies; beneath their lower lip were ivory pins. To Yusufu these frightened people with their prominent buttocks, swollen stomachs and rigid breasts seemed alien, but he volunteered that "they is woman, sir."

The first huts we came to were newly made with the bright yellow grasses of the early dry season. At our approach, a mother with a tiny baby strapped to her back quickly disappeared into a hut. All was quiet except for a persistent scratching noise: unfrightened workers unseen by us were tilling the earth and moving rocks with indigenous hoes. Further up we came to a clearing beneath a massive boulder. An old man left his seat on the rock, came forward and prostrated himself, feebly making a fist with his right hand and shaking it in salute. It seemed that he regarded the white shape before him as a superior in the cosmos. I gathered that he was the chief elder of the clan, and I was relieved when his abject welcome was done. Yusufu watched from a distance with an expression of amused tolerance.

From the top of the massive rock I heard a rustle of voices. A group of old men were weaving baskets in the deep shade. They continued the work but chattered at me cheerfully in their language. I talked back in English to which they responded with laughter and additional elaborate greetings. With pointing and gestures we carried on a cheerful conversation. I could have stayed in this Arcadian scene longer, but I knew we had to get back. I waved goodbye—my friends on the boulder delightedly copying my wave, and the more protocol-conscious chief once again got down on his hands and knees in farewell.

Back in the rest house Dixie was several beers in and well into an erratic discussion of the plebiscite with the Smalls. He chided me for disobeying the rules of the "unsettled district," and the Smalls were surprised at my taking any walk at all. They said they had never been outside the house except by car or when Mr. Small had plebiscite duties.

Dixie waxed enthusiastic about the pagans as we took the road south. "Ah, they are good people, very hard working. Good mimics too. You don't have to be in Gwoza a day before a group of them will start walking the way you do and imitating the way you move your face. They can do every white man in Gwoza. Now they call me the oldest resident of the place because I've been here so long. There is only the DO and the Coopers and myself—Cooper is the man who has the job of persuading the people to come down off the hills and settle in the plains. He's been here for years, and he's managed to get 200 of them down, and there are 20,000 just in the hills around here. And then there was Major Holmes. Did you know him?" Dixie assumed that I knew everybody he was talking about. "I miss him—he was the engineer in charge of the road construction and a real pukka sahib—you must have known him." On a market day at the height of the road construction Major Holmes organized the first and only meeting of the Gwoza Sports Association. He put up £100 worth of Becks beer as prizes and piled the bottles in the middle of the sports field. There were potato sack races, relays and all the usual field events. "But then we had a 100-yard dash for the women and the place blew up." Dixie's narrative swirled into the turmoil of the lack of sportsmanship among the unfortunate girls, the

amorous forays of the male contestants, and the bounty of the limitless brew, leaving me to imagine the finale of the Gwoza Sports Association on its first and only day.

Dixie delivered these nuggets as we headed south along a recently completed section of the road, wide and smooth. To the left—east—was the range of mountains, slopes covered with great square boulders and thickly terraced by the farmers. To the right was the Bornu plain stretching to the western horizon. Very few of the hill people had moved to the plain; there were only about a dozen of their huts in the villages we passed at the foot of the hills. I had to slow the car for people heading to the Sunday market at Gwoza. When I pressed the horn the heavily loaded women leapt unnecessarily wide of the path of the vehicle accompanied by hoots of laughter from Kyari and Yusufu in the rear seat.

Gwoza market

Gwoza, the chief market town of the area, is also the headquarters of a district under the jurisdiction of the Emirate of Dikwa in Bama, though none of the population in the hills is Muslim. The district office is a solid brick building containing a jail and a dispensary; the NA office is close to the slope. Looking up revealed a panoramic view of the mountains, the ridges etched against the sky.

English missionaries run a hospital just beyond the town. They, the ADO, Mr. Cooper, the Gwoza resettlement man, and Dixie are the only permanent European residents since work on the road ceased. The African population at the edge of the plain is the kind of motley collection that can be found in towns near borders dividing religion and tribe. Here are the adventurous tribesmen who have left the hills and accepted Islam, now wearing long rigas, but sharing views of the supernatural with the people they no longer outwardly resemble.

Ibos, who come from the Eastern Region, hundreds of miles away, trade and operate canteens in the town. Other southerners are mechanics and shopkeepers. The men in khaki shirts and shorts, the women in Western style dresses, energetically trade here, selling a variety of items and living hard in the hope of making enough money to return home and buy a house. A frontier place like this with a newly developed highway and a mishmash of population offers a promising location for enterprise.

The market at Gwoza was dense with nakedness, the rich black of hundreds of bodies packed into the small concourse of a country market. Women squatted by calabashes of corn and millet, shoppers and onlookers walked about chatting. In the shade more traders displayed trinkets, soap, mirrors, candy, to a throng that was more interested in looking than able to buy. Young girls wearing large rings in their ears and bones piercing their upper and lower lips responded with graceful coquetry as I approached. They looked me over carefully, but with eye contact they giggled and turned away. My path through the market was opened up by the curious who stopped to stare, and when I turned around I discovered I was being followed by a score of captivated children and adults. In the throng there were more women than men, but I saw several splendid patriarchs, one whose bearded face and gnarled features could have served as a model for an elder in the Old Testament. Another fine-looking patriarch proudly walked about in an orange housecoat that had belonged to an English housewife in the 1940s, sold to him by traders who vended discarded European clothing by the bale. It may have looked foolish to outsiders, but he walked about proudly, the orange framing his nakedness.

Dixie invited me to visit his house, a simple mud and brick structure between the market and the hills. This day there was a continuous stream of people heading to and from the market. Dixie extolled the friendliness of the people and told of gifts of food left for him in the past. While he was on plebiscite duty the house was occupied by Mr. Bradburn, an engineer, and his wife. Bradburn rose to greet us from a dining table littered with mystery novels. His wife prepared drinks, beer for Dixie, squash for me. She had arrived from the UK a week or two before. Once the drinks were passed she sat in an armchair, with a desolate expression that reminded me of what I'd seen once in a geriatric ward. Like the Smalls, the Bradburns' faces were untouched by the sun. As we sat saying little or nothing in the shuttered house I found myself remembering the radiant blackness of the market, and, now that my thirst was quenched, it prompted me to go out again. I made the excuse that I would have my lunch outside. Bradburn thought this peculiar, but Dixie suggested a rest house about six or seven miles down the road where I could have a good view of the country from its porch.

I fetched Yusufu from the back of the house where he was visiting the Bradburn servants and headed south along the main road.

At a sign reading "Gwoza Resettlement Scheme" I took a bumpy track to a waterhole set deeply into the earth and surrounded by low hills. A herd of cattle stood about it drinking their fill. Yusufu pointed out the rest house on a knoll overlooking the water. It consisted of two sturdy round huts with thatched roofs joined by a mud-walled corridor. We walked up to it and sat on a shaded stone terrace with a good view of the water hole below and the nearby slopes. While I ate the homemade bread and sardines that Sarke had prepared, I saw human figures moving among the huts on the nearest hill and heard the cattle drinking at the waterhole below. I leaned back against the bole of a small tree rejoicing at the view, the dryness of the air, and the gentle sounds. A cool breeze came up from time to time, adding to a feeling of idyllic peace and refreshment.

A pagan woman with a small calabash on her head like a helmet approached the water. One of the cows, owned by a Muslim herder, stirred slightly and the woman fled into thick reeds. A Kanuri woman, surely by her carriage one of the leading wives of the neighboring village, came to the water to bathe, her stately ankle-length gown rustling as she walked. At the edge of the water she took off her black stole and yellow dress to don a white robe. She stood in the shallow water bathing herself, a Bathsheba.

A gigantic tree on the knoll nearby not only provided shade, but its enormous, twisted open roots made easy chairs, hammocks and backrests for the elders of the village. Several men had come there to sit and talk, although the chief attraction was the white stranger on the terrace. Yusufu identified these as Fulani, eastern members of the famous nomadic tribes whose territory stretches across the savanna lands of Northern Nigeria and west to Mali. After a time, with the help of Yusufu, I paid my respects to a distinguished-looking old man in a deep blue robe at the center of the group. We talked about the weather, the harvest, the plebiscite, mountains—about anything that came to mind. He obviously enjoyed the chat, and I observed an interested, humorous expression on his handsome face. Here on this hillside in restricted "pagan" territory his eloquent speech and bearing suggested a cosmopolitan outlook that was worthy of an experienced diplomat.

In mid-afternoon I took a walk along the track past the village. The light was brilliant and sparkling as on a late September day in a temperate clime. A boy was waiting for me at the car with a bowl of eggs, a generous dozen of them. He said they were the gift of the headman, my distinguished friend of the afternoon, who had ordered them sent to me with his greetings.

When I returned to the Bradburns, Dixie was still drinking and Mr. Bradburn was still sitting with arms crossed at the end of the book-strewn table, his wife remained in the armchair. Dixie said that he had business to do in his depot just up the road before heading back to Bama, but wasn't quite ready to stir. I left to look for Malam Kyari and found him in a compound near the school. It was the house of his friend, Malam Shettima who reclined in an ancient deck chair as he chatted with Kyari. Between them was a box of sweets and a squash-like cold drink thick with glucose which they described as their "feast." Shettima gave me a warm handshake, and forced a handful of mints in his hand when he bade goodbye to Kyari, conveying warmth and affection.

Abba Kyari was delighted with his visit and the expedition. "I could stay here many days and never tire," he said. "I want to see all my country—there is so much to see." During the rest of my stay in Nigeria we took several trips together, and there could be no more passionate and proud tourist than gentle Kyari.

Dixie finally got to the car after vociferous goodbyes to his hosts. We motored to his maintenance depot, quiet on a Sunday afternoon. He promised he would have native beer prepared for us in a few minutes, and left to look at a couple of old Land Rovers that he might bring up north for the plebiscite. When he returned he escorted me through the workers' quarters, past waving children and men who greeted him with smiles. In a large hut, in what Dixie said was the storekeeper's (supply clerk's) compound, we came upon an exceedingly thin old man wrapped in a red and black checked cloth. Dixie introduced him as "Par, the storekeeper." Par indicated chairs and invited us to be seated; in front of us on a tea crate were three tall glasses. Deliberately and delicately Par poured a thick milky brew into the glasses from a teapot with a wire mesh on its spout. The wire mesh kept falling into the glasses, and with a long finger he repeatedly pulled it out. It took some time before the glasses were filled—during which Dixie began a running account of how much of this one could drink without feeling it, how quickly the locals became drunk on it, and folklore concerning other Europeans who drank it. He kept assuring me it was quite harmless, something seemingly confirmed by its innocuous appearance and smell. When the glasses were full, we each held them ceremoniously while Par offered a toast to our health. The brew was almost tasteless and had a faint sting from fermentation, nothing that would encourage or discourage one from having more. Par turned to me gravely and informed me that Major Holmes, he of the Gwoza Sports Association, had always taken this beer in the evening "because it liberated the bowels in the morning time." The major had also affirmed that it made food taste better.

We were joined by two men who drove up noisily in a police Land Rover. With a wry smile, Par asked them to be seated and Dixie boomed out orders that they be given beer. One of them, Dan Fulani, was dressed in RAF fatigues with an RAF cap back to front. He was a handsome fellow in the manner of his tribe and projected a devil may care attitude. He bowed deeply in greeting us, clearly a boon companion to Dixie. "What roguery are you up to now?" Dixie asked. Dan's companion, in the smart-looking blue and gray flannels of the Nigeria federal police, fingered his Enfield rifle nervously, watching from the corner of the hut and refusing any drink. He was Constable Rafael and clearly the proceedings were not appropriate for a policeman on duty. Dan Fulani teased him as a goody-goody and loudly kept up a refrain that "everything" would be all right if he would only "take it easy." Constable Rafael remained standing in the corner with his conscience.

It was a while before Dixie felt like stirring again, but we managed to get underway to reach Bama just before dark. He chortled about "my beer" on the way, but my attention was on the mysterious boulder-strewn mountains in the evening light.

Back to plebiscite duty

Monday at 8:00 a.m. the few AROs who had stayed in Bama over the weekend assembled in the plebiscite office to receive a high official of the UN supervisory staff. If we were asked where the others were we were coached to say that they had "urgent business in the provincial capital" or that they had already gone to the bush. A few minutes after eight a shiny 1959 Chevy station wagon drove up, flying the blue flag of the UN from a pole on its fender. A lesser official came first. He wore dark glasses, canvas shoes, white ribbed trousers and a jersey with a yachting emblem on it, an outfit suggesting a day of tennis rather than an official tour. The high UN official who followed had been an Iranian diplomat. He wore "easy" clothes—a blue sports shirt worn California style outside his belt, maroon trousers and elegant woven leather thong sandals. He doffed his dark glasses as we stood to greet him and smiled a half smile suggesting a relish of life and its challenges. He did not take note of our small numbers and motley appearance but launched into an inspirational talk on the nature of work on plebiscites, something that he enjoyed. "I hope you find this both as interesting and enjoyable as I do. You are not in an area where great delicacy is required, but, nonetheless, the careful handling of this will be a great achievement. Next year we have a plebiscite in the delicate atmosphere of the southern Cameroons. I hope all of you experienced gentlemen will help us there." In conclusion, he paused and smiled his smile again to wish us luck. He then bestowed the blessing of God upon us—I think we all bowed our heads—and in a twinkling was back in the Chevy to visit another sub headquarters.

During the talk a UN Jeep had driven up with Mr. Williams and another observer, a South Korean. Williams quickly attached a flashbulb to his Rolleflex and began snapping the scene; his companion did the same with a Kodak.

To the border village of Banki

After the UN officials left there was scant time for farewells as we were about to leave for the assigned bush stations. At Ali Roz, I found that Sarke had already organized the loads and stowed them on the Land Rover that Pembleton had assigned to take us to Banki. Sarke and I shared the broad front seat; Yusufu perched on a box in the open back. Aliyu, the driver, a tall and dignified man whose massive face was deeply engraved with tribal marks. He had driven the Land Rover from Kaduna, several hundred miles away, and regarded Bama and perhaps me and my party as altogether bush, that is, provincial, inept. He treated us with a slightly exaggerated ceremoniousness, doubtless recognizing that I was a neophyte.

We left the main road directly east of Bama and beat our way cross-country on what was little more than a path made by feet and hooves. The surfaces alternated between soft sand and a tough dried clay that shook the Land Rover despite our weight. Aliyu aimed for speed; at any even stretch he accelerated until forced to brake when the vehicle shuddered onto heat-baked furrows. I feared for the eggs and the crockery—needlessly, as I was to find that Sarke packs so skillfully that nothing ever broke. I didn't know this then and without success encouraged the imperturbable Aliyu to slow down. However, there were times when I could put my feet up on the shelf and enjoy the landscape. The flat country alternated between cultivated fields and profuse thorn scrub. Occasionally we descended a few feet to cross a dried-up riverbed. The villages we passed through appeared well-kept and prosperous, each with a wide main street (*dendal*) shaded by two or more enormous neem trees. Lanes led to family compounds enclosed by fences of woven grass. Children screamed delightedly at the Land Rover and chased it through their villages. When they heard it coming, women ducked into the nearest abode remaining only partly visible as they peeked out at us.

Men dressed in white or blue tunics and women in long dresses worked the fields. The most common crop was guinea corn, although here and there were fields of little white puffs of cotton, a cash crop recently introduced. Outside the villages goat and sheep grazed on the shrubs and drying grasses. Naked small boys tending stringy-haired sheep and small goats waved their sticks and shouted greetings as we passed. When the animals bolted the boys' cheers became commands to restore order.

For stretches there were no cultivated fields, and the flatland seemed to roll on without limit beneath a cloudless sky; with no hills or structures to give a sense of scale, the landscape seemed limitless. The grass was a fading russet; some patches were merely bristles coming out of white sand. Aliyu, seemingly enjoying the obstacle course, left the path frequently to weave around thorn bushes and four and five foot ant hills.

I wondered how this land could maintain stable villages given eight months of dry heat. I'd been told that the soil is unusually fertile, making a yield from a crop grown during the rainy season large enough to support the local population through the dry season and leave some for sale.

Ahead was Banki, the village where I would be spending the next two weeks. Pembleton told me that it had been difficult to select a site for the *rumfa*, or temporary "rest house." The best shade, he explained, was in the new market, but that was too busy and noisy; there was shade across the unmarked border in French territory, but that would be international trespass. He and the NA District Head (DH) chose a spot for the rumfa "right in the town, unfortunately." He said to check in once in a while as he was concerned that I might not be comfortable. (The only means of communication from Banki to Bama was by messenger on horse or foot or by asking a trader with a lorry heading in that direction to take a note.) The DH had ordered the village head (*lawan*) to lay on all necessities for my stay, the hut, food for the staff, horses, guides, firewood and guards. "If you don't get what you need, you give orders. Remember, in the bush, as far as the village head is concerned, you are the DO." I was to remember that, but I never could summon up the confidence to play the part.

Banki, like Bama was within the Kanuri-dominated Dikwa emirate in the Northern Cameroons and administered similarly to Bornu, the NA divided into districts each of which had an appointed head. Here was the system at work: the British colonial officer "advising" the local authority how to run the plebiscite. The NA officials knew about the plebiscite, and there had been no word in Bama of resistance or controversy.

Reflections from the metal roofs of its market sheds showed that Banki was imminent. The path at this point was smooth, and Aliyu put on a burst of speed for our entrance, taking the vehicle through narrow lanes, past thatched roofs covered with green pumpkin vines, stopping at the entrance to a large compound at the edge of the village. An old man at the entrance gate told us that this indeed was the lawan's house, but that he was waiting for me in the "old market." When we arrived there I saw that this space functioned like a village green. The principal village water well attracted a steady stream of women and children. Two neem trees provided deep pools of shade enjoyed by men returned from the fields. Marking one side of the open space was a canteen (shop) with mud walls and a corrugated iron roof, the only modern building in the village. Nearby was a cluster of grass huts that Yusufu told me were drinking and gambling dens, all on the "French," side of the unmarked border. Grass fences defining family compounds lined the opposite side with an open passage leading to the new market. In the center and in the shade of two smaller trees were huts made of woven yellow grass, the rumfa, my home for the next two weeks, in full view of the villagers going about daily routines. At first I was uneasy at the location, but I came to value being at the center of the village life.

The Land Rover pulled up next to the huts and there I was greeted by a loose-limbed man, the lawan, who was making a show of inspecting the construction, resting his stick of office behind his shoulders. Many villagers were watching—the men in the shade of the large trees, small boys, always curious but here kept at a distance by the elders in the lawan's party. I began with an elaborate greeting, but he launched directly into the business at hand. This was to be my rumfa, built by his order he announced in a preemptory tone. I responded that I brought greetings from Mr. Pembleton, and I inquired about the harvest and would have continued, but he clearly wanted to leave me to my own devices. His bearing and impatience showed that he regarded the imposed guest as an annoyance, and I detected the trace of a mocking smile. What did this foretell? His cooperation was essential to the job. Should I follow Pembleton's advice and "give orders?"

I had to settle in. The rumfa consisted of three small huts to be the kitchen and sleeping places for Yusufu and Sarke and two larger huts for me. They were beehive in shape, walls and roofs of thick grass matting. I requested that my two be connected by matting to form a corridor between them. The lawan seemed to consider this peculiar, but clapped his hands, and four workmen appeared with stakes and matting. When I told him they had done a good job, he turned to Yusufu and told him that, "if a white man says it is good, then I know the work has been done well." I took this with the grain of salt with which it seemed to have been delivered, the hidden note of mockery coming through again. I asked him to show me around the village later in the afternoon. This he met with a brisk nod and told Yusufu he would wake me, turned on his heel and left with his entourage.

After the plebiscite Pembleton told me that he had laid out a plot beneath one of the large trees. The lawan instead put it beneath the insufficient shade of smaller trees, hence the shifty, mocking manner. He had played a trick on the DO, perhaps sign of the impending change.

As soon as the loads were off the Land Rover, Aliyu headed back to Bama. I was on my own, with Sarke and Yusufu. On Sarke's advice, the darker of the larger huts was to be the store room and larder. One of the lawan's women came bearing an earthenware pot of water; this we sank into the sand in the dark interior where it kept the eggs moderately fresh and made the drinking water slightly cooler than the air. In the other hut I put the cot, suspending the netting from the matted grass ceiling. The only furniture pieces were the folding table and an aluminum framed folding chair with red canvas that would have been suitable for a suburban patio. It was not long before Sarke covered the table with a blue and white embroidered cloth and served lunch, a steaming dish of hearty soup and an Irish stew. Through the matting I could hear the buzz of the village, animated by the sounds of this strange official and and his party.

When Sarke announced the lawan at four o'clock, I willingly left the hot rumfa to join him and an entourage of about half a dozen village elders. He led us at a brisk pace, shouting back to Yusufu descriptions of what we were seeing.

The new market was a large field with three newly built sheds whose roofs provide shelter from sun and rain. On market day the country people sit beneath the open sky beside their calabashes. The large field and the new sheds witness that Banki had become the market center for an extensive area, but there was something else. A colleague had told me that Banki was one of the only markets where he had seen armed villagers.

With gestures the lawan told us that people also came to the market from French territory. On the "English" side lay the orderly Kanuri village, on the "French"side was the strangers' quarter, a collection of gambling and drinking huts organized by renegade Muslims and people from the hill tribes. Beyond was another small hamlet, also in French territory, which Yusufu described as the "place where the people waiting to go to Mecca lives." Pilgrims to the holy place walk their way across the continent, taking several years for the journey. Those who run out of money stay here for a time, working as agricultural laborers before continuing through Chad and the Sudan to the Arabian Peninsula. Their Imam was a steady, if strident, announcer of the dawn during my stay.

At a far edge of the village the lawan waved his stick to show the extent of the land under cultivation. Women with head baskets filled with flame-shaped cones of guinea corn came from the fields and stopped to kneel to the lawan. Soon we arrived at the dye pits—clay lined holes in the earth where the village dyers dip yards of cheap white imported cloth to transform them to a rich blue. There we were joined by a plump Kanuri woman dressed in a long red robe with the full helmet hair style identifying her as a matron. She smiled as she came up to us, bowed repeatedly and seemed to wordlessly gush. This was startling as I was accustomed to the reticent public behavior of the Kanuri women in Bornu. She joined our tour, a step or two behind the lawan, smiling at my comments. "She is the head of women," Yusufu told me, and hence the only female privileged to walk with the elders. She was in charge of all women's activities which from further questioning, meant that she regulated the activities of the village prostitutes and the parties of the young people. "She regulates the price of the harlots, sir, for a night's company." Other officials included the head of young men, head of the warriors, and heads of other groups that composed the elaborate web of Kanuri society.

A plebiscite Land Rover stood near the rumfa when we returned to the old market. I walked ahead of the lawan to greet its occupant, a large man dressed in a voluminous blue gown who promptly told me he was from the NA on official business. On his upper lip he sported a mustache, the ends of which twirled finely into invisibility. He referred to himself as the "Council for Redevelopment and many other things," punctuating his fluent English with raucous laughter. I told him I was pleased by the rumfa that had been built but had made some changes. He replied that all the lawans in the district had been informed about the plebiscite and would cooperate fully. Turning to the lawan of Banki, who seemed to have shed some of his aplomb merely by being in the presence of this official, he bellowed out a vigorous speech in Kanuri. The nearby villagers began laughing uproariously as the lawan pulled a handkerchief full of shillings from beneath his robe and handed it to the councilor who, laughing said that, "this is in payment for the wood staves that the Forestry Department has provided for the building of your rumfa." He wrote out a receipt and held it out to be countersigned. The lawan had no taste for this and shied away, but the Councilor forced it on him, and he made a quick scratch with a pencil. With a roar of mocking laughter the visitor showed me the line that was all that the lawan could manage for a signature. As he mounted the Land Rover he gave further orders among which was that the rumfa be surrounded by no less than six guards through the night, and that I was to pay no more than seven shillings a day for the two horses I would need.

The vehicle roared off into the fading light; the lawan smoothed his ruffled feathers and bade me good night. The crowd, who obviously enjoyed the display of power, dispersed. The NA visitor had publicly humiliated the lawan, unpleasant to witness, but I could not feel sorry for my intransigent host. In any event, the six guards never materialized, even later when circumstances made their presence necessary. Each morning I found an old man fast asleep on the ground outside my door, wrapped in his gown, like a log beside an extinguished fire.

The First Trek

The next morning I was awakened by the call of the Imam and the braying of donkeys. The rumfa was a spot of quiet amid the sounds of people who are born, work, age and die within sight and hearing of one another. In this moment I lived in public; I stepped out of the hut in a blue bathrobe to look at the dawn. Women from the strangers' quarter and the pilgrims' camp were already at the well to draw water. One jackass chased a female with brays sounding like creaking gates and with pathetic little leaps constrained by his hobbles. Servants in their sleeping robes like shrouded corpses prodded these animals to move them to their masters' houses. Women were starting the days' fires. An unhappy dog, scurried from the kitchen where Sarke had left an opened tin for him. Men stretched by the doors of the huts across the border. The sun rose from beside a large bump to the east in French territory, northernmost of the mountain chain that extends from the southern Cameroons. Framing it were swatches of yellowed grasses on the far bank of the dried-up riverbed.

I enjoyed the contrast between the vastness of nature and the intricacy and warmth of the human life in the village. No one took notice of the stranger in pajamas and dressing gown, a sign of acceptance.

This morning I was hesitant, much less used to Banki than it to me. I didn't know how much I could be outside or how much I should keep to myself. Back in the hut I was confined by its darkness and the exclusiveness that surrounds the European in this land. Sarke brought morning tea, steaming in its aluminum pot. I drank cups of it and opened my notebook to resume notes interrupted over the past few days by the conviviality on the Ali Roz porch.

The morning was comparatively cool, enjoyable in contrast to the searing heat of the middle of the day. The custom of the country is to travel in this coolness, leaving the hot time of day to rest. I wanted to use these early hours for writing and told the lawan to bring the horses after 9 AM. He had received this with a critical look, and so he was teaching me a lesson when the horse arrived at 7 a.m., and I heard the horse boy greeting Sarke and Yusufu and the animal leaping about, whinnying and snorting as though preparing for a great occasion. Could I take him on? I had not ridden for over two years.

Sarke announced that this was the party for the day's trek all was ready to start. I went out to bid good morning and to observe the horse making the spirited sounds. He was a jet-black stallion, not tall, as is usual in this country, but with a fine wide chest. Just as I came out, the horse that was to carry Yusufu arrived, and the stallion leapt as if given an electric charge, all four hooves left the ground at once. He began another powerful series of whinnies and snorts, waving his head back and forth in grand style. I asked the horse boy about him and admitted that I was not an experienced horseman. Mustapha was a short, lithe man who assured me everything would go well and that this horse was obedient, true enough as I was to find. The sharp native bit can control him. This is an unpleasant looking piece of steel that when the reins are pulled its sharp edge cuts into the horse's mouth. Though they prance and jump about, these horses fear the cruel bit and will only go so far. The Kanuri are great horsemen; they ride in a flashy manner pushing the horse to perform. Their most famous trick is to gallop at top speed towards a person to whom the rider wishes to pay homage; just before running into him, they pull hard on the reins to make the horse stand nearly erect on hind legs and paw the air over the honored person. This skill is achieved by the cut of the bit into the horse's mouth.

I gingerly mounted and sat in the enormous seat, which resembled an American Western saddle. The stirrups have small metal platforms for the feet with sharp edges to be used as spurs. A blanket covers the saddle making it initially seem comfortable, but its framework tormented the pelvic bones until I got used to it. My anticipation of a balky ride was groundless; throughout the day the black stallion was as placid as a donkey.

We were to visit two outlying villages to lay out polling stations. Our guide was Wakilie, assigned by the lawan, a man in late middle age with prominent front teeth and a ready smile. He walked barefooted with a slight limp, using a steel tipped spear as a staff. Mustapha, the horse "boy," followed on foot with his gown thrown over his shoulder, a joy to watch him go on mile after mile for all his middle years as lightly as a young boy. Third came Yusufu wearing a wide brimmed straw hat that looked like a sombrero. He sat round-shouldered and listless on a brown and white horse, but when the occasion demanded, he showed himself a capable horseman. Next was the barefoot bearer carrying a box containing manuals and forms for the plebiscite. I called him the Porter, a heavy-set man with a bushy mustache in the manner of a Victorian bar keep. The previous afternoon this fellow barged in as I talked with the lawan to offer his services as a bearer. Imitating the military, he saluted at a brace repeatedly as he waited for my reply. He was also skilled at executing brisk, military turns and about faces, though his body leaned at an angle as his feet were slower than his torso for the maneuver. The lawan had laughed at the suggestion that he be my bearer. Hiring him was probably another joke played on me, but if I had been experienced enough to reject him, I would have missed the fellow's good humor and enthusiasm—at least until drink got the better of him. He carried on his head a cardboard box labeled "*SS Fiernfiord*–STOW," a reminder of seas and temperate lands. In addition to plebiscite materials it contained a thermos flask of hot tea (which in later days I changed to fresh lime juice or water), two wine bottles of water wrapped in a towel, and a Tetley Tea box. On this last was an artist's conception of "our Ceylon tea plantation," showing men in pith helmets weighing and inspecting tea leaves brought by half naked workers from the fields. In this Sarke put two homemade rolls stuffed with crab meat or sardines for my lunch. I brought up the rear on the black stallion wearing US Army combat boots, khaki shorts (until my knees became red from the sun), an ancient shirt, and a gray rollaway hat from Moss Bros., London. I tried to hide the uncertainty I felt and appreciated that the diplomatic Mustapha and Wakilie took no apparent notice of it.

The day was sunny with a layer of blue haze on the horizon. Through this blueness the hills to the south appeared to be distant mountains, always to be a welcome sight on the home journey. The sky was streaked with thin clouds, as though a filmy substance had been stretched delicately across its surface. From the plain came a breeze that offered relief in the sun and made the shade delicious. On that flat land the sky took on a vastness that reminded me of the sea.

We headed for Tamawa along a track bordered by fields of tall guinea corn stalks set to dry. Villages showed up on the horizon like islands, the light brown of the corn and the scrub interrupted by a patch of dense green, the trees shading the dirt streets. Just so Tamawa appeared in the near distance, and villagers working the fields looked up at the strange procession and waved us on.

The main street seemed deserted, though as we passed women and children peered from compound doors. At the lawan's gate a young man welcomed us and went to fetch our host. Mustapha unsaddled the horses and let them roll in the dry sand while Yusufu and I waited in the shade. The lawan, an energetic old man, greeted me with great politeness. We shook hands, and he touched his breast in the Islamic custom. After each of my translated sentences he spoke the Kanuri version of "all is well" and clapped his hands in assent. He led us to a tree just outside the village, the only shade beyond the main street. Using the plan in the plebiscite manual, I paced out the polling station, defining the area to be fenced in as a waiting area, and siting the booths to be used for casting the ballot and another for searching voters if needed, both to be framed in to ensure privacy. As the election officers would be on duty throughout the day, their booth needed to be roofed. Construction required wooden posts and grass matting, the latter standard for village fencing. The lawan's workers vigorously attacked the soil to make the post holes. As this began Yusufu and I were shown to a small, low hut to "rest;" this was the rest house surviving in many villages originally put up for touring officers in the heyday of colonial administration. Although it was cool and the sand soft and clean, the dark interior was confining, and I resolved next time to take "rest" (always expected from hosts) beneath a tree.

When I'd had enough "rest," Mustapha saddled the horses and the procession resumed. The lawan escorted us to the edge of the village and wished us a safe journey with more of his gentle clapping.

At Mageribu its lawan seemed to have qualities of discretion and leadership beyond his years. The elders came along as I laid out the polling station beneath a magnificent tree at the edge of the village. These elders were noble looking farmers, faces molded by the labor and regularity of their lives. They listened attentively as I explained the voting procedure, but they looked concerned. One old man spoke up to request a new well. "At present the women must walk five miles for water during the dry season and because of this lack of water people are leaving the village." The lawan, aware that I had nothing to do with such matters, and no doubt embarrassed by the outburst, gestured the man into silence. (I mentioned the complaint to the DH the next day. Later I learned that he had immediately dispatched a messenger to reprimand the village lawan for permitting such an outburst.)

I spent the middle of the day beneath the tree chosen to shade the polling place, seated on a mat the lawan had sent. He extended to Yusufu, Mustapha, Wakilie, and the thirsty Porter the hospitality of his compound where the servants laid out mats and gave them sweet water and corn meal. Beneath the tree I enjoyed the dry breeze that carried away perspiration before it could bead. I took off the heavy boots and sat cross legged on the mat to eat Sarke's rolls and drink the filtered water from the *SS Fiernfiord* box. I noticed a pair of children peering at me through stalks of guinea corn. I shifted position self-consciously, but a little girl went into her hut and returned with a knife which she used to cut down the stalks to see me better. Her mother rushed out to pull her away, not before the better part of the stalks were down.

I read in the shade until the middle afternoon when the party reassembled. The lawan presented me with a most-welcome half-dozen eggs, which I added to the *SS Fiernfiord* box for the return. We set off to Banki, this time with the opalescent mountain to the south a beacon.

A mile from Banki my mount, hitherto lazy, began switching about and whinnying. He bucked when I reined him in, tentatively applying the knife-like edge of the native bit. I gathered up courage and decided to let him have his head. Off we went at a gallop. With one hand clutching the pummel and the other holding my hat, I'm sure my face showed intense concentration. The horse mingled the gallop with plunging and noble sounds. There was no consistent rhythm, nothing to do but hold on and suffer the pounding. With a flourish we tore into the old market of Banki, and my horse, realizing we were home, pulled up in front of the rumfa to the cheers of the men beneath the trees. Sarke "master now do savvy horse," and took the animal to a tether. I walked about a bit to stretch my saddle bound legs. I would not again be timid about riding.

The rumfa was hot so I brought the chair outside and sat reading and sipping squash until nightfall. The village paid no notice, which made me think I had been accepted as a temporary fixture. I watched the evening activities, the women's visits to the well, children with their hoops, animals being driven. I sat in the dark until the trader who sold French cigarettes and candy near the canteen blew out the lights on his table. It was time for a wash and dinner.

Sarke brought a pan of hot water, and by the light of the pressure lamp I took the sponge bath that was all I could manage, not equipped as the old timers were with a portable bath. When I was through with my wash, Sarke brought in his version of brown Windsor soup. Over dinner I read back numbers of English newspapers and, later, Basil Davidson's recent book on the history of the ancient African kingdoms. I noticed that Sarke was avoiding something on the floor as he came in and out in bare feet. With a broad grin he told me, "They do be plenty little frogs, plenty!" The rays of the pressure lamp had attracted scores of tiny frogs. They formed a circle beneath the lamp to catch insects that fell, burned by its heat. I soon became accustomed and too avoid stepping on them—a few handclaps would clear a route.

That night I dreamt that a small man in a black robe was doing all in his power to oppress me. He had almost succeeded in dominating me until I joined him in battle. I stabbed his eyes with my knife; he disappeared and my knife was left sticking into two frogs.

A REGULAR MARKET DAY

Wednesday was market day, drawing from villages in English territory and from across the border. At dawn people streamed past the rumfa, women bent under loads of foodstuffs, boys pulled goats and long-haired sheep and men prodded heavily laden donkeys. Animated noises filled the air. The night before three lorries had rumbled in, their motors sounding like slowly descending airplanes. These were the first lorries of the dry season to reach Banki, the tracks had been too soft for large vehicles for the past five months. They brought traders peddling candy, pomades, beer, tools, and other manufactured items.

After breakfast, I started to make notes before trekking or visiting the market. Shortly Sarke interrupted, announcing that "the emir" was outside to see me. I was surprised that so important a person had come to Banki with little fuss, but outside I realized this was the chief NA official of the district, the District Head (DH). Sarke used the august term to mean an influential man. The DH was short and slight, filled out with yards of blue cloth embroidered with yellow thread on the front and back. His retainers discreetly moved away to allow us to talk. He accompanied a greeting with a nervous laugh as he took off large reflecting sunglasses in which I briefly saw myself. He had a welcoming expression and began a stream of speech in excellent English, punctuated with laughter and accompanied by delicate hand motions. He told me with an engaging smile that he had attended courses at the Institute of Administration at Zaria. "Oh, yes ... twice." He recited the development projects for the district, the market sheds in Banki were prime examples, and he spoke with pride of the excellent education offered by the school at district headquarters. (I later learned that the school had been burned down some time before and was run by a drunkard.) He said he came every week to Banki to regulate disputes that took place on market day, leading me to the chair he used to dispense justice beneath the great tree. He then summoned the lawan of Banki to come up to us; before his superior the lawan barely altered his slightly mocking expression. The DH proceeded to give orders concerning the care to be taken of me, all of which he repeated in English. One was to place six guards around the rumfa at night; others had to do with supply: horses, water, and food for my assistants. Without changing his expression the lawan agreed to everything. (There never were the six guards, and later I had to push to get adequate food for Sarke and Yusufu.)

The DH ended our meeting by announcing that he needed rest before sitting in council. He handed me over to an elderly man, introduced as the lawan of Buduwa, the first village I would visit that day. The old man bowed and clapped his hands in appreciation of the forthcoming visit and said he would escort my party.

To Buduwa and Mbaga, conversation,
chance encounters, splendor

The lawan of Buduwa led our procession on a handsome brown stallion. The winds rising off the plain excited his horse into bursts of speed; at times the *lawan's* turquoise robe, billowing behind him became a distant mark. My animal realized he could be lazy with me and plodded along at a pace that made me envious of the grace and assurance of the elder on his mount.

Buduwa was farther than the villages of the day before. We followed a narrow track through scrub savanna to reach it by late morning. The elders were assembled and gathered in a circle around our party. They greeted with gentle applause nearly every word that Yusufu translated. The lawan's son was an exceptionally tall young man who made me think of the giants that by legend preceded the Kanuri near Lake Chad. With him I laid out the polling station at the edge of the village, and he supervised the construction.

Back at the lawan's compound I found one of the locally made deck chairs being readied. This one seemed to wobble under its own weight; its canvas had been replaced by mangy-looking cowhide. I knew that as a European guest it was my duty to sit in such a contraption, and I did so, after which an elder pulled out the footrest, and I stretched out to "rest" under the watchful eyes of the senior citizens of Buduwa.

After this public rest we moved on through deserted bush to Mbaga. Quite suddenly by noon the sun feels immensely strong; the heat pulls energy, and despite myself I sat listlessly on the horse and let him plug along. There was not a word of complaint from Wakilie, the Porter, and Mustapha, though they surely knew that it was foolish to travel in the middle of the day. They took long strides, barefooted on hardened clay that must have been searing to the skin. The route alternated between desolate scrub and tiny oases of deep green that indicated water near the surface.

Mbaga was deserted save for a few children and the lawan and his retainers; everyone else had gone to the Banki market. The lawan was a powerful-looking man whose expression indicated intelligence and humor. He had been expecting us and invited me to spend the midday day rest in the village rest house. I looked into the dark interior of the hut and told him I preferred to sit by his compound to catch any breeze that came. If he was surprised, he made no sign, and soon a servant brought out a mat. Then two servants gingerly brought from the compound a deck chair, kept available for a European visitor. As I carefully sat, the skins ripped and gave way. I told the lawan I would sit with him, cross legged on the mat. And, to give my feet a rest, I took off my US combat boots. Through Yusufu I chatted with my host, asking about the harvest, water, the track we had taken, the DO and other European officers. He knew a good deal about the district and the movement and characters of the plebiscite officers. "There is one old man at Kumshe, he no be happy. He no like bush." Aha! Williamson was at his station. When conversation failed we communed in silence in the deep shade of a neem tree with a light breeze from the *dandal*. Children peered out of doorways at the stranger; at the end of the street a naked little boy rolled a barrel hoop, the only animation in the village that afternoon.

Refreshed by the shade and by the lime juice and water from the thermos flask and the old wine bottles, I leaned against the fence that surrounded the lawan's house, feeling at peace, reflecting on how remote I was from modern life and its ever present combustion engines. Then came just such a sound, and shortly an Opel station wagon moved slowly down the dandal. My reverie was done, I got up to look. The car was tipped back on its rear axle, heavily loaded with boxes and Jerry cans for gasoline and water. It stopped at the unexpected sight of a white man suddenly appearing in this village; on the front seats were three young Frenchmen in short shorts, tennis jerseys, sandals, and dark glasses. Through the open window the driver told me that they had come from French Cameroons following the dried up riverbed by this village. And before that? They started in Brazzaville in the French Congo several hundred miles away and were heading to Algiers across the Sahara. The first bad road conditions they had met were in the last 15 miles in "English" territory. The driver never stopped the motor; we shook hands all around, and I pointed out the track to Bama. Off they went on the next segment of a journey that would cover two thirds of the continent. They may have been as surprised to get directions from an American as I was by their sudden appearance in Mbaga.

Shortly there came the sound of another vehicle. A Land Rover pulled up bearing the logo of the Muslim NPC, the dominant political party. Five imposing Kanuri men descended, led by a tall, sallow man, who spoke excellent English. In a slightly mocking tone he told me that they had been on a tour through the hills behind Gwoza and had taken a back way to Bama. They were politicking—no speeches, he said, consultation with the village leaders. He looked me over, eyes taking in my bare feet, and concluded I was a neophyte. "You must be suffering if you have been touring and are unused to the bush." I replied that I was enjoying myself. The others, who had been talking with the lawan, announced that they must leave to reach Bama before dark. In the back of the Land Rover I saw an impressive lineup of shotguns. Are these for game? There was a neutral "yes" in response. The driver started the vehicle with a roar, ratcheted up the gears as he rushed the vehicle out of the somnolent village. These are very important people, the lawan told me through Yusufu.

It was now the late afternoon when the sun casts its rays across the land. The shrubs, huts and trees resumed three dimensions after being flattened by the sun directly overhead in the middle of the day.

Yusufu told me that the lawan wished to accompany us part of the way to Banki. As his entourage gathered outside his compound, I noticed that one man carried an ancient muzzle-loaded flintlock musket; a powder horn hung from one shoulder and a pouch filled with lead shot from the other. When I asked him if this gun had ever killed, he replied with a smile "many things." Another carried a long spear in one hand, a bow slung over a shoulder with a quiver of arrows.

On horseback the two armed men led, I following on my black stallion, restless in the distracting new company, then the lawan and four of his elders, all in their best robes and riding handsome steeds. Wakilie and the Porter with the *SS Fiernfiord* box on his head followed and Yusufu brought up the rear, riding confidently beneath his wide-brimmed straw hat.

The angled sun invested the savanna with rich color, sharp shadows and heightened detail. My companions seemed to glow as the light brought out the essence of the colors of their clothing and equipment. Their dark brown skin, always handsome, seemed imperishable. Everything bespoke grandeur and nobility, a momentary revelation of Africa's beauty.

We passed Mbaga villagers returning from the Banki market. Women with baskets or calabashes on their heads moved to one side, gave me a quiet greeting and knelt to the lawan. After what sounded like a ritual exchange of courtesies, he shouted out hearty jokes greeted by the women's laughter. Among the returning villagers were men with spears and bows and arrows and a few with muskets like the man at the front of our column. As a colleague had told me, it was only in Banki that he noted villagers coming to market armed. If thieves were watching the motley procession from the shrubs they stayed put. At he halfway point, the lawan took his leave. I felt honored that he and his men had chosen to accompany us, adding to the bond formed on the convivial afternoon visit on the mat by his compound. I looked forward to seeing him again when inspecting the completed polling station in a few days.

My horse nearly danced the last two miles, whinnying fervently even at a donkey coming from the market and breaking into a sideways step when another horse passed. When Banki came into view he began a leaping gallop, which, despite my attempts to slow him down, carried me exuberantly through the nearly deserted market with no damage to person or property. As the day before, he halted without bidding at the rumfa.

After changing clothes I moved the folding chair outside and sat sipping lime juice and water, exhilarated by the day's experience. African tableland with apparently insignificant vegetation can be surpassingly beautiful in the evening light. I treasured the long afternoon and the often-wordless visit with the Mbaga lawan and the splendor his retinue leant to our return.

In failing light the last of the market people headed across the border, laboring under sewing machines, pulling reluctant goats and cattle. Some traders stopped for the pagan brew in the huts across the way. Arguments and scuffles sounded through the night.

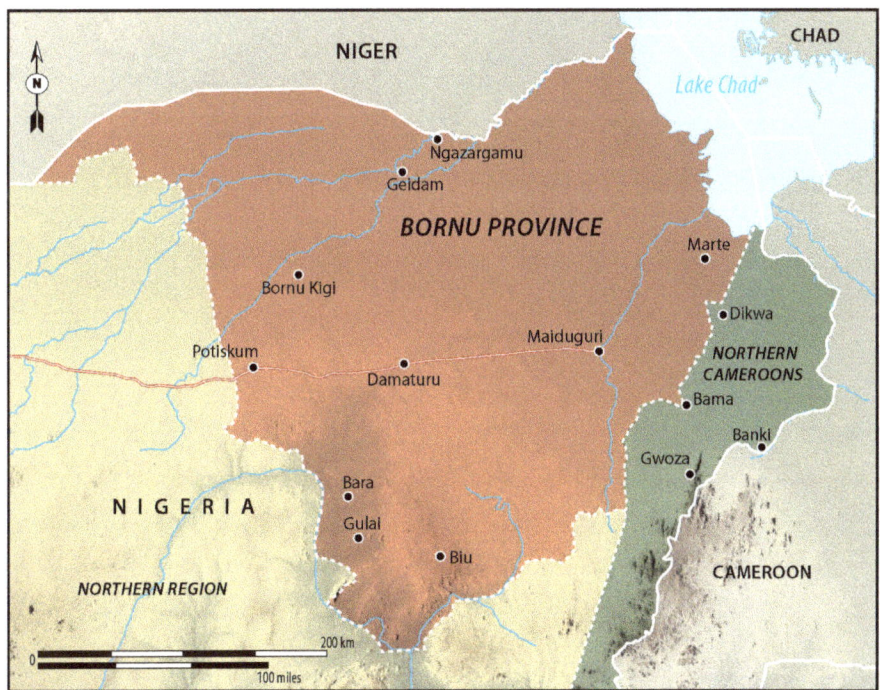

An international expedition

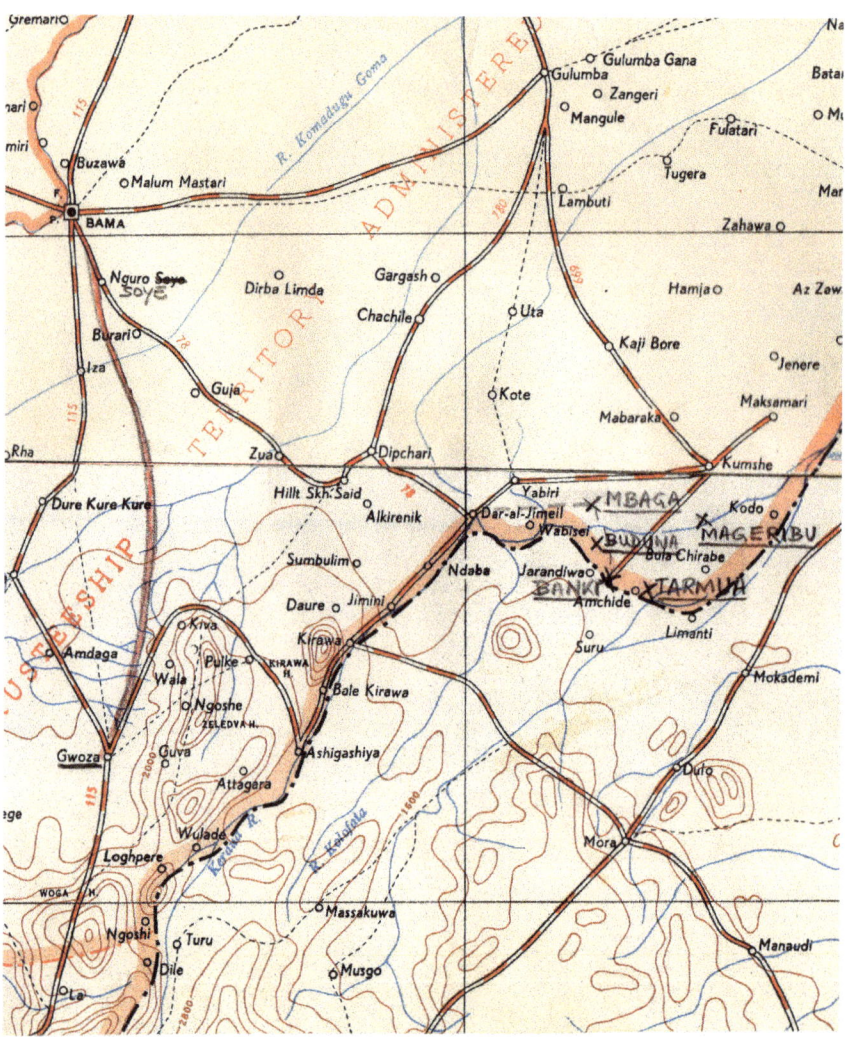

This is the map supplied me in Bama. The heavy line shows the border between "English" and "French." At the lower right is Mora, the nearest French town. The border with French territory follows a riverbed. This section of a much larger map was almost unusable. I relied on local guides to get to the villages whose names were underlined.

The next day I crossed that unmarked border to "French" anticipating exotic cultural differences. What do national boundaries mean in Africa? None of my colleagues had crossed the border, and only knew hearsay. According to Yusufu, there was some danger involved; villagers told him that the savanna between here and Mora, the nearest inhabited place in "French," was known for its thieves. Locals would not pass that way unarmed and never at night. The plebiscite officers in Bama had agreed that I might cross over but at my own risk, warning not to "get knocked on the head."

We started just after sunrise heading to the southwest along a path made by feet and hooves through desolate, uninhabited country. We were the same trekking team, Wakilie, Porter, Mustapha, and Yusufu and me on horseback. The path was beaten hard as concrete by the sun; great cracks in the surface showed the quagmire it had been during the rains when there could be a foot of water above saturated soil. Now the sun had evaporated all moisture, leaving large fissures. The path skirted trees, but there were thickets, a few so dense that I had to dismount so as not to be scraped off the horse. Most of the country was open, and I looked in vain for the animals whose tracks crisscrossed ours in all directions.

The only human we came across was a man seemingly contemplating a dead leaf in a thicket. According to Yusufu he had dropped his bow and arrow and assumed the disarming pose when he caught sight of us. So at least we had glimpsed one of the promised thieves.

By midmorning we reached a north-south road, broad and scraped smooth by heavy mechanical equipment. It was shown as a straight line on my map, and I headed south toward hills outlined on the horizon. The road was mostly level with slight undulations, easy walking but now beneath a relentless sun. We kept on for an hour without seeing a person or a vehicle. I dismounted from time to time to refresh muscles stiffened and hurting from the punishing native saddle. At last there were people, an old man and a boy burning brush by the side of the road. Yusufu tried many languages to find out the distance to the nearest village. The old man was uncomprehending, and I realized we had crossed into a territory where none of our tongues was understood. So the border meant something; it seemed magical, a few hours at a walking pace brought us to a foreign land. We shortly came to another burning party, people smaller-limbed than the tall Kanuri. One had a few words to exchange with Yusufu, although the report was confusing. The man had never heard of Mora but, even so, "it is too far." (Yusufu may have been editing his own feelings into the translation.) In any event, it was time to have a break. There was shade beneath one of the few large trees we had seen in this benighted landscape.

The horses were thirsty and tired, but my companions showed no sign of flagging. I was desperately thirsty. We passed around the filtered drinking water. I drank what may have been a quart, but my companions took the water moderately, seemingly only as a courtesy. I noticed that old Wakilie was staring intently up the road. The speck was a solitary person walking toward us; with the binoculars I saw it was a woman, clad in black, striding along with a calabash on her head. Although she was nearly a quarter a mile away, and it was time for us to resume the march, I decided to hold up. Someone who could stride so briskly under the midday sun was worth waiting for. When she was within a few yards, Yusufu exclaimed, "That woman be Shuwa." She came into the shade, put the calabash down and squatted beside Yusufu and Mustapha. She had the sallow skin of the Shuwa Arab and scars from the tribal markings on both sides of her face. Her hair fell around her head in the loose strands fashionable among these far western cousins of the Arabs. She smiled at my greeting, not shy or surprised. Yusufu found language in common and told me that for the past day and a half she had walked from Kala, about 30 or more miles to the north. She intended to sell the contents of the calabash in French territory. The next village was "not far," and we could get the information we wanted there.

I will never know why this strong woman had left her people to stride across the deserted plain to a small village in the French Cameroons or if she intended to return. She was strikingly independent, and I sensed humor in her exchanges with Yusufu. It was humbling to realize I would never know who she was or where she was going or what she thought of her life, much less her response to this chance encounter. We resumed at a faster pace, and I looked back several times at the resolute walker as her silhouette gradually faded. I felt deprived when a slight incline hid her from view.

"Not far" turned out to be a distance that dried my mouth and thoroughly cramped the joints that gripped the belly of my flagging mount. Shortly after noon, on a rise by a rocky hill, I saw a reflection from what must be a metal roof. Here at last was a place where there would be shade and water for the horses and a settlement. A boy came toward us on a bicycle, only the second traveler we had seen on the magnificent highway. I spoke to him in French, and he answered with the same. Yes, this was the border village. It was not Mora, but there was a customs house. Yes, there is a European who lives here—his house is near the reflecting roof.

The next quarter of a mile was not easy, but it was forgotten when I reached the cool shade of the customs house porch. As soon as the saddles were off, the horses rolled luxuriously in the dry sand beneath the trees of the *Douane*; I distributed shillings to Mustapha, Wakilie, and the Porter for food and drink.

The village was a small place on a rise; its chief function was customs control. Directly above us a hill was littered with angular rocks like those in Gwoza, tumbled by the centuries; to the south hills multiplied into the distance. Nearby beside the barren road were three or four concrete block commercial buildings and a few straw huts. The village center was indicated by two trim concrete buildings, one marked *L'Ecole* and, where I sat, *Douane*. The tricolor of France flew from the flagstaff in front of the porch. No pedestrians or vehicles awaited inspection in either direction.

The four customs inspectors seated at their ease on the porch waved me to join them. They were Cameroonians from the coastal south wearing US Army khaki uniforms with French emblems of rank on sleeves and breast pockets; their snappy French pillbox hats sat on a table, unworn due to the heat and an absence of traffic. All four wore large dark glasses, ceating the look of a movie festival. Their French was excellent, and we struck up a conversation that was as lively as my halting ability in the language could make it. They had barely heard about the plebiscite to be held a few miles from their post and knew nothing of the choices involved. They had all been to *lycées* in the south, and were otherwise politically knowledgeable and *engagè*. The youngest of the group deplored the recent victory of the Conservative party in the British general election. He asked me to help him understand "how a people could reject socialism in a time like this." He went on to condemn Britain's role in the world today. The senior of the four, a mild-mannered fellow, smoking a long iron pipe, questioned me me carefully about the traditional Muslim rulers of Northern Nigeria: were they not "reactionary, feudal?" All spoke contemptuously of *"la guerre politique"* going on in the south of Cameroon, but viewed with equanimity the independence to come in January. Our congenial talk didn't break up until early afternoon. These knowledgeable (and underemployed) civil servants were a striking contrast to their sleepy NA counterparts in Northern Nigeria. They were *évolué*, speaking and thinking like Frenchmen as their education had encouraged.

The young socialist offered to take me to a cotton factory nearby which was run by a European. We drove to a large open shed sheltering a modern cotton gin in the process of installation, workers sprawled about on lunch break, machinery and building materials awaiting installation. My guide took me to the house nearby, a rectangular white concrete structure, canopied by a new aluminum roof whose reflection we had spotted earlier. He doffed his splendid Gendarme cap and dark classes to knock on the door. A short, elderly Frenchman opened the door, greeted me and invited me in without acknowledging my guide who went off with my thanks. Inside were Europeans, two men, a woman and child seated at a table, concluding lunch with bread, cheese and wine. The room was white and cool, I could have been in the south of France. I shook hands all around; the men were engineers setting up the cotton gin, the woman the wife of one, her daughter, a pretty child of about eight. The man who had opened the door introduced himself as *"le patron"* and told me twice that he came from Paris and only spent a few months of the year in Africa. The woman put into my hands a metal cup of deliciously sweet lemonade and laughed with the others at the speed with which I drank it. She gave me all I could drink. When the door of the electric refrigerator opened it displayed a variety of fresh vegetables. It seemed miraculous; nothing like this was available in Bornu. She made me a Roquefort sandwich while I told the company what I was doing and how I happened to drop in. The cheese was the first I had eaten since leaving French territory on my way to Nigeria weeks before—it tasted the rarest thing imaginable. My French seemed to improve at once.

Soon the engineers left and the patron offered to show me around the factory. He was delighted to learn that I was an American as he announced proudly that the cotton gin came from the state of Georgia, and did I know of its manufacturer? He described each step of the carding process as it would be performed and proudly pointed out that local men, referred to as "peasants," had built the shed and were assembling the machine under the supervision of the engineers; no laborers had to be imported from the more advanced south. He enthusiastically showed off the machinery and almost tiptoed in awe of a gigantic steam turbine in a separate room whose flywheel evoked an earlier industrial age. "This was a bargain, outmoded in France, but splendid here!" The patron was so pleased by my interest in his project he commanded a young African waiting outside to bring around his car to drive me to Mora. "*Oui, patron,*" corresponded to the "yes, master" of English Africa. The patron was happy to send me to visit the *sous-prefecture* of Mora, "although you will find very little there to interest you." "An English car, too!" he said with a twinkle as a splendid long Land Rover pulled out of the garage. "I much regret that this gin is so small. I wish I could send you 76 km south where there is one that is *formidable!*"

The patron instructed the chauffeur to show me the post office, the dispensary, the school, and the market—though the last was not open today. Curiously, I found I was as excited by the prospect of seeing this sous prefecture as I had been when visiting a new city as a schoolboy.

It was only a few kilometers to Mora through barren and deserted land. We passed a small group of naked hill people making their way on foot. There was only one horseman on the road to remind that it was still the north. There were hills on each side with great loose rocks scattered about on slopes scraped by a mighty river in geologic time, or at least that's how I imagined the transformation. After the narrow lanes in British territory, the untrafficked road was impressive, laid out on a continental scale, mastering the landscape in its broad sweep.

Mora lay at the base of one of the ancient hills. In its center were official buildings designed in the Moorish style with arched porticos.

These backed onto the slope, giving the place the feeling of a mountain barracks town.

It was now 2:50, the hour when officials in "English" would be driving home from their offices for drinks at the club and an afternoon nap, but French officialdom took the siesta during the heat of the day, and the buildings were still closed, looking strangely as if they had been empty for months. Soldiers in US Army khaki shorts and short sleeved shirts lounged about. They looked trim and potentially alert, but I suddenly missed the decaying old men in long robes that hang about the administrative buildings in Bornu. The bulletin boards on the walls of the sous-prefecture were covered with laws and edicts on many subjects, assuming a high level of literacy. Mora was a border town, an administrative outpost in the hills, and after the concentrations of humanity in the Muslim cities of Nigeria, it seemed cold and lonely.

The town's layout was splendid, however: great avenues lined by trees; a sports field and concrete signs identical to those on national routes in France. I had only a few minutes so I followed a sign to *L'Ecole*. About 100 boys and girls aged 8 to 12, were playing in front of a pair of single story classroom buildings. There were no uniforms; they wore their own clothes, some fairly shabby, about an equal mix of boys and girls. I asked for the headmaster and was shown to a small office from which emerged a young man wearing a loud sports shirt, short shorts and a pilot's dark glasses. He led me from classroom to classroom: "here the children study geography," the maps and photographs showed that the Mediterranean was the subject of the week; "here is history," on the wall a poster of Chennceaux glowing in autumn light; the language room had Fontaine's fables as text, and so on.

A bell rang somewhere, and the children's play quickly ceased. Three young teachers appeared dressed in the same style as the headmaster and conveying an air of nervous energy. They marshaled the children in lines by class who on command marked time in the military manner, marching in place, singing vigorously. At another command the classes smartly marched to their respective rooms, led by a teacher. It showed high spirits and drive, as I told the headmaster in thanks, a lively display of French colonial education.

It was late in the afternoon, and we had to leave if we wanted to reach Banki before dark. At the cotton factory *M. le Patron* sent me off with another reminder to visit the cotton gin 76 km away, "that would be really worth the trip." Mustapha and Wakilie had the horses saddled; the Porter was just off the boil, and though he swayed a bit beneath the *SS Fiernfiord* box, he was able to keep up. The party moved along briskly, no longer contending with the sun.

We started too late. Darkness overtook us in the wasteland between the road and Banki, I was confused by the crisscrossing paths picked out by the flashlight on our route, but Wakilie always chose correctly. Riding into the African darkness is not an experience for the eyes alone; the dark envelops everything; one's whole being in its embrace. There are no vehicle lights or reflections from cities to dilute its darkness. On this night there was light above: the sky was covered with stars.

At the dried-up riverbed in Banki a horse neighed; it must have been a mare, as my stallion, suddenly revived, jumped in the soft sand and whinnied. From the village came domestic noises—animals, cooking, chatter, and laughter. Yusufu rode ahead; all of us ahead of the Porter, who staggered along in the darkness. Observing my companions as they crossed the sandy riverbed beneath the sky with its pinpoints of light, I remembered a picture in my bedroom as a child. It showed three Arab men armed with long, slim rifles, watering their horses at a stream. The image had inspired my child's longing for faraway places and people.

Sarke greeted us with a chuckle, "people here do say you be lost, taken by the bandits!" I paid Mustapha and the exhausted Porter and gave them added "dash" for their resolute companionship. The Porter went off to a den across the border for more of his favorite brew. My sore knees and thighs were welcome reminders of a journey full of surprises at every turn.

Running into into a Durbar of a Day Off

The days in Banki begin at six with the first invocation of the imam in the pilgrims' camp. There is harsh braying from the village donkeys who are tightly hobbled for the night, tormented males noisily trying to break out at the sound of a female. I moved slowly this morning, stiff after the international expedition. The native saddle takes getting used to, the pommel is a convenience for long rides, but the wide saddle pushes the knees outward. In the early light I stood outside watching others go about their morning chores as I enjoyed the tart taste of one of our remaining grapefruits.

There was no plebiscite work this day, and though most of my colleagues would be heading back to their homes for the weekend, I looked forward to a trek to Kumshe, a larger village beyond those I was responsible for. I was on my own; I had no word from Pembleton, and the only news of any colleagues had come from the lawan of Mbaga.

Thus far I had little sense of how villagers were thinking about their plebiscite choices. I asked Yusufu to report any talk about the plebiscite; what he came up with were observations such as: "the peoples they will vote for English, they says no vote for French because of police," and "some Shuwa, they vote for French, because less taxes there." There was of course no way to vote "for French;" the alternative to joining Nigeria was to put off the decision. We AROs were required to keep a strict impartiality. This was hardly necessary since most of us had little or no opinion on the outcome of the plebiscite. Everyone assumed that the Muslims would vote for joining with Nigeria. We were, however, to be on guard for evidence that local leaders were applying pressure to influence the vote. In Tamawa on an official sign announcing the plebiscite someone had handwritten in Kanuri, "Deposit your ballots in the white box [to join Nigeria]." As no one in that village could read I did not report it.

The horses arrived just after seven. Somewhat subdued, the team started out, Wakilie, with his long spear, limping a bit, Mustapha, Yusufu, and the Porter, whose snoring I heard during the night as he slept on the ground by the rumfa. Our destination was Kumshe, the district headquarters where the DH had what he called a "palace." When asked, Banki people disagreed as to how far Kumshe was. Some said seven miles, others nine miles, others "very far," but all agreed that the road was passable and that Kumshe was a fine place. My joints accommodated to the saddle with less pain than I anticipated. We headed into a gentle north wind lifting off the land from Lake Chad. This was promising.

The road could have been driven by car, though broken up in places where the sun-dried surface cracked. Several bicyclists passed shouting cheerful greetings. In the cultivated fields on both sides of the road women plucked ears from the local corn and men cut down the stocks with locally fashioned iron machetes. In the villages children and old people wove grasses to make mats for the floors of huts. This was the busiest time of year; the fields will not be worked again until the rains, five months away.

The larger towns appear as islands of green in the yellow and brown savanna. The party had separated because with growing confidence about the route I had cantered ahead. Just as a large green canopy of neem trees came into view signaling a town, the horse broke into a gallop; I lost control and hung on to the pommel. On the breeze I heard snatches of music, drawling and the nasal piping of native horns. I reined in, but even the cruel bit could not restrain my mount's excitement. We broke into a wild gallop, a jolting experience unless the rider relaxes enough to hover just above the rear end of the saddle. The native riders do this routinely, but I bounced away in a state of mild panic. We tore into the town through crowded streets. The villagers cheered my derring-do—this would have encouraged me if there had been time to think about it. We reached the dandal leading to the DH's compound, it was packed with people quite evidently in a festive mood. The native horns blared out their brilliant, monotonous cadences, several drums were going at rapid tempo, and women were cheering with the high pitched "ai-ee-ai," "ai ai ee ee" ululating sounds used to celebrate favorite warriors. I had unknowingly chosen a moment to arrive when a *durbar* was in progress to honor the arrival of a distinguished visitor, someone else.

The welcome I received at Kumshe was intended to greet the Dikwa Emir. The finery worn by the horses and their behavior was as I saw in Maiduguri a few weeks before.

A procession of horsemen came from the "palace," their mounts rearing and turning about, excited by the music and the female cries. My animal got into the spirit of the occasion and raised his forelegs high into the air and waved them in greeting. Before he knew it, I slid off and gave the reins to the first man I could reach who smiled and said, in words whose intent I understood, that he would take care of the animal. (Traditional Muslim hospitality provides for visiting horses in a villager's compound all day.) Dismounted and no longer part of it, I could now watch the celebration.

The DH's compound—or palace—was visible through the dust, revealing a clay wall and an entrance gate, an imposing presence compared to the nearby grass huts. As I took this in, a phalanx of 20 odd horsemen galloped down the dandal with spears held high shouting greetings to the enthusiastic onlookers. Village boys jumped as close as they dared, brandishing sticks. Behind the phalanx the DH rode, astride an animal as big as a Percheron workhorse, elegantly dressed as before and with reflecting sunglasses in place. His mount was giving him trouble: it reared and turned full circle several times during the progress, and I saw him pull hard at the reins with little apparent effect. The horses accompanying him were brightly caparisoned with sheepskin trappings that had been dipped in an orange dye; there were colorful tassels, decorated straps and halters like the mount in a copy of an early Renaissance painting that hung in my room as a child. The procession moved slowly while the riders showed off their mounts by prompting them to rear and paw the air, making partial turns and raising dust in huge clouds. Beneath the shouts of the warriors and the onlookers' cheers were the fervent sounds of the wind instruments, more strident and biting than any English horn, yet with a similar timbre. The drums maintained a steady beat. That madcap ride had brought me into the midst of a medieval festival procession. It dawned on me that it had been triggered by my arrival, mistaken for that of the expected honored guest.

After the DH and his entourage swirled past, three young men of the village, done up in their best robes, came up to me, doffed their sunglasses, and one after the other extended a hand in greeting. They spoke a stilted English and laughed with a brittle intensity. "How do you do, sir? Welcome to Kumshe. It is a fine day, sir." Each in turn repeated these phrases with a ridiculous formality. One of them approached me boldly as if trying to see how matey he could be in front of his friends. Startled by this deviation from the usual Kanuri dignity and courtesy, I withdrew my hand, even though I could see that I was offending him. I did not discover the cause of this somewhat aggressive behavior until later.

Yusufu, Mustapha, Wakilie and the very weary Porter came up at this point to report that they had arrived. They seemed delighted at my enthusiasm for the goings on in the village, and I gave them a few shillings to celebrate. Yusufu stayed by me to provide a running commentary. "The peoples here is having a feast, the emir to come soon to talk to them about the plebiscite." And he continued, never complaining at my frequently repeated requests to "tell me what the people are saying."

We walked slowly up the dandal to a shady place just outside the town. As usual, a European attracted attention, although happily the durbar was competition. A collection of naked small boys followed, watching carefully my every gesture. Old women selling kola nuts, native candy and groundnuts grinned a greeting and laughed when I replied with a traditional raised fist salute.

I was not entirely sure that my presence would be welcomed in a day of celebration; the nervous DH might be uneasy at having me around. I found him seated under a clump of neem trees near a burned-out building that I took to have been the school. His people milled about waiting for something, the horses had been distributed among the trees, each held by a servant while the chief warriors disposed themselves in a circle around the DH.

"You saw, of course, that I had trouble with the horse," the DH said. "He is not used to these ceremonies, but I bring him out in order to please the people. It satisfies them to see me ride him. Yes, it is all right if you stay here for you will see some of the native ceremonies. We are expecting to do homage to the emir in any minute." As he said this, he averted his eyes, and appeared extremely nervous. I became anxious and assured him that I would watch the dancing and would like to walk around. He first seemed to take no notice, then, "you will excuse me, because my people want me to return to them. Very shortly I will take you on tour through the facilities of the village."

I sat under a tree with Yusufu, drinking lime juice and water from the thermos flask, delicious but slightly sour. I had a piece of native candy, a white chewy substance made of fresh sugar cane to give strength.

I had not been in Africa long enough to have perspective on the DH's assertion that the arrival of the emir was imminent. For a while I kept checking the road for a sign of his entourage. There was nothing, and I turned with delight to the dancing and storytelling that was going on under the trees. In front of the DH's canvas chair was a small band, a drummer, another percussionist who shook gourds full of seeds or pebbles to make a rhythmic comment on the persistent drive of the drums, and a native horn player whose cheeks bulged out to hold the prodigious amounts of air necessary to propel his instrument's haunting sound. The musicians shuffled about the gourd shaker who often broke into dance steps by himself. Some maidens of the village came forth, distinguished from the matrons by their youth and hair set into three high ridges, in contrast to the massive helmet form that signifies a matron. These girls were just past puberty, wearing special dancing gowns, multi-colored sarongs wound tightly about their bodies, covering breasts but leaving shoulders bare. They formed into a circle and began a dance with a slow rhythmic walking step; at a cue from the music each girl moved her bust and her bottom smoothly front and back in time, but with no change in facial expression. Through repetition it became an artful and convincing voluptuousness. This went on for an hour or more while the DH watched solemnly. From time to time a man would join the band to sing the DH's praises.

Under another clump of trees was a more popular group, the leading harlots of Kumshe (as Yusufu termed them) led men and women in a dance of the Shuwa Arabs driven by a pair of tireless drummers. The dancers snaked around in a circle, slowly putting one foot forward then the next, occasionally singing, always dignified in bearing. It was mostly an elegant shuffle, even aristocratic, interrupted by moments of sheer exuberance when, at a signal from the drummer, the dancers turned and did what the English call a "bum wiggle" with a sideways motion amid wild laughter. The champion was the one whose bottom could move furthest and quickest.

A large proportion of the townspeople were on the streets, scores of children and the entire population of men. Some of the more daring or outward-going wives were on hand too, leaving purdah for this celebration. The children crowding in among the dancers were kept in order by a giant with a shaven head, a household slave of the DH. He wielded a huge whip to restrain the more daring small boys. The richly caparisoned horses, held by servants, stood in the shade by the dances, their dismounted riders seated by them, creating pools of rich color from their their spreading robes. A few remained mounted and joined in the high points of the dance with screams and waving spears.

Suddenly a shout went up from the road. The dances broke up, the warriors leapt on their horses, and all rushed onto the dandal, yelling and waving weapons. The DH once more mounted his great Percheron which reared and whirled in the midst of the mob. "The emir is here, sir," announced Yusufu enthusiastically. Through the crowd milling about the road I saw a small white Jeep approaching. As it neared, Marshall Williams of the UN staff leaned out a rear window, a movie camera to his eye. It was a UN Jeep, no emir in sight.

Dancers and spectators crowded the roadway, horses and people tumbled together in dust and noise. The DH attempted to swing his mounted entourage into some sort of order aided by the giant servant who cracked a whip from atop his horse. A cry of jubilation and welcome went up from the crowd as the white Jeep came closer. When the warriors and the crowd realized that this was not the emir, the noise abated, replaced by animated chattering at the appearance of yet another European stranger.

Mr. Williams hopped out of the jeep and met my incredulous greeting matter-of-factly. His first concern was that he had run out of film in this shot of a lifetime. The DH dismounted and walked toward us to meet the stranger. I introduced the representative of the United Nations as the curious and now fairly subdued inhabitants of Kumshe looked on.

"Would you take a photo of me while I am on top of that fellow's horse?" Mr. W. asked me. Remembering the performance that the animal had put up that morning, and also thinking of the easily injured pride of the DH, I suggested it would not be appropriate. "I know what you mean," said Mr. W., "my father would never let anyone even touch his horse back home in Texas." He contented himself with asking the warriors to pose on their horses, which they did with pleasure. Between shots he told me that he was on a swing through my part of the plebiscite territory, and that he expected to be able to visit all stations before the vote. The plebiscite preparations were proceeding smoothly, although he was not as willing to predict the result as he might have been a week ago. "I'm keeping my ear to the ground through my excellent interpreter here."

By now the crowd had redistributed itself among the trees, rather disconsolately I thought, and I bade Mr. W. farewell as he left to swing through Banki and Mbaga. The DH was obviously hurt and confused that the welcome for the emir had been intercepted so unexpectedly by the stranger in a Jeep. I felt obliged to explain what Williams was doing, but nothing could shake the DH's gloom. The UN was a vague concept. He brightened slightly: "Now I shall take you on a tour of the installations of Kumshe." Cocking his head to one side he began reciting like a love poem the plans the NA had for his district, the market sheds that would be built, the wells that would be sunk. He pointed to the shell of a building beneath the trees, the school before "hooligans" burned it down. The primary school—the only one in the district—now held its sessions in a grass hut not far away until there were funds for a substantial building. I thought of the difficulty elegant Abba Kyari, a Kumshe school teacher, had in grasping even the simplest of the polling formalities, casting doubt on the quality of the instruction in that school.

The one other building that stood out in Kumshe was the dispensary, like the school, the only one within many miles. Such facilities were run by an assistant, usually a local man who had been sent to one of the cities in Nigeria for a six-month course in rudimentary medicine. I understood that the skills varied from village to village; sometimes the assistants retained what they had learned and were able to give relatively clean injections of penicillin, dress wounds and report cases of leprosy. Because in this vast country it was difficult to maintain a satisfactory inspection system, many of the dispensaries fell into disorder; the assistant sold the drugs and neglected work. The people then turned back to native medicines and doctors.

The DH proudly showed me the interior of the dispensary, though it appeared to be a shambles. Bottles were overturned on the tables, the floor was filthy, there was no order, and little olfactory evidence that antiseptics had been used for the floor and walls. The assistant was the young man who had been so matey to me in front of his two companions earlier in the day. He bustled about, clinking bottles in an effort to appear busy, eyes hidden behind dark glasses. He was clearly drunk, probably from medicinal alcohol. The DH, however, added a note of pride to his usual winning smile as he showed me the books that recorded treatments. His indifference to what was going on was as depressing as the sight of the drunken assistant. I politely refrained from comment and smiled in gratitude for the tour. He returned me to the glade where the dances had resumed.

I later learned that the DH's equanimity in the dispensary was superior acting. One of my students told me that the moment I left, the DH ordered the drunken assistant to be taken into custody and brought before the emir that afternoon. He was made to "swear on holy Koran that he would never drink again." Following the vote in the plebiscite, I learned that there had been trouble in this district. The preceding Emir of Dikwa had been exiled by the regional government and replaced by the man who was expected this day. It is possible that the actions of the "hooligans" had been a consequence of the government's action. Likewise, the nervousness of the DH could have reflected an insecure position under the new emir.

The villagers had spent a good deal of energy in abortive welcomings, and by early afternoon most of them sat quietly under the trees. The young dancers had returned and were bumping slowly in a circle in front of the DH, but the lively renditions were over. A court storyteller—or so I presumed him to be—was telling humorous stories while I munched a sardine roll for lunch. Thanks to Yusufu I got the gist: tales of adultery mimed by the storyteller, received with raucous laughter.

The heat of the day had arrived; there was a somnolence in the air despite the willingness of everyone to spring up at a moment's notice. I dozed off during one of the storyteller's complicated intrigues. Suddenly the sound of a distant car horn woke me up. The emir was finally upon us! The DH leapt from his folding chair, the horsemen roused themselves, villagers resumed the ardor of the early morning and poured onto the road, crowding around a light blue Ford Fairlane, 1958 model, whose driver was blowing its resonant horn, barely heard through the cries of the warriors and the women. The horsemen wheeled about, heedless of those on foot, brandishing their spears in barbaric salute. The car rocked slowly along, touched and pursued by dozens of little boys. In the back seat I saw a scholarly-looking man wearing horn-rimmed spectacles and a white turban. He raised his hand nonchalantly to acknowledge the tumult as the car edged forward. Behind him came a truck bearing two gigantic Muslim horns and their musicians who blew raucous calls to the crowd. With them were three or four nondescript men and a pair of energetic harlots, "the Emir's bodyguards," as Yusufu explained. Their cheers added to the melee.

I rushed ahead of the car through a surging mass of bodies and horses and dust to take a picture, wondering what the Emir would think of my white face in the midst of it. The scene reminded me of a photograph in *Seven Pillars of Wisdom* showing the entrance of Feisal into Damascus—surely it could have looked something like this, absent the Ford Fairlane.

America's most popular business car, robin's egg blue, led the way to the DH's palace, followed by the splendidly outfitted DH's guard and accompanied by ecstatic drumming and wailing from the bands. The Emir dismounted to spend the rest of the day as the guest of the highly attentive DH.

Most of the townspeople then dispersed. Curious boys stood or sat by the exotic car as the driver napped within. The village became quiet. I ate another sandwich, drank as much water as I could allow from the dwindling supply in the bottles, and settled in for a nap in in the quiet shade where there had been such vibrant activity only a few moments before.

In midafternoon Yusufu woke me to tell me that "there be European in rest house." What had this person been doing during all the excitement? I walked over to the rest house area—the house, like the school, had been burned down, and in its place stood two substantial grass huts. I called hello and the thick, hoarse response was unmistakably Dixie, who soon emerged, pale and puffy around the eyes. He gruffly commanded his boy to bring chairs and tea. What was all the excitement about? After I told him of the celebrations, his only comment was, "so the little fucker had a durbar for himself. I'm a friend of his, but still he's a foolish little fucker who's going to get himself into a lot of trouble one day." He didn't go on, and I didn't know whether he referred to the DH or to the Emir.

The tea was served by a bright-looking lad that Dixie claimed he had trained from pagan simplicity to cook, keep house and speak with a slight Scots accent. We sat in comfortable canvas folding chairs in the shade. I watched the light begin to transform into its late afternoon radiance and gathered strength from the tea for the trek back to Banki.

Dixie seemed in low spirits. I asked him about his eyes, bloodshot and weary-looking, beyond the usual hangover. "It was that frigging Spanish Communist from the Spanish Civil War," implying that I knew who that was. He explained: "They found a Spanish communist at the border two days ago—trying to get to French territory to stir up trouble down there where the pastors are killing one another. Randall [of the federal police] put him in the frigging native jail where he got hold of one of those pans of food and began slamming it against the walls of the cell. Christ what a racket. I told Randall I would go in to shut him up, but the tear gas thing blew up in my face when I pulled it on him." What was the Spanish communist doing on the border in this part of Africa? "The fucker was crazy," which summed it up for Dixie. I'll never know.

Mustapha and Wakilie appeared with the horses—having found and saddled them and come to the rest house on their own. Dixie began rambling, more animated than in the lugubrious account of the tear gas burst. He told of his efforts to ride horseback in Pakistan and "EyeRak" and on his sister's farm in the Highlands. He looked my horses over approvingly, but I was relieved that he decided not ride back with us. I mounted, and Dixie told me to come back soon. "Check in with me from time to time," as he waved me off. He had no news from headquarters in Bama.

The Porter carried the *Fiernfiord* box at a rakish angle at the head of our procession. We were not a quarter of a mile from Kumshe when he staggered and fell, groaning beside the path. "No pay attention to him, master," said Yusufu, "he drink too much beer today and never can walk." Wakilie lifted the box onto his old shoulders, and we left the Porter to return to Kumshe with an extra shilling for a night's lodging. My employment had been too much for him. He returned to Banki a few days later, but he was committed to drink, and on the firm advice of Yusufu he left our team.

The miles to Banki went quickly as I tested my horse's various gaits. We arrived in the rumfa at a tearing gallop, sweaty but satisfied after the eventful day. Sarke quickly fetched me a pint mug of squash and some ground nuts to keep me until dark and dinner. I told Yusufu to inform the staff that the next day would be one of rest. He remarked with a laconic smile, "We do travel too much, sir."

A DAY OF REST

I woke at the usual time, but fatigued and pleased it would be a rest day, time to make some notes in the relative cool of the morning.

I enjoyed the beginning of the day in Banki—after Sarke cleared breakfast, I sat at the rickety table, its spread legs digging into the sand, and wrote letters that I owed to friends and family. On the market day a lorry driver had handed me a packet from Pembleton which contained a half dozen memos, welcome letters from home, and a pile of rich reading material, the London *Observer*, the onion skin edition of *The New York Times*, *The Economist*, and *West Africa*. The happiest task was to answer the letters and to be in touch for a time with the busy world that seemed so far from Banki.

TAKING STOCK OF FOOD

We had been in Banki for a week. Sarke's supply of tinned foods was dwindling; the grapefruit was "finished," and the local vendors had no fruit or vegetables. Even eggs were difficult to find. The Banki lawan had not fulfilled the commitment to provide food to my assistants. Yusufu came to me at the end of each day to complain that the lawan had not sent sufficient food for him and Sarke. "The lawan loves money" and claimed that he was keeping a share of what the plebiscite paid him for our support. As for myself, I had planned to live on what the local economy offered; I scoffed at the piles of expensive tinned foods that my colleagues brought with them; I expected that I would do just as well with the native fruits and vegetables. This had worked in Bama where there were vegetables and fruits in the market and delicious papayas and limes, but Banki was a desolate spot. The sole fresh vegetable available was the native cucumber, but Sarke insisted that I would not like it. There were groundouts and corn which Sarke used to make thick brown bread and one evening he brought Shuwa butter to the table. This may be healthy, but it smelled rank, and I'd heard that the Shuwa women preserved it using their urine. Shuwa milk likewise had an almost suffocating rank smell that lingered in the room. It would doubtless have been strengthening, but I didn't partake. Sarke managed to find a few eggs from the scrawny local chickens and regularly bought cow meat for his standard dish of Irish stew with a few old carrots that had survived from Bama. Possibly more important was the thick soup, served nightly, rendered from the flesh and bones of some animal after a long day's boiling. There was one delicacy to enjoy, a tin of gooseberries that Sarke found deep in the kitchen box toward the end of our last week in Banki. I couldn't recall anything as delicious. When we returned to Maiduguri I discovered that Sarke had saved a good many tinned items because they were "too dear" to use. I also discovered an unopened bottle of Black & White that he had packed but not brought out, "too dear" to use!

A northern Nigerian day in the early dry season (October-November) begins with promise, a light wind from the north and a touch of freshness. In a temperate climate this freshness typically has a touch of moisture, but here it is totally dry. The coolness is relative, the day begins in the eighties, by midday it is 180degrees farenheit in the shade. But the temperature varies in a 24-hour cycle, reaching its height at midday, declining in the late afternoon and early evening and staying warm at night. Perspiration dries instantly and is not noticeable except where clothes touch a surface. At 9:30 a.m. the back of my shirt begins to stick to the canvas of the chair as the heat accumulates; at 9:52 when I stand up the back of my shorts is as wet as a freshly used bathing suit, the chair canvas soaked. At 10:10 the flies arrive. And it gets worse. Because of its diurnal variation the heat seems tolerable, but in fact it it is insidious; I found my energy level declining, sapped by the sweatless dry heat. Attention and concentration wander, initiative depends on sheer will.

There are billions of flies in the Western Sudan and the dry season does not diminish them. Millipedes and earwigs disappear after the first dry month; the number of moths decreases in the hot season and even my companions, the frogs, thin out in preparation for their yearly retreat from the hot winds. But the fly population remains constant, sucking moisture from skin, open sores on humans, and from dead animals. They may look like houseflies in a temperate clime, but their behavior differs, beginning with willpower. They cannot be brushed aside, they return directly to the same spot. Skin by itself is a target, but if there is a break, the flies will cluster; if brushed away they will come right back. In the space of an hour any given morning three score flies will be gathered on the table and on my legs searching for moisture. What begins as a tickle becomes an annoyance; to shake them off keeps the legs in constant motion. I became envious of horses' ability to twitch the skin independent of the joints. A trace of marmalade on the table will bring a dozen winged diners. I swat and swat. My copies of the *Economist* and *West Africa* are smeared with little bodies, but more escape than are killed. In the midst of it all a fly will land on the tip of the nose, brushed off, it returns to that precise place again and again. There is nothing to do but endure until the night.

To me in my rumfa the flies were an annoyance, but to children, the infirm, and animals they are a menace. Many small children in the villages have runny eyes and some have untreated sores. The flies cluster to feed unhindered and pass along infections. Every piece of meat on display in the markets has its regiment of flies. These creatures become monsters on continuing acquaintance, giant black hairy monsters with delicate wings as in nightmares. The villagers seem to accept them as facts of life and ignore them except where there are servants to wave them off with cow tail whisks.

This Saturday morning I accepted the flies and heat and enjoyed reading about books in the *Observer* with Sir Harold Nicolson and gardening with his wife, Vita Sackville-West; there was news of the London theater season, the latest films, and analyses of politics in an Africa unrecognizable from my current vantage. The middle of the day brings claustrophobia; the heat deprives incentive for a walk unless there is a critical job to do. Not until three or four will it be feasible to take a stroll. The best way to pass those hours is the traditional one, a nap.

The polling officers arrive

My siesta was interrupted by the sound of a lorry approaching and coming to a stop by the rumfa. Off jumped the polling officers, my students from the Bama training. They were understandably frazzled by the bumpy journey on the open lorry in the heat of the day. Abba Kagu, his usual smiling self, carrying a copy of the regulations in English in one hand, came forward as their spokesman to formally announce that the presiding and polling officers were pleased to be in Banki, and he greeted me on their behalf. In return, I invited them into the rumfa where they sat in a circle around the table and Sarke served nuts as a welcoming "feast." We went over the book of rules for the nth time, and it was still true that my team had only a vague idea of what to do under anything other than routine circumstances.

They then posted to their stations: Abba Kagu went off to Mageribu on his bicycle with his assistant, Mustapha, walking behind. Baba Wakilbe walked the short distance to Tamawa; Kyari Shettima, my prize pupil, dressed in pure white robes as before, headed off to the venerable lawan at Buduwa; Abba Kyari, resplendent in his black felt hat and blue *riga*, and as uncomprehending as before, left for Mbaga where I was sure the knowledgeable lawan would guide him. Friendly young Malam Gimba is to be here in Banki, likely to be the most difficult polling station because of its relative size, proximity to the border, and Shuwa in the nearby bush. He is earnest and anxious to do a good job, but easily rattled. But I will be here in case he needs help, an arrangement agreeable to him because he wants to practice English. As he is a Kanuri, he could be a more effective informant than Yusufu about political views in the village.

In the posting each presiding officer was accompanied by a laborer carrying on his back the orange and white ballot boxes tacked onto a board. I wrote out a quick note to Pembleton acknowledging the arrival of the men. This went off to Bama with the lorry driver along with the letters that I had written that morning. For a moment I was in touch with headquarters and by mail with the larger world.

Evening, a ride, a walk, Moral Rearmament

By five the land had cooled a few degrees and the sun was low in the west. After the lively expeditions of the previous days, staying in and near the rumfa made me restless. I asked Mustapha to bring the horse for an evening ride. The animal was rested and took me on brisk walks and a fine canter across the river bed into the badlands in French territory, returning just as the sun disappeared behind the blue mountain. I then strolled through the village at the magic time when the candles and kerosene lamps of the vendors and home cooking fires mingled in the dusk.

Yusufu caught up with me: "There is man by canteen wish to speak with you; he know French language." The canteen at the edge of the field near the rumfa was a mud-walled building roofed with iron sheathing, cloth the main item of sale. At its door I found the concessionaire talking with a man in traditional Kanuri-Muslim dress with a face heavily scarred by tribal markings. He was tall and powerful-looking, smoking a *Gaulois* held between his lips as he talked. He introduced himself as the DH of a French village across the border. He took my hand in a strong clasp and began talking in fluent French. He started right in with an account of the French native administration of which he was a part, pointing out that in his village, only two kilometers away, there is a primary school and the language of instruction is French. He was contrasting this with Banki, which had no school, and with the practice of using the local language for instruction in Bornu primary schools. "Oh yes, French administration, it is very interesting," he concluded, then asked me, "Have you ever visited Europe? I have just returned only a month ago from Geneva."

"Geneva? It is very beautiful there among the mountains, is it not?" I said, groping for some way to express my surprise and to draw him out. "Oh yes, very beautiful and very interesting. My time there was excellent and well spent. I intend to go there again for a longer time."

"Why were you visiting Switzerland?"

"You have heard of *Rearmament Morale*, have you not? *Bien.* I was at the castle of that group. They are very, very interesting, the people of *Rearmament Morale.*"

I agreed that they were very interesting indeed, to which he replied,

"Now, I must be going, but you will come one evening to my village with me, to visit the school and the dispensary and my house. And we can discuss the very interesting ideas of *Rearmament Morale*." He squeezed my hand with a smile and leapt upon his horse, spurring roughly with the iron stirrups and galloped across the border scattering chickens and raising the dust. The pleasant young fellow who ran the canteen smiled, proud of having brought us together. I mingled surprise and amusement to have met someone in the remote village of Banki who spoke excellent French and had been a guest of Moral Rearmament in Switzerland. In college I had heard mention of the morality-based, self-improvement Moral Rearmament organization and its proselytizing. Now its reach extends to sub-Saharan Africa.

The night was unusually close and muggy, a variation from the usual dryness. A thin cloud cover hid the stars and kept the heated air on the land. I tossed on the camp bed for most of the night, half suffocating in the close atmosphere, any slight breeze diminished by the mosquito netting.

Inspections on the Buduwa-Mbaga circuit

On Sunday we were on the move again; shortly after seven Mustapha arrived with the horses. Wakilie told me that the treks of the past days had injured his foot so that he could no longer walk with us. The Porter had disappeared into the drinking dens with his earnings, so Mustapha and Yusufu were my companions. I strapped my notebook, a flask and one bottle to the saddle which should do as we planned to return to Banki in the early afternoon. The stripped-down procession lacked something in color, but it was adequate to inspect the polling stations and to visit the polling officers on site.

At Buduwa Kyari Shettima was supervising the lawan's laborers as they drove the stakes for the waiting area fence in the places that I had set. The grass matting was ready to be put into place to make the huts for the presiding officer's desk and the polling booth. In order not to trap local sheep and goats, the waiting area would be fenced only on the day prior to polling. In this final week a 24-hour guard will be posted in the polling area to keep goats from eating the huts.

In each of the villages the presiding officers are considered important persons: they are there in an official capacity and recognized as literate. I noticed that the lawan had made Kyari a guest in his compound. Except to supervise the construction and watch over it, there was not much for the officers to do in the week that remained before the voting. I had no worries about Kyari. I gave him permission to come into Banki on Wednesday for market day.

I pushed on to Mbaga and since I knew the route, it was an opportunity to exercise the horse on the hard-dried clay of the badlands that seemed less formidable on this second track, and we arrived before noon at the great tree outside the village well. Beneath it we found Abba Kyari, his hat off and slightly sweaty. He was puzzling over the plan for the polling station while the laborers rested on their haunches awaiting instructions. As he laid it out the waiting area could have corralled 100 sheep; it stretched 200 feet on each side in a crazy trapezoid. The footprints for the office and the polling booth were far too small. With his habitual frightened look, Abba watched me pace out the boundaries. With that same fearfulness he assented to all my suggestions, but I couldn't tell how much he understood.

It was time for a rest. The lawan had placed a large mat for both of us in front of his compound; I joined him to chat through Yusufu. Would I like to see his son? In a few minutes a boy of about six with a light complexion and wearing a robe extending to his feet was brought out by one of the women. "His mother is a Shuwa," the lawan told me with pride. The child seemed terrified by his father and the stranger; the lawan roared with laughter at his shyness, and summoned a naked little lad who was playing in the street nearby. "He is a good friend, and will give him courage." But the young prince would not be reassured. In another effort to relax him, a servant came out with a brightly colored mechanical train. The boy refused to play with it, but the lawan and I dragged it back and forth across the mat to the wonder of the elders. The lawan said it recently came from the Switzerland, and, yes, brought by *"Rearmament Morale"* whom I had met the previous night.

Finally, the boy was allowed to return to the women where he would be content, and, after a discussion about plans for his son's schooling, I bade the lawan farewell and headed back to Banki where Sarke had a bowl of soup and sardine salad waiting for me in the heat and darkness of the rumfa.

The Tamuwa-Mageribu circuit;
absent officers, a bitten ear and a purported adultery

The next day was the Tamuwa-Mageribu circuit. At the former I found Malam Baba Wakilbe in a singlet lounging in the polling booth hut. He roused himself and with the fine old lawan, showed me the polling station. All seemed well save for minor adjustments in the booths. Baba has five days to rest, partake of his host's hospitality, and guard the mats and the plebiscite materials.

At Mageribu Abba Kagu and Malam Mustapha, his assistant, were absent. According to a confused account by the lawan, as relayed by Yusufu, one of them allegedly tried to seduce a village woman and had been wounded by the aggrieved husband. Both young men had gone to be treated at the Kumshe dispensary. I left a note for Abba, chiding him for leaving his post and the precious ballots and ballot boxes and, unfairly, as it turned out, berated him for playing around with a village woman.

That night, back in Banki, a messenger brought me a note folded in a larger piece of paper addressed to "I/C Polling Station, Banki, Area." It read:

> The P. H. Judd
> returning officer
> of Banki Area,
>
> Sir,
> I have the honor to submit here with my few lines of reply your note for this morning. The case was happened last night and it was not present of me, I was sleeping.
>
> In the morning, while Bulama [the Village head] explained to me the matter, the man try to park his goods to another village.
>
> So as soon as I saw him, I (immediately) quickly go to the DH to report him.
>
> Mustapha himself blood coming out in his body so I take him on a bicycle to dispensary and also to acknowledge to DH.
>
> If so the man will run away in the village, go to French.
>
> That is the only reason of my going to leave the polling station.

The one side of polling station will be take off, as I already know. The reason leave it like this, we use to go there and rest, and weather become hot.

Therefore I beg your honor to not be angry for this.

Yours obedient servant,

Abba

After dark Abba rode up on his bicycle, out of breath and eager to explain himself. I was satisfied by the excellent letter, but he had more to say. The outraged supposed husband had bitten Mustapha's ear, and the man was now trying to "park" his goods in another village before escaping to French territory, he was a troublemaker and Mustapha had not been attentive to his or any wife. (The origins of the dispute that led to the biting of the ear remained mysterious.) The explanation ran on long after I told him I entirely accepted it. He left to attend Mustapha's wound and assured me he would seek justice from the DH.

The toy man; Mountebanks

Tuesday was another day of rest, begun with a brisk ride followed by catching up with the papers and notes. By noon the heat in the rumfa was uncomfortable, and I looked for relief. There were sounds of activity outside where a crowd had gathered in the shade of the large village tree. Upwards of 50 adults and children were in a circle around a man demonstrating an ancient carnival device, an iron bar with a seat on either end balanced on a fulcrum; chips of red paint from the past evident. A young Hausa turned a crank attached to the base of the fulcrum, and the bar with two small boys on its seats turned slowly around, dipping in the course of a circuit, the boys' faces rapt with wonder. Their friends crowded around, wide-eyed, admiring their courage. The going price for a ride was one penny for two people.

The man turning the crank accepted the pennies, clearly enjoying the children's excitement and the admiration of the adults. Sarke told me that he had seen him a few years ago in a town nearly 500 miles away. "He be the toy man—he travel all over the North of Nigeria—all over everywhere!" He wore light tan riding breeches and was barefoot. The main attraction was this merry-go-round made of heavy cast metal, but he offered other delights. Malam Gimba, who had joined the circle, pointed to a box on the ground. "In that box, sir, are the splendid things, ostriches, giraffes, and all things like that." He put down a penny and looked into a hole in the box while the toy man pushed a little button at its side. He offered me a peek, and I saw, dimly illuminated by a flashlight bulb, a postcard of the self-government celebrations in Kaduna the year before, showing the Emir of Kano's entourage mounted on camels. Images of the major African animals slowly went by as the man turned a wheel on the box. He next opened a chest to display the mechanical toys, a strutting ostrich, a kicking donkey, and a duck that perpetually chased a butterfly. These were somewhat battered, but they performed their motions to cries of delight from the little boys and wondering comments from a growing number of adults gathered around.

It was a large crowd and abruptly two men leapt into its center screaming self-advertisements to attract attention. They moved violently and jerkily and pounded their chests as they shouted, faces colored with red and blue dye. They launched into a chant to gather people to see their show. One of them held a string high and commanded a toy castle on the ground to rise and fall along it, as though at the will of their incantations. "Those are medicine men," whispered Malam Gimba in awe, although for my sake he managed a halfhearted deprecatory chuckle. The shorter of the two, with boastful gestures and talk, thrust an extremely long needle up his nose; holding his head back to show how deeply it had penetrated, he chanted of the achievement. His companion, after an elaborate introduction, broke a piece of bottle glass and thrust the splinters into his mouth and vigorously chewed them. He stuck out a tongue encrusted with splintered glass, keeping a guttural chant going the whole time. These actions done, the men took out knives and stabbed or pricked themselves on arms and breasts, shouting to all that none of the instruments made a mark, their skin was so strong.

All this was prefatory to sale of the magic powder that had made these feats possible. From a trouser pocket one man produced a dirty handkerchief full of the powder that had strengthened their skin against the knives, making the body impervious to pain from glass or from a wire through the nose. This powder would preserve a man from injury, delay his death, cure impotence, and keep him from sickness. The old men crowded around to buy. Malam Gimba gave three pence for a small handful. When enough pennies were collected, the mountebanks, leaping like young horses and chanting, ran to the pagan drinking dens to spend their proceeds.

Dances in the evening

At dusk I heard a rumble from the direction of Bama that I first thought to be an airplane and then realized that it was once again the traders' lorries arriving with their weekly loads for the market next day. I asked Yusufu to accompany me on a walk through the town. The drums had begun an incessant beat, calling the people to "play" as Yusufu turned it, meaning to dance. We made our way into the darkness of the village streets where dimly visible shapes brushed by almost like bats. Occasionally a vendor would have a lighted candle on his stand, and there was subdued talk from the compounds. The dance was at an intersection lit by three kerosene lanterns hung on the fences of family compounds. Children were dancing to the beat of the drums and the wailing of pipes. In a rough circle older ones tried to ape adults in dignity; the younger leapt about haphazardly. Yusufu said that "this be night for young people to dance," and pointed out one man whom he said was "head of the young people." The large lady who had been so friendly on my first day in Banki, "the head of women," smiled in greeting.

The dance developed chaotically as more and more of the village youth and traders, many drunk, displaced the children, swaying as they walked, swinging imperiously from one hip to the other. Some of the youth held cigarettes on their lips, impairing the dignity of the slow dance, a contrast with the dances in Kumshe a few days before. The leaders could not keep order, and the dance degenerated into a pushing and shoving session. Yusufu and I headed back to the rumfa, guided by the yellow light of my nearly exhausted flashlight. At intervals during the night I was awakened by the drumming and the boisterous sounds of the horns.

Market day

The presiding and polling officers had permission to come into Banki on market day. Some of them complained that they were bored in the villages, "nothing to talk about with bush people." They welcomed a day in Banki with the market and traders from relatively far off places. At about 10 a.m. the lads assembled at the rumfa for a feast, kola nuts and sweet water while I reviewed the procedures with them for yet another time. My familiar questions were still met with a blank look on Abba Kyari's handsome face; Malam Gimba flinched at each question, even if not directed to him. Nothing could be done now, so I urged them to read and reread the pamphlet. About responses to the plebiscite in the villages, most had little or nothing to report. Kyari Shettima said that everyone was taking seriously the emir's orders not to tell people how to vote in the plebiscite; though all agreed that villagers would vote exactly as their leaders wanted them to—for integration with Nigeria. Abba Kagu, as cherubic and smiling as ever, laughed condescendingly at the notion of the villagers exercising independent choice. Our meeting broke up before noon, and Malam Gimba accompanied me on a visit to the market. Already there were five or six hundred people, and more were arriving. The traders from Bama showed their wares on tables sheltered from the sun in the sheds that the DH had so proudly pointed out. Nearby were smaller shelters, usually mats placed on sticks to shield the goats and other livestock from the sun. The ironmongers created spearheads from pieces of petrol tins heated over red hot coals and beaten into shape. One variant had vicious-looking turned-up prongs designed to keep the metal embedded in the flesh of the animal. Near them Shuwa and Kanuri women sat on the open ground with milk, nuts, herbs and soup materials on mats in front of them. They kept up a constant chatter amid redolent smells from the herbs.

After about 20 minutes walking through the market I returned to the shade of the rumfa, almost dizzy from the sun and the glare from the sandy ground. I was glad to be inside despite the hundreds of flies. Sarke had to serve me a couple of pints of lime juice and water before he rested.

At about one o'clock I heard a motor outside, and Dixie marched into the hut, his Anzac hat canted to one side. He told me he had picked up a Land Rover in Bama and had driven here to see how the road was. The rumfa had no chair for a guest, so I sat on the sand, leaning against a pole for support, while Dixie took the chair. I did not then know that Sarke had hidden the Black & White among the kitchen supplies, so I had to give Dixie the bad news that there was no booze and hoped that lime juice and water would take care of his basic thirst. I was glad to have some news from the plebiscite staff in Bama embellished with Dixie's colorful comments. After an hour he put on his Anzac hat and drove off in the Land Rover.

At late lunch in the rumfa I became aware that the market noise had risen and changed character, but I attributed this to the growing numbers in an already large assembly. After lunch I went out and confronted serious disorder, men and women with goods and animals fleeing the market, running past the rumfa, many crossing the border. Curious, I walked to an area where I could see the noisy mob by the market sheds while staying clear of the fray. Women were no longer sitting by their calabashes; men and boys were untethering their animals and leading them away; most of the lorries had disappeared, the last were heading out of the village on the Bama road, followed by people on foot. The weekly market is a key feature of the rural economy, subsistence depends on the exchange of grains and animals. It was highly unusual that the market had broken up in chaos. People were obviously frightened and I didn't know why.

Were the plebiscite officers and I and the process itself in danger? What could I do? I had no transportation, no radio. A schoolboy in a white uniform ran past shouting, "Flee, master, flee!" I decided the only tactic was to remain in place, stand by the rumfa calmly. In the confusion there was no time to think of alternatives—if there were any—and overall I experienced this bizarre and frightening disturbance with a kind-of hallucinogenic quality.

"Hide, hide!" Malam Gimba shouted as he passed by the rumfa and then ran away. Malam Abba Kyari appeared and gestured drunkenly to the crowd to stop them as if on my behalf. I told him to find a hut where he could sleep it off in safety. He headed for the stew pots over the border, but out of a misplaced sense of loyalty he shortly returned, weaving through the crowds, his robe and hat spotless as always.

An unarmed NA policeman came up to me to explain in limited English that he was on duty escorting a prisoner from "French." He pointed proudly to a man whom he said was his "brother." Whether this was the prisoner I could not make out. I asked him to escort Abba Kyari to safety; he started to do so, but as Kyari broke away, he saluted me briskly several times and disclaimed further responsibility. Absent anything else to say, I asked if he had been in the Army. He clicked his heels and saluted repeatedly and launched into a recitation of his name, serial number and unit, saluting at each item. When Malam Kyari Shettima came up and castigated him for not helping protect the DH in the market, he again saluted and clicked heels. He fixed his gaze on me and continued saluting with added relish as though I was commending his behavior. It was clear that this symbol of authority would be of no help if the situation worsened.

Perhaps the French Cameroonian policeman I saw at the border watching the people stream by could help. He seemed to be ready for service, a trim figure in short shorts, a short-sleeved khaki shirt with a French emblem of rank on the breast pocket, and an American army overseas cap placed rigidly on his head. He came to me as I approached. We shook hands, he bowed, said *"enchanté"* and turned on his heel heading into "French." Why he was at Banki I had no clue, but trim and alert as he seemed, he also could not help.

Fleeing schoolboys, readily identified by their white shirts and shorts, had some knowledge of English. On the run one of them told me that the disturbance began with "trouble with Shuwa." Tension between the nomads and the settled had broken into a fight.

I looked for the DH and was surprised and relieved to see him in the market amidst a throng of gesticulating men waving spears. Suddenly a Land Rover drove up heading out of the village, Dixie Deans in the passenger seat. The driver stopped. Dixie remained inside, I could see he was trembling. He shouted out the window: "Get the frigging well out—far out of here." The Land Rover pulled away as an NA policeman opened a passage through the spearmen and was soon out of sight. None of the angry men had so much as noticed me, much less threatened me. I kept up the confident manner and returned to the old market and the rumfa. The noise of the crowd continued.

I found my team of election officers gathered about; they urged me to order a Land Rover, but there was no radio or telephone connection with the plebiscite office in Bama, and there were no vehicles in the village. Maybe there would be some help when the news reached Bama through the bush telegraph or from Dixie.

The DH moved in our direction away from the market, a few NA police preceding. At last, here was authority. He went to the large tree where he typically held court. Suddenly the posse of NA policemen, along with several of the DH's mounted personal servants, made a concerted rush across the border and surrounded the drinking and gambling huts. In no time they returned dragging a man seized in one of the huts. Malam Gimba suddenly appeared and pointed to one of the policemen to tell me that he had the most powerful medicine of all, "No spears or bullets can touch him." That was off the point, but I surmised that the seized man was the prisoner that the first NA policeman had been escorting.

Suddenly, my acquaintance, the "*Rearmament Morale*" DH of the village in "French" galloped across the border, a *Gaulois* hanging from his lips, a screaming mob brandishing spears behind him. He protested to the DH that the NA police posse had illegally trespassed on French territory when they dragged the man from the huts. His followers took hold of the man and *Rearmament Morale* wheeled on his horse and repatriated the prisoner across the border. It was an international incident.

Following this drama, an old pagan, the worse for drink, approached and cursed me in Fulani, because, as Malam Gimba interpreted, "English bring trouble like this in the market—French people be good." He raised his arm with fingers outstretched to denounce me. My young colleagues treated him with the disdain the Kanuris reserve for the unfortunate hill people who come to the market.

After these bizarre events, the market was deserted, and the locals retired to their compounds leaving only my group in the field by the rumfa. According to the lads, "a fight started by a group of Shuwa" precipitated the riot that broke up the market. The Kanuri have "a great hatred of the Shuwa people." Any excuse will serve to ignite tribal feeling. I was in danger too, as "they would shoot you only they are not sure whether you have strong medicine against bows and arrows." Another of the lads gave a current political dimension to the conflicts. He had heard that the Action Group (the political party based in southwestern Nigeria) could have contributed to the tension. "Action Group people told the Shuwa that if the white box won [join with Nigeria], they will be oppressed by the Kanuri just as in Rabeh's time."

I requested guards for the night from the DH as he stood beneath the great tree. He nervously agreed to provide them, but evaded any discussion of the market breakup. The field by the rumfa was deserted by evening. Sarke lit the Tilley lamp and served dinner on my camp table outside under the stars, visible to unseen eyes, and I read until bedtime. It was a show of confidence that I did not fully believe, but what else could I do?

I slept secure in the belief that the rumfa was guarded. When I looked out at dawn I saw three figures wrapped in blankets fast asleep on the ground. The DH had provided guards as he had promised, but these old fellows were not about to spend the night awake. However, there was no evidence of an attempt on the rumfa.

The next day I chose to test what Malam Gimba called my magic and trekked with Mustapha and Yusufu to Tamawa and Mageribu. There was no sign of trouble. A schoolboy told me when I returned that this display showed I did have magic, that the Shuwa knew I was impervious to their weapons.

In the early afternoon I heard the sound of a motor, and a long Land Rover drew up. From its insignia, I saw that it was the Nigerian Army. An English officer about my age descended and introduced himself as Lieutenant Pierce. At the command "Dismount," half a dozen smartly uniformed soldiers with rifles jumped from the open back of the vehicle and dressed into a line. The cavalry had arrived! The news of the market riot had reached higher authorities and prompted this show of military might. It was the federal army, an unfamiliar presence in these parts, a modern force whose jurisdiction extended beyond regional boundaries. On the hood of the vehicle was a dead baboon. In response to my wondering glance the lieutenant told me they had seen it *en route* and shot it to demonstrate the squad's capability. There are many eyes and ears in the bush, and news travels fast. I knew that Shuwa and

Kanuri alike would be aware of the demonstration. I assured him that Banki and the villages I had just visited were quiet and that I and the polling officers were going about our business without interference. At a command, the soldiers smartly remounted the vehicle which briskly drove away with the dead baboon on the hood, a sign of what force could do.

The next day at noon a plebiscite Land Rover with driver arrived to be at my service during the election, a sign of support that greatly pleased my polling officers. I used the vehicle to take several of them to villages on the way to Kumshe, now a quiet place without the excitement of a *durbar*. While there I had a cup of tea with Mr. Williamson at the rest house. Not surprisingly, he was delighted that there was only a day to go before the voting when he would be released to more civilized parts. My ride back to Banki was comfortable and quick, but I missed trekking by horse with Wakilie, Mustapha and Yusufu and the Porter.

THE VOTE

The voting went off without a hitch. With the Land Rover I was able to visit my four village polling stations during the day and attend to Banki. I heard of no challenges or disturbances. The officers did not have to use the painfully learned procedures to deal with questionable credentials or unruly behavior. The voters, dressed in their best, lined up before the polls opened and patiently waited their turn. An hour after the polls opened, nearly all votes had been cast. The polls stayed opened and empty of voters for hours.

On Saturday evening November 7 in Banki I celebrated in my journal the achievement of the vote: the first anonymous paper ballot election in that part of the world had taken place peacefully and involved almost all men of voting age:

The plebiscite is done. Three of my five sets of ballot boxes lie safely at the foot of my bed, trussed up in wrapping paper. I will fetch the other two by Land Rover early tomorrow morning. I am proud of the performance of my presiding and polling officers—they handled the tasks more efficiently and quietly than I expected from the training sessions. Even Malam Abba Kyari in Mbaga got through the day without difficulty. Young Malam Gimba, here in Banki, though flustered, managed the accounting better than anyone else. I helped with a final accounting at night on my table illuminated by the Tilley to put the completed station report forms in the appropriate folders. The voting was well disciplined, though I expect that the result may be more variable than some people thought in advance.

Sarke, Yusufu and I returned in the Land Rover to Bama with the sealed ballot boxes. Mine joined those from other districts on tables in the large room where we had the training sessions. In a formal procedure designed to prevent tampering or miscounting, my colleagues and I opened them, sorted and counted the ballots, and swore to the tallies. There was only a short time to swap stories as we all departed soon after the tally, Sarke, Yusufu, and I headed back to Maiduguri in my Opel.

The final tally for most districts in the Northern Cameroons confounded expectations. The voters in the Kanuri districts overwhelmingly chose to drop their ballots in the box in favor of the ambiguous alternative to delay a decision on the future of the trust territory. All of my colleagues assigned to plebiscite duty had expected as a matter of course that the Kanuri majority would choose to join their fellow tribesmen in Bornu. Instead, the voters chose to put off the decision. There was nothing in the small scraps of opinion I heard in the bush to indicate such an outcome.

Back in Maiduguri at the request of David Williams of *West Africa*, I wrote an article offering a number of implications of the surprising outcome that I had heard locally after the voting.

- The choice by the majority of the Kanuri farmers in villages signified resistance to the NA which had supported the choice of joining Nigeria.
- As the NPC, the leading political party, had supported union; did this mean a weakening of its appeal with possible implications for the federal election coming in a few weeks?
- Did the Kanuri voters calculate that a "delay" vote would allow the popular exiled Emir of Dikwa to return?
- Or did the delay imply that the British would fund more infrastructure projects?
- Did the farmers simply want to stay under the British authority that they were used to?

We'll never know why the vote went as it did because there was no polling and no open campaigning. In less than two months the same voters gave the NPC an overwhelming majority in the federal election. A year later a second plebiscite was held with precisely termed alternatives, yea or nay to joining Nigeria. It resulted in overwhelming approval of joining Nigeria—the majority (Kanuri) in favor, the minority (hill people, some urban dwellers) against. It was a conclusive re-run, with no hypothetical alternative. The Northern Cameroons peacefully left UN Trusteeship to face the future as part of Nigeria and Bornu. The voting was honest, the white box alternative to put off the decision was inept.

The Northern Cameroons plebiscite of 1959 may be a tiny footnote in history, but for me the three weeks in the bush were revelatory. I had been part of a well-planned and fair election within the special circumastances of a largely illiterate electorate. I had been part of the soon-to-be dismantled British colonial system, met admistrators (Pembleton, the overburdened Mr. Lawrence) and specialists at work with a range of character and perspectives (a way to celebrate Dixie and Williamson among the others). I was in in Bama long enough to experience walks along the riverbed as the light faded, in a settlement where there was no electricity, walking through the town with the flickering kerosene candles pon vendors' tables, passing shadowy figures, catch a glimpse of the shrouded royal wife on horseback guarded by a warrior with an unsheathed broad sword. The weeks in the border village of Banki surrounded me with the traditional life of family, farming and local trade. It too was full of character, the shifty *lawan*, the "head of women," the maligned drinking and gambling dens across the invisible border, *Rearmament Morale* please his stay at the castle in Geneva, my trek to "French," the customs inspectors on the highway, *le patron* and his cotton gin, the briskly chanting school children in Mora. The treks to and from the four polling stations meant meeting other village heads, in particular the strong non-verbal connection with the *lawan* of Mbaga. I felt common bonds with the polling officers, so eager to please, rallying around after the market riot and coping with a process entirely new to them.

Africa revealed itself in the late afternoon, in the depth of its darkness, the soft sound of talk in the village. It revealed itself also in the wild juxtapositions, my unexpected and accidental welcome in Kumshe, *Rearmament Morale* riding across the border to seize a man and drag him across the border. I had that moment of recall of the picture of the Arab horsemen on my childhood bedroom wall as we crossed the dry riverbed at dusk in Banki, and trekking by horse with a bearer carrying a load, like explorers I had read about in boys' books. I shared with the intredid explorers of those books the challenge of dealing with information from the interpretation of tongues I was entirely ignorant of with repeats of "what are they saying? What does he say? Who is he? She?

It was an adventure, yes, but there was the added dimension of responsibility. I had a task requiring organization, diplomacy, endurance, and in that market riot, a cool head that I did not know I had. I had been searching for an advneture. In a few weeks I'd find it again in an even more expansive set of encounters.

Chapter Three

Interludes:
a visit to Lake Chad,
perceptions of past and future in Bama

There was less than a month between the plebiscite and the federal election in December. After the expansive experience of the plebiscite, I felt confined in the suburban GRA, and dissension continued in the staff room. The visit of a senior education official from Kaduna promised change, but nothing came of it. The antidote was to go to the bush, which I did on a 36-hour weekend to a village near Lake Chad where I saw fishermen at work and enjoyed the company of a hydraulic engineer and his wife. On the return there was a chance encounter such as Africa so often awards, this with a hitchhiking Belgian journalist. Shortly thereafter two academics observing the preparations for the federal election visited me, and I took the historian of them to Bama to meet DO Lawrence for a discussion that included prescient (and mordant) predictions for the future. When I was told I would be an ARO in the upcoming federal election I knew it would be a different challenge with a motor, but how enthralling it was is the subject of the next chapter.

Back to the school and the GRA

I called him Alhaji Trader. On afternoons over several months he set up his wares on the porch while I was napping and when I got up he would tempt me to buy with gentle, sibilant words until I bought a flyswatter or a little capped basket.

How one's feelings change and lag. I returned from the plebiscite determined to "stick it." Next I was equally determined to ask for a "touring job;" now, perhaps because of the greater relaxation in examination period, I'm back to "sticking it." Because I am beginning to have some idea of what I am teaching, I feel more confident of finding my own place here (or level as fellow teacher LL puts it, implying that it will be a low one). Here, despite my distaste for this segregated white community, I am feeling something of the elation that comes with taking hold of a challenging situation.

The staff room, particularly REU [an English teacher], is excited about "the Jelf visit." Jelf, the Permanent Secretary of the Education

Department, whom I met in Oxford, is due next week to inspect all the education facilities in Maiduguri. REU debates whether to ask for a transfer and speculates about who will be moved; we are all curious about the "G succession." [A possibility that the headmaster would be transferred.] Such are the voices of government service—but the speculation along with the cool weather gives some genuine energy to the staff room that helps other of my thoughts. [The visit of the senior official resulted in no changes and I knew the backbiting in the staff room would continue.]

The pace of national politics grows. Today I overheard in the NA Reading Room the librarian and another who looks like a northerner, talk about the arrival on Monday of the Action Group helicopter. "They asked permission to land near the market, and the NA refused, but they say they will drop leaflets on the town." Last week the Bornu Youth Movement (BYM) signed up "everybody" from here to Damaturu. [As *Wikipedia* describes: "The party was founded by young radicals of Kanuri heritage who were indignant with the administrative course of native authorities in Bornu and wanted to reform the authority." In the upcoming federal election the party is affiliated with the Action Group.] On Monday the NA rounded up all of them. The conversation continued: "Force will never do—the people will vote against the NPC this time." "But they will lose their position by trying to intimidate people."

It took about two weeks after the release of the plebiscite for the pressure of Maiduguri to build up within me. I have completely escaped the social world, and I am with myself—-and alone. I've not been for a social visit in almost two months except for an evening with the Landers last Saturday when we had drinks and supper and listened to a Haydn divertimento, *The Devil's Trill* and Chopin's *Impromptus*. At this stage, I do not see what there can be for me in the GRA, as I don't fit into the "white" social life. The system is a vice—the limited curriculum, the emphasis on hard-to-achieve essays, I find more and more confining. I tell myself that this is a peripheral concern, yet I expend much of my evenings on anger at the system and at my colleagues rather than on something constructive. It is what Mrs. Benkert [mother of a friend] called "morbid scrupling of which we must be aware." I sense a heavy current of melancholy turning within to bitterness or a stronger, corrosive, emotion which takes over in these times of loneliness, "when the sweetest thought is turned to the awareness of death." I see no meeting with this society, yet feel trapped by it; there is no repose, no softening of the light. There is no God to pray to in order to throw the pettiness of these problems into a proper perspective.

On the Southern Shore of Lake Chad

Yesterday Saturday, left Maiduguri at 1:15 p.m. after loading the car with the absurd pile of materials that seem to be required here even for one night away. Sarke, as always, was willing. Malam Kyari, my companion in Gwoza two weeks ago, came with us to translate and sightsee. The morning had been spent in a steadily complaining chatter in the staff room that left me somewhat enfeebled. I thought that I was a fool to pack and set off for only a day and a half away, but the thought of what a weekend in Maiduguri is like drove me on.

The road to the north is not a good one, and loose sand made the car veer about like a toy boat on a stormy lake. During the first hour every hard bump, and there were several, served to remind me how foolish it was to undertake this. But desperate situations need desperate remedies, and after arriving, settling in and having one of Sarke's dinners followed by an evening pipe and above all, being in the bush again, I knew I had done the right thing.

Sunday:

What shall I do—now or next? What have I accomplished? Have I lost myself in confusion again? Where can I find a job that will give scope? Why do I mind so much? Why am I at the mercy of such trivia? I feel that I am back again in the same old situation of claustrophobia, desperately inhibited, confused, unable and uncertain how to break out.

The crisis *is* about one's work, not about other things. My dissatisfactions here and in other places are due not only to the frustration of the right impulses—one's ideals, one's wish to give, and so on, but doubtless also to other impulses set up long ago as to one's place in society, position & prestige (of the "right" sort of cause). For proper analysis of the roots of my restlessness it is necessary to scrape down.

What is the desire I have for comfort, for peace, for satisfaction—for something soft to care for and nourish? This counters the ever present discipline of hardness, firmness and, above all, aloneness and independence which refuses to touch the soft creature. But one looks to the darkness and feels that to go there would be to be lost completely. Always there is the expectation that at the next crossing, at a bend in the road, finally will come an answer. Is there nothing between this North and South?

But there is this moment. I'm seated in a small summerhouse, really a galvanized roof over an area enclosed by (successful) mosquito-proofing. The wind blows strongly from the north with the steadiness of a sea breeze. In the early morning the flat, russet-colored land with its few trees looks like Tuckernuck [island next to Nantucket]—I can see the lake from where I am, this, with the wind, gives me some of the refreshment of the sea. This is settling the spirits.

At seven a.m. Malam Kyari came with the *Serkin barake* [rest house custodian] and two horses. Mine was a young stallion, untrained and almost off his head with a desire to get at Kyari's mare. We rode to the encampment of the fishermen about a mile away. The elders came up to shake hands with the *baturi* [stranger]. Kyari tells me that the people here are extremely prosperous. They seem far more sophisticated than my polling officers at Banki. Some of them took us on a large dugout canoe for a ride on the lake. Such a vessel is worth £40 or £50 according to Kyari. Other local boats are made of reeds, with graceful gondolas like prows. One motorboat was named "The Northern Mail." We observed boats with fishermen and their belongings heading for other villages on the shore or islands in the middle. Kyari says it takes two days of poling to reach the lake's open water.

I walked back from the village after giving the *serkin barake* three shillings for the use of the horses—a generous fee, but to my surprise he grumbled a bit. The harmattan blew all the heat away even at high noon. I was elated by the feel of that wind. Sitting in the screen-enclosed house, I enjoyed an hour of the clearest thoughts in many weeks.

Lunched with Mr. and Mrs. Wilkie and baby at the other guest house. Grace before the meal followed by a lively conversation with an edge of wit, a rarity here. Sympathetic people, he rather awkward, ginger-haired, she, Celtic face and a lilt in her accent I took to be Irish but she was from Edinburgh. He is working on a survey for the Lake Chad irrigation project. The plan is to bring water from the lake to grow guinea corn and perhaps some rice. After the planning and some preliminary work it was discovered that the water of Lake Chad is too saline for the guinea corn. There is also the problem of inducing the people to work harder to increase their income. Some of the fishermen are perfectly happy with what they get now by going out for two months and living the rest of the year on their earnings.

Visited the French *sous prefect* in Gamboru, the Cameroon border village—he limping badly due to an auto accident. He wore an army uniform and lived in a mud house at the edge of town; no suburban GRA for the Cameroon administration.

Drove back into the sun. The wide-open spaces of the north changed gradually to thick thorn bush near Dikwa. Breaking through a convoy is an arduous task. The trucks, some battered beyond belief, plunge through the sandy road bed and often make so much noise that the driver does not hear my horn and does not pull over to let the private car pass. Or, he willfully stays in the middle to avoid being enveloped by dust in his turn. Many of our miles were passed in a cloud of dust so thick that I could not see the lorry 100 feet ahead. My hand stayed steadily on the horn. One driver kept us in torment so long that when I finally pulled by him I blocked the way with the car, and Malam Kyari and Sarke, only slightly more furious than I, got out to vigorously "abuse" the man. (Local usage: "abuse" equates to berate.) He protested ignorance of our presence, which Kyari and Sarke denounced as a lie. Near a small village Sarke asked me to stop while he ran out to catch a small boy who had thrown a stone at the car—he shook him vigorously.

M. Cuypere from Belgium

In the near darkness just outside of Yenuwa not far from Maiduguri I passed a white man standing on the road waving at the car. I backed up to this unusual sight, and he introduced himself as a Belgian journalist. He wore sneakers, blue jeans cut off above the ankles, an Australian Army hat and carried the whole skin of a monkey as a bag for his belongings. He was completely bald, even the fringe was shaved—his was a Walloon face, as in Netherlandish painting. He explained his situation in loud French. He was on tour for his journal, three months to explore all of Africa very cheaply, interested in the *indigènes, les nouveaux, le folk lore, et des preblèmes social.*

Fearing Sarke's response to a request to prepare dinner for two on our return, I took M. de Cuypere to the Raceourse Hotel in the canteen area. The Action Group political campaign team had arrived that afternoon, and the hotel was full of Yorubas, many drunk, all walking about or dancing Highlife by themselves on the ballroom floor. I explained to my new friend that these were the members of a leading political party. He observed the press of party activists about the bar. After a time he turned to me: "but these are not mature people, they have not a mature political philosophy do they?" He did not comment on the glorious, and unheard of, anomaly at the bar of two Kanuri women in evening dress drinking Tango. He had brought his monkey skin with him to the restaurant much to the wonder of a droopy eyed Yoruba from Lagos who asked him what it was. *"C'est un singe"* was the laconic reply.

M. Cuypere slept the night in my spare bedroom. Sarke was confused and tardy about serving two breakfasts, and during the wait my new friend boomed out his thoughts. "I see you have your books, but you must lack the spiritual refreshment that comes in Europe with its concerts, the theater, congresses—it is a sacrifice to come out here." He appeared to be somewhat deaf and could not hear my halting French, but the conversation continued in that vein regardless.

I left him at the local Barclays Bank at 7:30 a.m.—where, I was told, he introduced himself to the manager, had a chat and proceeded on foot to the police immigration office. On the street he cut a remarkable figure, his large pink head an object of comment by the Kanuri women. With his jacket over his arm, mopping his brow, he appeared at the school after breakfast. He was enchanted to meet each one of my startled colleagues. Later I took him to pick up his monkey sack and deposited him near a lorry which would take him to Kano at the outrageous price of £2. (over 300 miles, a 7.5 hour trip by car.)

Visiting scholars

A large, rather ponderous gentleman came to the staff room in mid-morning. He gave me his card reading, "Charles R. Nixon, PhD, Research Associate, African Economic and Political Development Project." He said that Henry Manigian of the USIA in Kaduna had sent him to me. He later came to my house for a drink with Charles Bennett of the Oxford School for Commonwealth Studies, a genial Englishman who had been sent to me by David Williams. This attention was flattering indeed! Nixon even took notes while I talked, making my meagre store of information appear even smaller. "The boys in your school tend to come from what particular class?" "What can you say about politics?" etc. Both visitors were surprised by how little I had to say of the tenuous political atmosphere here—tenuous because of the strain it puts on government officers to not get out of line by expressing opinions.

"Independence means freedom for the Native Authorities (NAs)," was the sentence Nixon quoted from his recent talk with the Resident. His and Bennett's analysis is that with self-government the central authority (Kaduna) will have less and less influence over the emirs and the NAs. These will then go on to do whatever they wish. The implication is that political repression will result, and the present system of graft and corruption will expand as soon as the authority of the European District Officers goes. Bennett: "Indirect rule as it has been practiced since Lugard was not the system he intended as one may see by rereading his 1922 *The Dual Mandate*. It was the intention stated there that the DOs should govern right with the emir and keep a firm hold on what was going on. His successors changed this policy—you then have the "Resident" living up to the title, an advisor, the DOs likewise."

Both of my visitors took note of examples I cited of the NA exercising undue political control on behalf of the National People's Congress (NPC), dominant in the Muslim North, which made me wish I knew more. But three months as a schoolteacher does not provide one with such details.

CHARLES BENNETT AND MR. LAWRENCE

I offered to take Bennett to Bama for the day. After a visit to the school and the NA reading room, we left at about eleven. The road seemed worse than when I returned from the plebiscite. The car suffered several hard knocks but mostly rocked and sloshed through the sand. Conversation was difficult over the bumps, particularly since a crate of stones I keep in the back began to rattle.

Bennett told me he had been in the Indian Army during the war and after went to Oxford to take up Colonial, now Commonwealth, studies. He is writing a history of Kenya and has done a good deal of work on India and Burma.

Bama was quiet and peaceful. We stood on the steps of the District Office to talk to a man whom I thought at first to be a clerk, but who turned out to be Malam Abubakar Kigo, the new ADO. I found him to be intelligent with a confident sense of English unusual in the North, though he repeatedly laughed nervously and gave one the impression of being unfocused. One wonders how this fellow for all his intelligence will stand up to the emirs and the NAs in the future. There was a looseness about him that was unsettling.

Mr. Lawrence appeared—said he was "rotten" and appeared to be in a state of battle fatigue. He motioned us into his office. It was in the same state of disarray I remembered, files piled around his desk, office supplies stacked on them or thrown into a corner. He sat down to write an urgent telegram, soon to be dispatched by a harried-looking southern Nigerian wireless operator. Outside sat and stood several people; every now and then Lawrence would interrupt himself to ask of his senior messenger in a combination of modern Arabic and English, "what does that gentleman in the yellow want?" or, "who is that, the man with the District Head's Land Rover?" ("We have to borrow the vehicle of a DH since we are so short for this election.") The messenger, an extremely tall man, carrying a staff and wearing a white turban carelessly on his head, shuffled out to deal with the petitioner in question—usually only to usher him in with his problem to be presented directly.

The emergency telegram completed, Lawrence turned his attention to Bennett. He plunged right in:

I came from the Sudan and I am no exponent of indirect rule. I feel all we have done here is to perpetuate and condone a corrupt system of government. The emirs and the NA counselors do nothing that will not benefit themselves, the courts judge only on the basis of how much they will be paid. I tell the emir—a nice bloke, about 40, intelligent—what happened in Iraq [where in 1958 the military assassinated the king and eliminated the monarchy], and that this old system cannot go on forever. But he does not seem to listen and goes on his own way. There are things that are happening here that could be called fascist—Gestapo techniques of arresting a man because he is your political opponent. Independence means that this sort of thing will go on unchecked. We are out of touch, there is too much paperwork. The secretary-typists in Lagos and Kaduna churn the stuff out faster than we can ever answer. But where is our authority? We must do what the NA wishes or be moved. Kaduna does not back up a DO any longer.

There is the case of the NPC candidate, Guduf, caught in the act of guiding people's hands into the white box [in favor of a union with Nigeria]—the wire we received from the Premier's Parliamentary Secretary, regarding the legitimacy of his candidacy, stated "if not nominated—he should be."

The point of this is not so much the loss of the white man's authority, but the weakening of the central authority. It is commonly believed that the Sardauna of Sokoto [premier of Northern Nigeria] will be unable to manage his own emirs after independence. The Sardauna is propelled to claim a self-government that he perhaps will not be able to maintain because of the pressure from outside Nigeria such as Ghana's independence and the ferment in other African territories.

Bennett:

Nations are created in struggle. When was Nigeria's? It is an impossible thing to say, but Britain should have been tough with Nigeria before she let her go. There are obvious reasons why she could not do this. Once Ghana was independent there was no stopping Nigeria. In India and Ghana there were genuine popular movements that unified the country in a cause. In Nigeria what is there but a collection of local interests.

Assigned to serve in the Federal Election

Yesterday a useless, chattering day in the staff room. On such days I long for a real job to mesh with. The difficulty is that after such a morning nothing is possible until the brain stops spinning in the afternoon.

By contrast I went for a drink in the evening with Peter Crews, Senior District Officer (SDO) in charge of the arrangements for the upcoming Federal Election on 12 December. This is the country-wide election that will select the representatives who will form the new government and take Nigeria to independence next year. My position will again be Assistant Returning Officer, using my Cameroons experience. In his agreeable manner, Crews went over my role in Fune-Gujba constituency in western Bornu. I will tour the polling places to see that they are set up as required and review procedures with the presiding officers and the village and District Heads. There are major differences from my role in the plebiscite. This constituency is vast, about 115 miles north to south and over 40 miles from east to west. For this I will have a driver and a Land Rover and another vehicle for support. The polling stations have been constructed and the officers are trained and in place. This is an election; there are three parties each to have a ballot box dedicated by color. There is an incumbent federal representative running for reelection on the Northern People's Congress (NPC) ticket and candidates from the Action Group and Northern Elements Progressive Union (NEPU). The NPC is the dominant party of the Northern Region supported by the Muslim population. The Action Group originated in the Western Region with its large Yoruba population; despite its name NEPU's strength is in the Eastern Region where Ibos are dominant. Since it is a contested election, and the two parties with southern Nigeria affiliation are regarded suspiciously by the establishment in the North, there could be difficulties such as suppression of the southern parties by the dominant NPC and the NAs, voting irregularities.

Peter Crews then briefed me on the materials I will be taking to the malams at the polling stations, the ballots, report forms, and items as humble as string and Bic pens.

Crews is a gentle man, shy, and I sensed lonely for his family, someone who seems half-crippled without his wife and children.

I am most excited at the prospect of this second expedition in the bush and by its scale.

A "Feast" at the School

Dr. and Mrs. Lander came for drinks. Afterwards we went to the school for a "feast." The boys were assembled in three squares around the football goal posts dining quietly from their bowls. The staff sat at a long table in front of the goal posts, also eating a gruel poured from buckets into bowls—a food that was not, I discovered later, pleasing to some of them. Section VI [Sixth Form] sat in the center as the party was in their honor. The setting had all the makings of a festive and even joyful occasion, and I looked forward to a bit of laughter and ceremony after the meal. There was a speech by Malam Alami and a reply from a member of Section VI. Following was a husky speech from the headmaster, recounting the administrative steps that led to adding a VI form level. The unimaginative dead weight of his account of the bureaucratic process crushed the event. When he concluded, the boys left in a twinkling, and the staff drove back to the GRA. There was no laughter or high spirits. I paced the floor at home for some time, restless and angry.

Speaking for a Military Career

At 10 a.m. a captain from the Queens Own Nigerian Regiment met with the boys in Section VI encouraging them to consider a career in the military. He spoke out of the corner of his mouth beneath a carefully trimmed mustache. He used "really" repeatedly for emphasis; another regular interjection was "what do you say?" followed by "infantry." The boys listened attentively; he urged them to become officers to protect their country and kinfolk: "It is not the man in the front lines who is killed, but the women and children at home." He spoke of the sacrifice of Army life—"you have not one life but many lives," but pointed out that the career of the officer was one of the quickest ways to a senior service position. After some questions, Ibrahim Bama brought the session to an end: "What happens when the Army takes over the government?" Embarrassed laughter.

On to the Federal Election

Pleasant tea with REU and his wife; they open up upon acquaintance. Evening "cram" session for the ten who are to take the General Certificate Examination (GCE). They were in an almost slaphappy mode, I could get nothing out of them except for a few good responses from Malams Gagi and Gimba. Felt depressed about what I had taught them—it seemed fleshless, and this session gave me no assurance about their prospects.

Tomorrow I will be off to the Fune-Gujba constituency in central Bornu to prepare for the voting in the Federal Election.

CHAPTER FOUR

From the savanna to the hills, preparing the vote, the Nigerian Federal Election of 1959

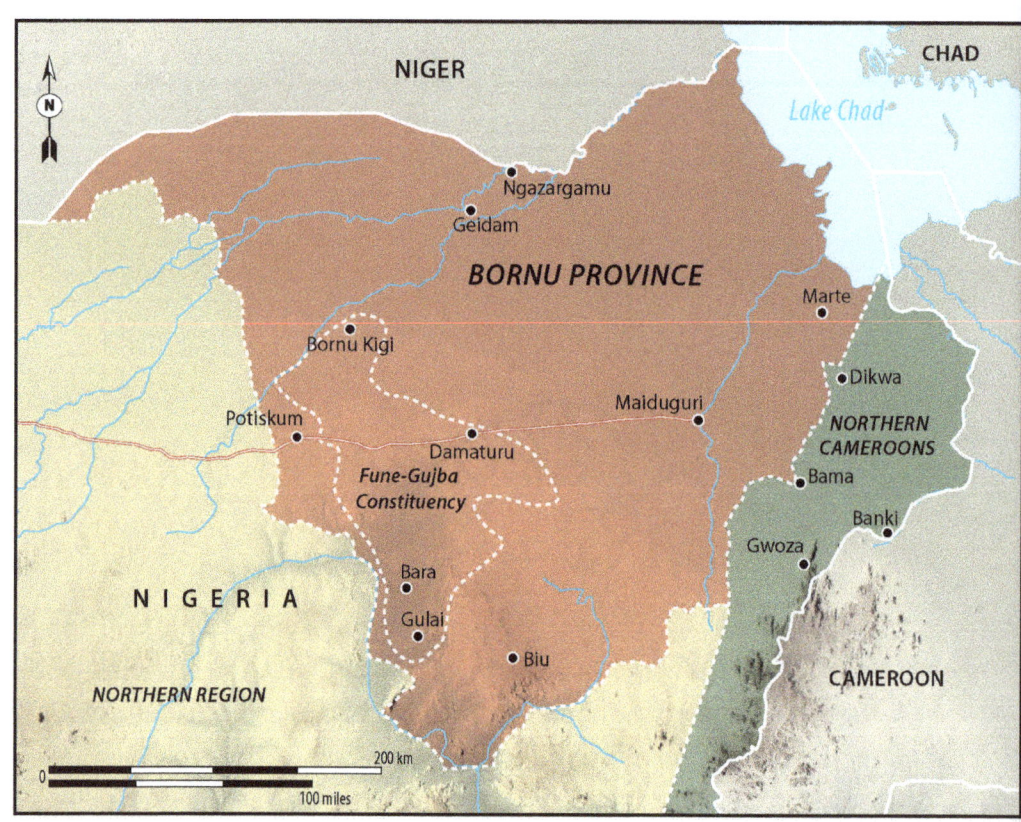

Loop outlines the Fune-Gujba Constituency within Bornu Province.
The towns with polling stations are circled in the survey map on the next page.
The constituency was over 100 miles North-South and about 40 miles East-West.

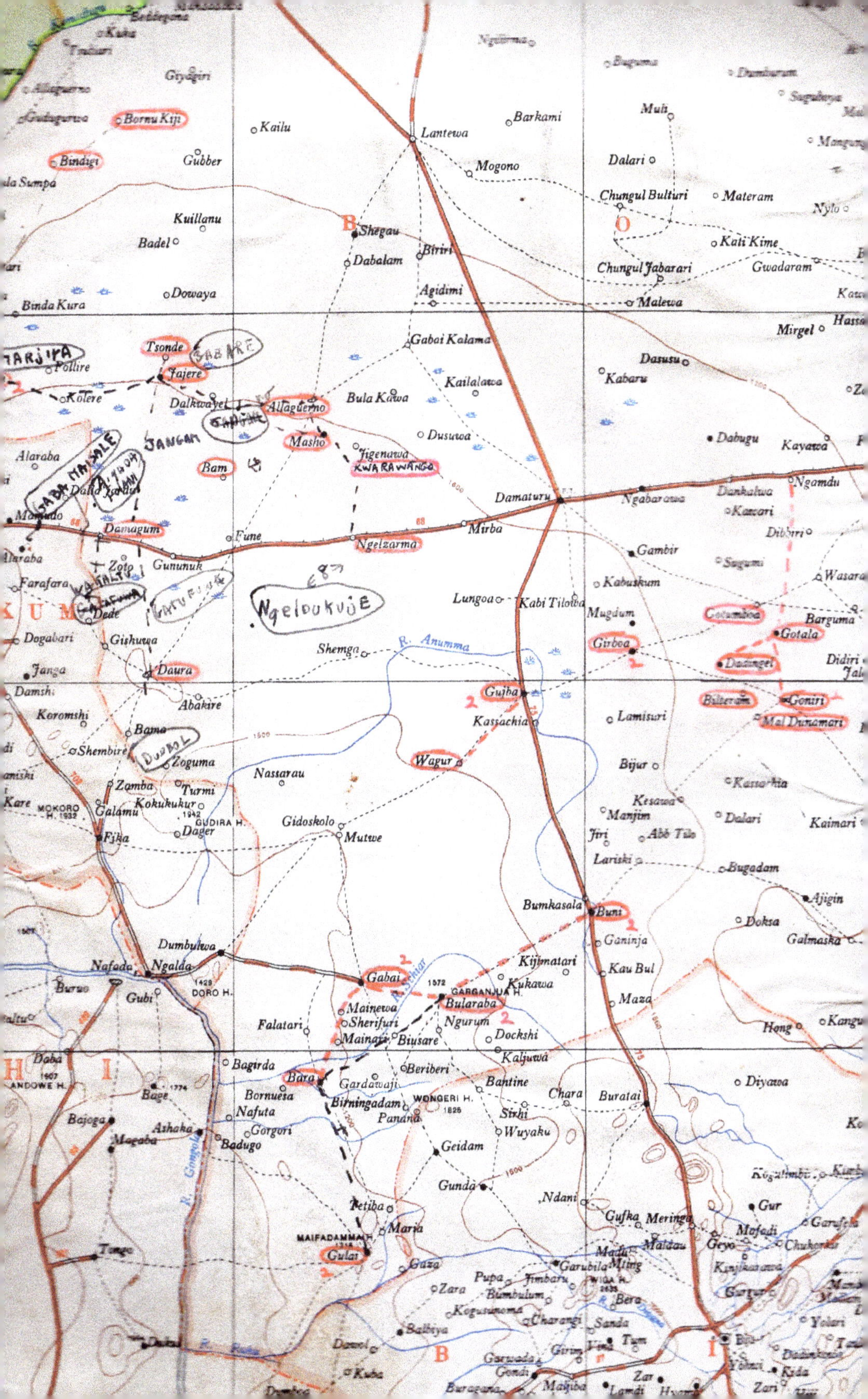

Bornu Kiji
Bindigi
Gubber
Kailu
Lantewa
Barkami
Mogono
Muli
Dalari
Chungul Bulturi
Materam
Kuillanu
Badel
Shegau
Biriri
Dabalam
Kali Kime
Chungul Jabarari
Gwadaram
Dowaya
Agidimi
Malewa
Binda Kura
Mirgel
Gabai Kalama
Tsonde
Pollire
Jajere
Kolere
Dalkwayel
Allaguerno
Bula Kawa
Kailalawa
Dasusu
Kabaru
Masho
Dusuwa
Dabugu
Kayawa
Alaraba
Bam
Jigenawa
KWARAWANGO
JANGAN
Damaturu
Ngabarawa
Ngamdu
Damagum
Fune
Ngelzarma
Mirba
Gambir
Gununuk
Zoto
Farafara
Ngeloukuje
Kabuskum
Lungoa
Kabi Tilowa
Mugdum
Dede
Dogabari
Gishuwa
Gotala
Barguma
Shemga
R. Anumma
Girbea
Janga
Daura
Dadingel
Didiri
Damshi
Gujba
Abakire
Koromshi
Kassachia
Bulteram
Goniri
Lamisuri
Mai Dunamari
Bama
Shembire
Wagur
Bijur
Zoguma
Nassarau
Kassarhia
Zamba
Turmi
Kesawa
Kokukukur
Manjim
Dalari
Kaimari
Galamu
Dager
GUDIRA H.
Gidoskolo
Mutwe
Jiri
Fika
Lariski
Bugadam
Bumkasala
Buni
Ajigin
Doksa
Dumbulwa
Ganinja
Galmaska
Nafada
Ngalda
Kijimatari
Gabai
Kau Bul
Buzuo
Gubi
DORO H.
Mainewa
Kukawa
Bularaba
Maza
Sherifuri
Falatari
Ngurum
Hong
Mainari
Biusare
Dockshi
Kaljuwa
Baba
Bagirda
Beriberi
Diyawa
ANDOWE H.
Bara
Gardawaji
Bantine
Chara
Buratai
Bage
Bornuesa
Birningadam
WONGERI H.
Nafuta
Panana
Sirhi
Bajoga
Ashaka
Gorgori
Wuyaku
Magaba
Badugo
Geidam
R. Gongola
Gunda
Ndani
Petiba
Gur
Maria
Gufka
Meringa
MAIFADAMMAH
Mafadi
Tongo
Gulat
Gaza
Garubila
Zara
Pupa
Jimbaru
Bera
Bumbulum
Charangi
Sanda
Salbiya
Dawel
Tum
Kuba
Gondi
Garwada
Buragaru
Mafiba
Zar
Lamdi
Zari
Yolari

A day or two after I met with Peter Crews his tall Fulanii messenger, Amadu, delivered a folder bound in official light green covers. I was assigned to Constituency 49, Fune-Gujba in western Bornu. The incumbent was the NPC candidate for reelection to the federal House of Representatives, Alhaji Musa Hindi, a scribe in the Maiduguri NA treasury. I was to cross paths with him and his entourage several times on my tours of the polling stations. Also running were Bukar Yoruba for the Action Group, a trader from Maiduguri, and Datti Ngelzararma for NEPU, also a trader, neither of whom I came across. It was widely assumed that the NPC was supported by the traditional leaders in the NA; support for the two other parties came from the southern Nigerians who had come north for trading and employment. As in the plebiscite, there was a possibility that local or tribal dissatisfaction with the NA-NPC establishment could lead to a protest vote for one of the other parties. Since the NA establishment was wary of competition, there was concern among election officials that there could be ballot tampering by the NA. We were to follow rules established by the higher ups that sought to reduce local officials showing favoritism for candidates. I was instructed to keep a watchful eye out and report any infractions.

For me the key information in the folder was the map of the constituency, a section cut from a copy of the Bornu survey map of 1952 and pasted on the back of the folder cover. With a red felt tip pen someone—maybe SDO Crews—had circled each village assigned a polling station. The detail in the map was bewildering. The villages seem to have been scattered across the land without any logic, unconnected to each other by lines signifying roads. The only apparent organizing features were lines showing the through roads laid out under the Protectorate. The east-west road with its single lane of tarmac that I used to reach Maiduguri was crossed north-south by lines suggesting comparable roads. In fact they were sand and clay tracks, but at least they would be passable by vehicles in this dry season. I could see that I would be crossing and re-crossing the east-west road to reach villages north and south. From the towns on the road I could both send messages to Crews and receive them by regular traffic or a wireless operator. Otherwise I would be dependent on a messenger and there were considerable distances between towns. It was daunting to see no connecting roads to most of the circled places. In the field, however, local people would point the way, sometimes providing a guide, as the map was only a general indicator of location with little or no guidance as to route. Mostly we followed informal tracks, and in the hills south we went cross-country. North of the main road and for a piece south there was open savanna with extensive land under cultivation including groundnuts, millet and guinea corn. To the south the villages were closer together and the contours indicated altitudes of up to 2000 feet and although the distances between villages seemed slight, I knew traveling among them would often be slow going.

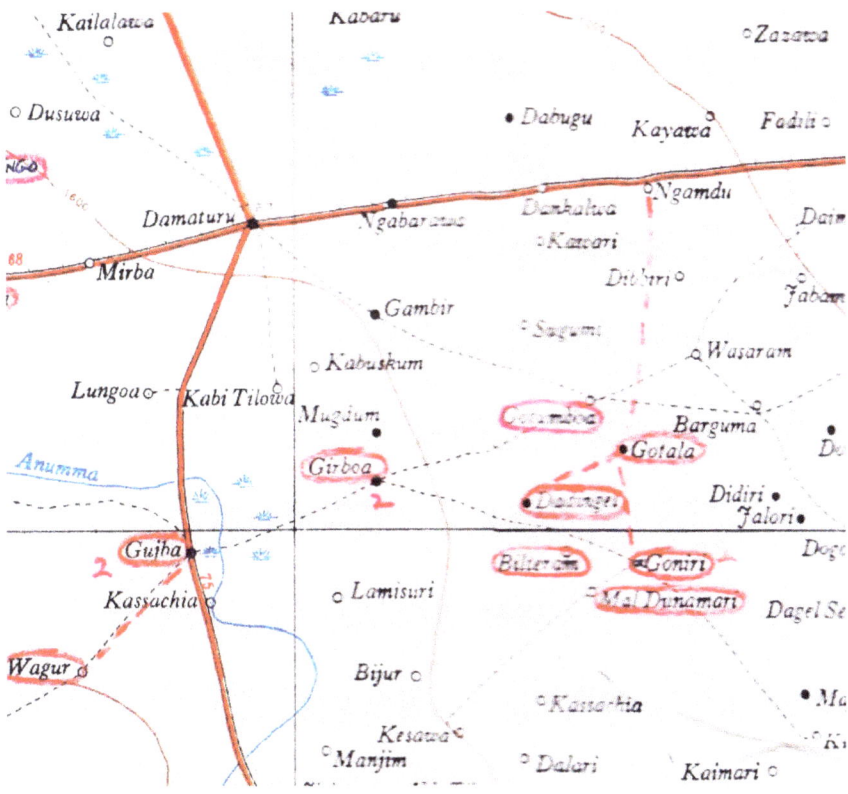

THE FUNE-GUJBA CONSTITUENCY IN THE OFFICIAL FOLDER. NOTE THE CLUSTER OF VILLAGES WITH POLLING PLACES AT THE BOTTOM IN THE HILLS. AS CAN BE SEEN, THE ASSIGNED VILLAGES WERE FAR MORE SPREAD OUT ON THE PLAIN. THE FARTHEST POINT INTO THE HILLS WAS BARA WHERE I SPENT TWO NIGHTS, WATCHED DANCES, AND FOUND A MESSAGE WRAPPED AROUND A STONE BY MY BED IN THE MORNING CLAIMING THAT THE VILLAGE LEADERS WERE SUPPRESSING AN OPPOSITION PARTY.

There was nothing in the folder about the ethnographic groups that I would encounter, only listings of the villages and the number of registered voters, though I was aware that I would find prosperous Kanuri farmers, Fulani nomads and their herds, villages of "settled" Fulani, and, in the hills, Bura and Ma tribes. Ibos and Yorubas from southern Nigeria were in the towns on the main road.

I invited Bukar Zoru, one of the best students in the VI Form, to be my interpreter. Fresh from taking the GCE, he spoke Hausa, Kanuri and fluent English. I was assigned two Land Rovers and drivers, one for the two of us, the other to carry election materials and to deliver Sarke in advance to set up for the overnights. There would be thirteen nights in the field, a mix of single and two night stays. In the villages closer to the main road there were rest houses for touring officers, but elsewhere I would put up in schools, meeting rooms, and, in one town, in a family compound.

From the scale provided on the map—one inch equals 12.4 miles—the constituency was 115 miles north to south and about forty-five miles east to west; meaning an area of 4600 mi.^{2} or about twice the size of Devon, the largest county in England, slightly less than the 4815 mi.^{2} of my native Connecticut. The most northern village was close to the border with Niger and the Sahara; in the hills to the south I found palms, fruit trees and soil that could be worked in the dry season, unexpected surprises.

The polling stations were in seventeen NA districts with 20,100 registered voters. The first task was to deliver the ballots, the boxes (three, nailed to a board), and report forms to the polling officers and review the procedures. The simple, everyday items I was to bring to each polling station were:

    1 ink pad
    1 bottle stamp pad ink
    1 box drawling pins [sic. Drawing pens?]
    2 lengths of baft (A colleague told me that "baft" is a rough cloth.)
    1 plank of wood
    1 pencil
    1 stick of sealing wax

1 Bic pen
1 bottle of gum
A quantity of pins
Brown paper

It would be a challenge to cover this area and be alert to tampering and campaign violations. Although I knew I would miss the close association I had with the villagers in and around Banki, the geographic reach was exciting, the Land Rovers would make it possible.

Monday, December 1, leaving for the Federal Election

Enormously excited about setting off. From 6 a.m. on we prepared the loads, rushed to town with Bukar to buy an extra box of kola nuts for the VI Formers to celebrate the completion of their GCE. The questions were not difficult, but the essays would strain the uncertain English of most of the class.

Bukar Zoru, fresh from the GCE, came with me in the car to Ngandu on the main road. We gave a lift to Maina, a student in the Senior Primary School, who will do various odd jobs for us. Sarke preceded in a Land Rover driven by a pleasant Kano lad named Yakopo. At Ngandu, about eighty-four miles west, Bukar and I switched to a Land Rover and headed south on a track twelve miles through the savanna to the Kanuri farming village of Gotumboa.

There the lawan himself was the presiding officer. When I asked him what he would do if a man ripped his ballot paper by accident he, to the delight of the villagers crowded about, responded, "I would arrest him." If a man came without his registration card, "I would tell him to go away." This clown presaged a chaotic voting day. A lawan's presence as presiding officer violated the province-wide decree by the Shehu instructing the NAs to be neutral and would likely discourage voters supporting other than the dominant NPC. Although the voting hut is fully enclosed, such secrecy may not be widely understood or trusted. In the present case I have no authority to disqualify the lawan in his role as an election official.

The area is agricultural, largely Kanuri, with villages close to each other. It was another ten miles to Gomri, entered through the inviting deep shade of an avenue of neem trees. Bags of groundnuts were stacked next to scales awaiting the lorries that now could use the sun-hardened track to the main road. There was an air of bustle in the village, even brightness, signs of prosperity. The women were more colorfully dressed than any I had seen outside of Maiduguri. In the late afternoon, the shade beneath the deep green canopy made Gomri, a large village of 1766 male voters, as inviting as any in the south of France.

We parked by the school where Sarke had already set up the kitchen and my bed and table. At 7 p.m. I held a meeting illuminated by the white light of the Tilley lamp with the three local presiding officers. As the discussion developed, I realized that this was a more conscientious and interested group than that of the previous village. When we broke up they thanked me for my help.

One of the group was a man who rested glasses on the tip of his nose and sported a peaked hat like that from 18th-century Prussia. It was likely a lady's hat, another instance of European castoffs finding a way into African society.

Earlier that day as we watched little boys gathered around the Land Rover Bukar commented, "the hope of the future," and added that very few of these boys would be educated—many parents did not want their sons to leave the farm and there were few places in the schools. He told me that when he was a child he and his friends would flee from white men as some of the people believed that the Europeans were cannibals.

Only one or two white men visited a year, usually the DO. "The people liked the DO because he was not corrupt." Bukar also discussed his choice of profession. He was not drawn to any of the "normal" professions—agriculture, army, police, etc. Would accounting be a good career? I strongly urged "further education" as Bukar is a top student.

December 2 Wednesday, first sight of the candidate

First stop Mal Duvanii, virtually a sister village to Gomri, only five miles south. The presiding officers were both farmers; one was waiting for us and the other came on his bicycle from the fields. It was a relatively small place with 287 voters.

In this dense agricultural area Dulturum was only five miles from where we had started that morning. There we came upon a campaign rally. From the back of a Land Rover with NPC signs waving in the wind, Alhaji Musa Hindi addressed a small crowd in front of the lawan's compound. The DH and polling officers were all there in support, and the polling officers were the village scribes in the NA, leaving no doubt that they favored the NPC. There was no question who supported this candidate, whatever the rule from the highest authority.

CANDIDATE REPRESENTATIVE MUSA HINDI AT A CAMPAIGN STOP

Musa Hindi finished his speech and retired to the shade of the school porch, sitting cross-egged on a decorated rug surrounded by an entourage. I introduced myself and chatted, while a member of the entourage, an old man with a speech impediment, gave forth a stream of words, a bizarre accompaniment to our pleasantries. Bukar later disparaged Musa Hindi because he had been merely an NA clerk when he was elected Federal Representative.

Although it was only about six miles to Dadingel, progress was slow and rough as the track challenged even a Land Rover. From heavy lorries bringing groundnuts to market and little or no maintenance, the road was nearly impassable. Yakopo cursed the man who sent us this way as our vehicle stuttered and danced over caked furrows.

The election officer at Dadingel was a young man who seemed conscientious, but he was the son of the lawan and thereby an establishment figure. This village was of moderate size with 444 voters.

After about a dozen miles on a better track we were back in Ngandu by 2:30 p.m. A mad goat stood in front of the lawan's house fulminating against unseen enemies, too paralyzed to do anything but stand perpetually in an aggressive posture, another bizarre experience that day. Bukar and Maina went for their prayers and stayed away longer than expected, prompting a dressing down from Sarke in Hausa that quite startled them. (The devoted and competent Sarke can be grumpy.)

It is about twenty-five miles east on the main road to Damaturu, one of the scrappy commercial centers that have grown up at crossroads of north-south unpaved roads. In the town we found the impressive Amadu, Peter Crews' messenger. He brought us replacement ballots and reporting forms—correcting printing errors—to be distributed to the polling stations. A note from Crews told me of violations at Damagum where the DH reportedly had been removing the posters of the Action Group. Many of the Yorubas who support that party live and work in the commercial towns along the road. Their party, like the Ibo-dominated NEPU, is regarded by the NA leadership as a threat, despite its supporters being a tiny minority. Crews included a telegram he received accusing the Damagum DH of "allowing Sawaba members to take away all election posters fixed in front of their houses. We want an immediate inquiry." [Sawaba was a small, activist Muslim party.] At the bottom of the note was, "Your baby," in Peter Crews neat hand. Anticipating controversies, another envelope contained instructions for notifying the police of violations of the campaign regulations.

TELEGRAM REPORTING A VIOLATION OF PRE-ELECTION RULES BY A LOCAL AUTHORITY THAT REMOVED SIGNS OF AN OPPOSITION PARTY. HAND WRITTEN NOTATION AT THE BOTTOM ADDRESSED TO ME BY PETER CREWS, SENIOR DISTRICT OFFICER: "YOUR BABY."

From Damaturu we returned through the bush to Gomri for a second night. We gave a ride to a Fulani Land Rover. Bukar told me that the Fulani set great store by their sticks. As compensation, the boy was thrilled by his first ride in a motor vehicle.

Agricultural Kanuri villages on the savanna near the main east-west road

Above: Village schoolhouse where I put up for the night

Along the main road, in pursuit of "my baby," meeting the Alkali and confronting the DH at Damagum. December 4,

In Gomri at seven I ate a hasty breakfast, wondering where my people were. I found them in a small knot outside the school waiting for me to appear. No need to wait for me, I told them, come to me directly. There was yet another electoral violation when the school headmaster came up holding the green box for the pro-NPC ballots. All ballot boxes should have been under the control of the polling officers, nailed to the board. The traditional authorities once again overreached. However, I saw no evidence of tampering and instructed it to be nailed to the board as required.

Back at Damaturu there was a new federal Land Rover assigned to with a cheerful Ibo, Innocent, as the driver. I bundled Bukar and Maima into the vehicle and we drove at breakneck speed west along the single paved lane of the highway. The first stop was Ngelzarma, a town about fifteen miles west of Damaturu, a large place, with 1600 registered voters, many Ibo and Yoruba among them—including the NEPU candidate—meaning a potentially volatile mix on voting day. There was a toughness about the place: the roadside commercial strip was a collection of shacks and outdoor tables, the few cars were randomly parked. Vendors in folding chairs sat by tables at the edge of the tarmac to sell candy and cigarettes to passengers in the lorries stopping for a break.

Malam Nalu Ali, the village scribe, was the presiding officer, a towering figure of over six foot with a large head and body. Impeccably dressed in a light blue riga with a fresh undergarment of pajama material, he was not about to be instructed by me—he claimed he knew all about the procedures, and briskly anticipated all my questions. He was also able to tell me the whereabouts of nearly every other presiding officer within 25 miles. I requested that they be on hand for a meeting in two days.

Back on the road the handsome new Land Rover suddenly stopped; it had lost its oil. We left Innocent with the vehicle and hitched a ride on a great trailer truck filled with groundnuts. It let us off in the center of Damagum, another big place—1600 voters—whose reason for being is the road, the commercial strip dominated by energetic Ibos and Yoruba. the majority in commerce, but governed by a Kanuri NA.

In addition to the "your baby" charge to find out about the removal of opposition party posters, Peter Crews asked me to look into a case of a person accused of tampering with a ballot box now being tried in the local Alkali's court. Bukar and I threaded our way through the market—mostly Fulani women to the court which was in a small fly-blown room in a mud-walled public building. The alert-seeming Alkali sat at a table piled with law books. Upon my arrival he summoned two waiting polling officers. The senior of them testified that when he was briefly absent from the hut where the ballot boxes were stored, the other had taken the Action Group ballot box to his compound. When he returned it, the senior polling officer discovered that bottom was moist. The Alkali admitted that did not know how to deal with the case and had referred the matter to his chief, with a judgment was pending. I told him that while the ballot box should not have been removed from the polling office, it had not been opened and there was no indication of a more serious offense. It was another breach of procedures, but minor. The Alkali closed the case.

Next, we headed over to the DH concerning the report that Action Group signs had been pulled down. The DH's compound is enclosed with a dried mud wall; through a courtyard we found him in a sparely furnished room, a large man with a scraggly beard, reclining on a lounge chair. Through word-of-mouth he already knew both that I was in the town and that the Land Rover had broken down two miles away. He rose to offer me a metal chair and reclined again to give his response to the charge of tampering. From his recumbent position he categorically denied any interference with Action Group posters and piously quoted a letter from the Shehu instructing local NAs to deal with candidates and parties impartially. His manner indicated neither truth nor sincerity, but there was nothing I could do but to instruct Bukar to give him a stern warning in my name not to tamper with campaign materials. That was how I didn't resolve the matter of the posters.

(I realized later that Bukar was uncomfortable translating my "stern warning" to an elder. Yusufu from the plebiscite would have enthusiastically pitched into such a charge, but Bukar is a schoolboy and deferential to Kanuri elders.)

The next task was to get the Land Rover moving again. I knew that the rest house here at Damagum was occupied by Mr. and Mrs. Lloyd, he of the Federal Public Works Department who could deal with a broken-down vehicle. Mrs. Lloyd, a pleasant, blonde young woman, was seated on the front porch reading a mystery story. She told me her husband was already on the road in the "tipper," or towing vehicle, looking for the disabled Land Rover. (Another example of the effectiveness of the bush telegraph; he had been alerted within minutes of our appearing in the town.) Mrs. Lloyd offered me squash, and I happily drank two glasses. I had Bukar with me, and I was uncomfortably aware that she did not invite him onto the porch.

Mr. Lloyd soon appeared, reporting that he had sent one of his men to look for towing rope, adding that the DH had suggested using chains from the prison. (I'd seen two chained prisoners through a grilled door behind the Alkali's court.) This bizarre suggestion was not feasible as the chains were too heavy, but in the event, towing wasn't needed as the Land Rover drove up. Innocent had managed to get the engine to retain oil, though how he did so he could give no clear account. It seemed prudent to have the vehicle inspected at the PWD garage in the large town of Potiskum. We headed there at less than breakneck speed.

Potiskum, the largest town between Maiduguri and Kano, was outside of the constituency, but its NA supervised the DH at Damagum. I had to report the matter of the removal of the Action Group posters to this higher authority. At the NA office the official I spoke to quickly pointed out that there must be a better case made before proceeding. He told me he supported the principle of non-interference, but he clearly was not ready to investigate the controversy. So, this was the final blank wall in pursuit of "my baby."

Potiskum, at the western limit of Bornu Province, is a comparatively cosmopolitan commercial center with a Baptist mission school, many southerners, and on this day, the first opposition posters I had seen. I checked in with the DO at the catering rest house and found him chatting with two other DOs about acquaintances in the service, distinctly different accents among them. They had no reports of electoral disturbances.

Back to Damaturu in the evening. Stopped for a beer at a Yoruba bar. Outside I saw Mr. Lloyd reading a newspaper spread out on the hood of his car. He had sent Innocent back to Maiduguri with the new Land Rover as there appeared to be something wrong with the clutch. With a loaned Land Rover Bukar and I headed south in the dark on the bush path to Gujba. Sarke was waiting at the school where, reliable as always, he had everything set up for us.

Into the hills: a celebration at Biusane Bara in the dark. December 4

I was up before dawn at Gujba, awakened by the heavy snores of the NA policeman on guard. Sarke left by nine, driven by Gilbert to set up our next overnight stay in the hill country to the south. Maina, Bukar and I stayed behind to sort the reprinted ballots into packages for each polling station according to the number of registered voters. This tedious chore done, we headed south on a straight track eighteen miles to Buni. This track had the almost unique distinction among the routes between villages in this constituency of being shown on the map. Buni was of moderate size with 700 registered voters. The DH, whose authority includes nearby villages and hamlets, greeted us from a seat on a mat in front of the lawan's house. After the usual formalities, he watched as Bukar and I went over the procedures with the assembled polling officers. After the session, Bukar and Maina had their noontime chop in a "bush" hotel, the first of these we had come across. I found a shady spot beneath a tree to eat my customary sandwich. In the shade beneath a Zana mat canopy I saw a half dozen Fulani men. In these foothills tribes mix, animists and Christians from the hills to the south, the Kanuri from the plain, and these nomads. Each wore an arm amulet and each a knife wrapped onto a bare arm; their sticks close by. With their almond-shaped eyes and light skin color they seemed strange beings compared with the tall and imposing Kanuri. I wondered about their perpetual wandering, and centuries of survival as a tribe with no fixed abode.

Buni
Ganinja
Kijimatari
Kau Bul
Kukawa
GARGANJUA H.
Bularaba
Maza
Ngurum
Dockshi
Kaljuwa
Bantine
Chara
Buratai
ERI H.
1825
Sirhi
Wuyaku
Geidam
1600
Gunda
Ndani
Gufka Meringa
Maldau
Geyo
Madu
Kinji
Garubila Mting
Pupa Jimbaru
WIGA H.
2633
Bumbulum
Bera
Kogusunoma
Charangi
Sanda
Tum
Garwada
Girim
Gondi
Zar
Mahiba

After lunch we headed southwest cross-country, leaving the savanna and the Kanuri agricultural settlements. The terrain became contoured, hilly, and the climate different: green leaves on the shrubs indicated a longer rainy season. The people are shorter than the Kanuri, with different face markings, and it is no longer horse and cattle country. The route was nothing more than an opening through the shrub created by previous vehicles. The floods in the rainy season cut deep furrows that form into concrete-like ditches. For some stretches we passed through land littered with black stones twice the size of a fist deposited by floods over the years. Though beaten down by the rainy season floods, the trees and shrubs are green, soft touches in a terrain that looked to have been battered for centuries. In the distance were hills covered with green, a marvel to Bukar who had not seen a hill in his nineteen years. We passed groves of tall palm trees in fields of yellowed elephant grass, nourished by a longer rainy season.

Bush Village head on mat

LOCAL LEADERS AT THE CAMPAIGN'S LAND ROVER

At Bularaba palm trees in the courtyards of the compounds create a feeling of an oasis—while we were only about fifteen rough miles from our start we found ourselves in a different landscape and among a different people. Bularaba is isolated from most trade routes as only four-wheel-drive vehicles can manage the track we took, yet it had 1102 registered voters.

After briefing the polling officers, we left the village on a track with declivities of hardened clay shaped by past torrents, abrupt inclines and descents. Around us was a jumbled landscape making me wonder at nature's intent. Fulani were the only people to be seen—and few except in the villages.

It was another bumpy fifteen miles to Biusane in the hills. Through the bush telegraph the villagers knew we were coming and had assembled to bid us welcome in grand style. Three drummers kept up a fervent beat beneath the obligato of a raucous horn, starting as soon as they heard the Land Rover motor. When we stopped, the horn blower brought his instrument within inches of my face in salutation, a fierce oboe sound; a singer beside him vigorously shouted out what I later learned were praises. It was a joyful reception, entirely unexpected. I clapped my hands in appreciation to shouts of approval from the villagers. The session with the polling officers was an anti-climax, but not surprisingly the officers were eager and attentive.

MY RECEPTION AT BIUSINAE

From Biusane the next stop was Gabai, with 1,094 voters, the southernmost village of the constituency, shown on the map to be at an altitude of over 1500 feet. The path traversed plowed land alternating with fields of hard-baked mud. There were six miles of this to Gabai where the villagers told us ours was among the first motors to arrive since before the rains, five months ago. The village was laid out on a hill, with streets descending in a fan shape from an open space by the lawan's compound to facilitate drainage. There were several massive trees with bundles of fruit, now leafless, conveying a wintery impression amid the semitropical abundance. What seemed like the entire village gathered around for my talk, and when I was done the fierce-looking lawan opened a bundle he was carrying to present me with an ostrich egg, a delightful surprise.

The sun was nearly down as we started back to Biusane and from there to Bara, about twenty miles in all. Night came as the Land Rover pounded through hilly terrain on a rough track, fitfully lit by the bouncing headlights. Sarke had preceded us, and the white light from the Tilley lamp streamed from the meeting hut onto a small square by the lawan's gate. A crowd of curious villagers filled the square in this small place of only 368 registered voters; the map shows its elevation to be about 2000 feet. As the elderly lawan explained through Bukar, we were among Bura people, a tribe long settled deep in these hills. He almost went down on his knees to greet me; the arrival of my party with the two Land Rovers was clearly an important event.

At the meeting house, Sarke and Gilbert were full of good cheer, congratulating us for reaching the village in the dark over difficult terrain. Gilbert, who drove my Land Rover, is a southerner from Lagos; and as Sarke commented, "he no savvy the bush roads," but he made it.

After a wash I felt refreshed; the air was cool, and I sat down to enjoy the accommodation, a hut within a compound enclosed by a dried mud wall; the only decorations were a printed notice introducing the new Nigerian currency and a touched-up photograph of the Queen.

I felt I was living a fantasy in this remote land with its isolated settlements and warmly welcoming people. I realized I was benefiting from a legacy established over the decades by trusted touring officers, as Bukar had told me. Here too it had been years since a European visited, contributing to the excitement.

There was sad news from elsewhere. On the onion skin *Times* by the lamp was word that the great actor, Gerard Philippe, had died. Early in this same year I had been an extra when he played the lead in the a French production of de Musset's *Lorenzaccio*. His films were part of my coming-of-age. How could it be that he is gone, the epitome of ardent youth?

Political protest; vegetable gardens, tribal dances. December 5

Awakened at dawn by an imam who, in the course of his call, transformed spoken prayers into chant. I noticed an object on the floor, a paper wrapped about a stone and fastened by string; it must have been thrown over the wall. On the paper was a message in Hausa informing me that the lawan was abusing members of NEPU and confiscating party cards. Here was yet another not surprising case of the local authority acting in defiance of the firm official policy of non-interference. I reported this to Peter Crews a few days later when I reached a place where there was traffic to Maiduguri. To raise the issue with the *lawan* on the spot could lead to reprisals, and, in any case, I had no authority to do so. The clandestine note showed that at least some in this minority tribe were bucking the NA establishment. If Yusufu had been with me he might have picked up more information on this from the locals, but Bukar is reserved and likely seen as a student. I admit I enjoyed the drama of a covert message thrown over the wall; I would like to have followed it up. The reality was that it doubtless was a genuine grievance and over time such resentments of the unrestrained NA would increase, as Mr. Lawrence predicted. (Post-election I heard no report of trouble in Bara, but the place was remote and news would have had to travel through Kanuri territory.)

We spent the next day visiting nearby polling stations, returning to sleep at Bara in our comfortable enclaves. The first was Gulani almost twenty miles west and further into the hills. Maina drove the Land Rover, Bukar and I beside him on the front seat. There was no defined route, and we had two guides with us, Azia, from the Bara polling station, and the owner of the compound where the drivers and Bukar are staying. The latter was dressed for the outing in an English woman's winter overcoat.

For a stretch we followed a riverbed passing through groves of palm trees amid lush green elephant grass. Leaving the riverbed we soon realized the guides were lost. People in the fields prompted by the rare appearance of a Land Rover rushed to look at us and gave us directions. There were many suggestions to which our guides added their own, making it impossible to keep on a steady course. Eventually a village boy volunteered and put on what looked like his best clothes to lead us to Gulani. The people we were among are Bura, some shouted "sama-ha," the NEPU slogan, publicly opposing the establishment NPC.

The boy guided us through a landscape littered with large black rocks that floodwaters had carried from hills miles away, a reminder of the scale and intensity of water here during the wet season. On a stretch along an exposed ledge we had a view of distant villages perched atop thickly wooded hills.

The Gulani primary school was on a plateau swept by the cool breeze of the Harmattan. There were well-tended flowers outside, in the classrooms photos of the royal visit and self-government celebrations. I asked the vigorous, young *lawan* if there had been political disturbances in or around the village. He denied any such, but unconvincingly as his face conveyed the opposite. A senior primary school boy came up to us to practice English, and introduced himself as Congi. In front of the unsuspecting lawan, he told me in English that there had been protests a week before.

The lawan took us to a garden outside the town and proudly pointed out onion plants neatly laid out in squares. The dark clay earth was soft underfoot, altogether different from the soil on the Bornu plain at this season. We watched farmers carry filled calabashes from the waterholes in the village to water the crops, greeting us cheerfully as they passed. Gulani was known for its deep well—the ropes that pulled up the calabashes had worn inch-deep notches in the wood that framed the well's opening.

Around us the green leaves of lime and mango and banana trees ruffled in the breeze; we were in a luxurious orchard. I asked the *lawan* if the tree plantation and the gardens had been developed at the initiative of an agricultural officer. "The gardens have been like this as long as anyone can remember." Except for a survey officer passing through, mine was the first white face they had seen since an education officer opened the school six years ago. Our Land Rover was the third motor come to the village since the start of the rainy season.

The lawan told me of a project "to clear the road to Bara, beginning Monday." Gulani had to make a start, he said, as the Bara lawan, "being old," was reluctant to commence the project. "The people will understand the advantages if lorries can easily come to us." The surface of the uncertain track we had just followed from Bara was V-shaped and baked hard; grading it with pick and mattock would be a long-term proposition. Nonetheless, as the *lawan* affirmed, he was set to start the project on Monday.

A crowd attended my instructions to the presiding officers, small boys banded together at a respectful distance, men and elders behind the *lawan*, all in the ample shade. There were 573 registered voters in and around Gulani. The officers were from the first class at the primary school six years ago; now they were farmers and uncertain about the procedures. The lawan, acting as a big chief, found it all too complicated and did not hesitate to express his impatience. Judging by his forward-looking road project, he was progressive, but he revealed himself no democrat. Later when I visited him in his fine mud brick house, he turned on a battery radio just as it broadcast a charge that "administrative officers in Niger Province [to the south] are interfering with the natural rulers." I too interfered and cited the policy that the NA not interfere with political activity. I was talking to the air.

In the early afternoon the lawan, accompanied by a few elders, led us up to a hamlet on the hill overlooking the main village. The slopes had been scraped by the rains over the centuries leaving great boulders, hard as granite, though they were reddish in color like sandstone. From an outlook we saw distant hills, and on this perfectly still day, smoke from fires in the bush rose straight up. The lawan pointed to a hill and told us that many years ago Gulani had been situated on its summit, secure against the marauding tribes from the plain. I reveled in the vistas and encouraged Bukar to enjoy his first ever view from a hill.

At 3 p.m. we left this fair place. The Land Rover lurched and bumped, hot sun on the face, dust through the window, sweat on the shirt. Usually on such a ride I concentrate on the bumps and brace when I see them coming. Not so of this journey, as there were landscapes and people to enjoy. We stopped to admire a grove of gum Arabic trees near three small villages and were wildly greeted by small boys who, alerted by the sound of the motor, had run across several fields for a close look.

At Yabani we took a break in a palm grove. The fruit of this tree smells like a mango, not a nut. Ali, the bright-faced young lad who had earlier been our skillful guide to Gulani, pulled a knife from the sheath he wore at his waist and cut one open, alas, not yet ripe. Bukar and I found a spot in the cool shade, the leaves overhead rustling in a light breeze. We talked with seven small boys who had been collecting firewood and formed themselves in a circle around us, their eyes wide in wonder. Whenever a man passed, usually a farmer returning from the fields, one of them repeated his name as if it were the most wondrous fact in the world, and so it was for us in that moment.

We reached Bara as the sun was setting. The Forestry Malam, a friendly junior member of the local NA, unexpectedly came up to tell me he was inspecting the polling stations on behalf of the DH. This presumably was his way of tactfully disguising that he was a political agent, for his riga was the green of the NPC.

When I asked the old lawan what he knew of the origins of his people in these hills, he responded that they came many years ago from the plains. He added that there is a mixture of tribes here, Ma, from the Fika hills to the west, Bura or Babur in this village and in the Biu country to the east, and a few Kanuri and Fulani. This prompted me to mention that it would be interesting to see dances from these tribes. "The villagers will show you tonight," was his quiet response.

During dinner I heard a ceaseless beat by apprentice drummers accompanied by shouts from the village children. By dessert the noise had gathered strength and purpose. I set up the folding chair outside my compound on the public square, framed by mud walls with lanes through which the villagers poured in. Facing me was the "lawan's gate," the most prominent doorway on the square. Bukar and the Forestry Malam sat nearby on the tailgate of the Land Rover. The crescent moon and several battery-powered torches cast pools of light near the dancers' feet.

The dance began with a number of young men and women moving slowly and rhythmically in a circle, chanting a long melody, first men's voices, then women's, regularly alternating. This was a Ma dance which I took to be a sowing song for it had a solemn joyfulness about it. The high-pitched, open-throated women's voices topped the men when they came to face us in the revolving circle. Next was a Kanuri dance: in turn a pair of girls from a group of over a dozen advanced towards us with delicate steps fluttering their sarong-like dresses with modest downcast eyes as they bowed low and returned to the circle followed by the next pair who did the same until all had come forward and bowed.

In a Fulani dance, girls in pairs approached from the far side of the square, advanced slowly to regular drumbeats. As they approached they stooped lower and lower until they kneeled before us. Their steps were as light and elusive as the Fulani themselves.

In another dance the younger girls did a bottom-wagging routine which gradually took on an aggressive sexual character. Each wore a cloth around the pelvis knotted in front; as they approached us they agitated the knot to make it appear to be a male member. One by one they came to us competing with each other to express sexual excitement; with the heated drumming they accelerated the movement of the pelvis and the thighs. A girl of about twelve outdid the others; with the single-minded intensity of a child to the cheers of the crowd she enacted an expression of sex that was both terrifying because of its exaggeration and moving because of her skill.

The finale came at 11 p.m., a Fulani warriors' dance. By then the small boys who had been bouncing around at the edges sat to watch. The men wore Fulani red skirts with jangling instruments on their ankles; they grasped each other in groups of eight, chattering as they moved around the square. With a ferocious stamping they alternated directions, raising a cloud of dust. They repeated this barbaric splendor several times, then it ended as suddenly as it began. I clapped and bowed in thanks and the villagers cheered. It was close to midnight when we warmly bade each other good night.

Leaving the Hills, Return to the Plain and the Main Road. December 8

Gilbert had given a pigeon to Sarke for my dinner before the dance. In the wee hours it turned out to be unwelcome. Despite aches and pains in the morning, I summoned up words of farewell and appreciation to the lawan and people of Bara. We bumped our way the thirty-six miles back to Gujba where I took a welcome break on the porch of its rest house. Mr. McLeod arrived after three, a teacher who warmly communicated his interest in Africa and Africans. As we sorted election papers, he told me about his well-run school in the regional capital of Kaduna.

We headed back to the main east-west road at Damagum where the self-assured M. Mali Azi, as promised, had assembled most of the presiding officers of Fune District, a large section of the constituency; Damagum itself is large with 1306 registered voters. It was a hectic meeting. I could not restrain M. Aziz from vigorously berating the presiding officers for any hesitant or mistaken answer to my questions. Little was learned; I saw clearly that small sessions on mats by the village lawan gates are far more useful.

M. Mali Azi is known locally as a "kind" man. In witness he put up Bukar and gave him meals. He gave me a bottle of Tango and an assortment of bonbons.

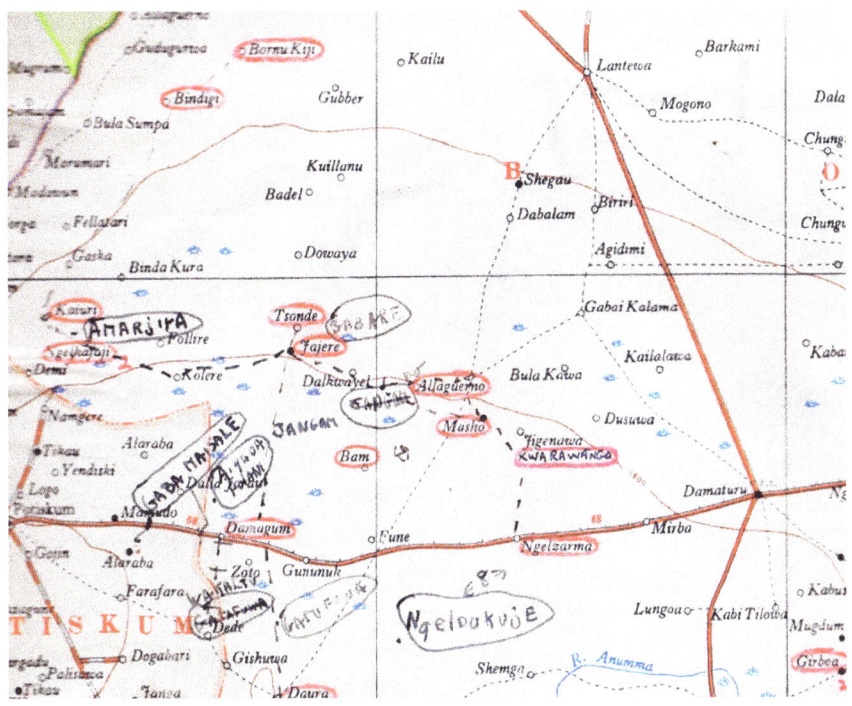

HILL COUNTRY IN THE SOUTH OF THE CONSTANCY.
NOTE THE CONTOUR LINES AS THE TERRAIN BECOMES MOUNTAINOUS.

Next we headed off on a dirt track through the savanna to Gatafuwa, our first stop at villages north of the main road. We were back in Kanuri country, on hard baked clay, amid shrubs and yellowed grasses. Along the route the villagers had set up posts with tiny paper signs saying "Gatafuwa this way." The presiding and polling officials clearly took pleasure and pride in their assignments, and I noted that they were living in the polling station to protect it.

Next we cut through the bush back to the main road and about twelve miles south to Daura with 586 registered voters. The village was built at the edge of hills, one nearby was particularily inviting. At my suggestion, a few of the villagers climbed it with me. To the north we could see the flat Bornu plain we had come from, its unvarying vastness apparent from the outlook. To the south were the Fika hills at the edge of the constituency.

At Daura I spent my first night within a compound in a Bornu house. Sarke set up the table in the master bedroom and made up the bed. Beyond the door was the purdah area, Bukar and the others put up in huts within the compound. The bed collapsed when I got into it, but apart from that, it was a pleasant stay. After dinner the villagers put on a Kanuri boys dance and dances for girls in pairs. The moon was nearly at half.

Back to the Savanna. December 8

From Daura it was a few miles north onto the main road again, the air chill and sweet. At Damagam. One of the polling officers later told me that he "makes us tremble and confuses us." No wonder the meeting the day before had been so unsatisfactory; he would browbeat them out of their wits. Happily he wasn't there, and I went over the procedures with M. Liman, the presiding officer at Aigadi Fulani near the Niger border to the north. He had come down to check in with me; his village is the most remote in the constituency, some fifty miles from the main road, too far to visit, a day to get there and back. He is one of the primary school boys recruited to serve as election officers. We gave another senior primary school boy a lift through the bush to Masho where he will be the presiding officer, he spent the time exchanging news with Bukar and practicing English. These boys are pressed into service as there are so few literate men in these northern villages.

SAVANNA LAND

Once again, we were on the great plain, Kanuri and Fulani villages and numerous Fulani tending their herds peppered the landscape. Masho, with only 271 registered voters, is a pleasant place with cool shade and locally grown fruit. It is far enough from the main road not to be a way station, but close enough for trading and marketing of crops. I found fresh limes to squeeze into my water.

For lunch Bukar and Ibrahim, our driver for this segment, asked me to join them; the meal was *dawa*, a porridge made of cornmeal and sour milk, pepper and sugar. Much to their pleasure, I joined them in taking the food from a large spoon made from a gourd. "Have you ever eaten from a spoon like this?" they asked. I found the porridge tasty and filling, although a bit monotonous.

Allaguerno with 456 voters we reached by a level track a few miles further north. The lawan was young, sturdy and athletic looking, with a forceful manner. While I went through the procedures his young daughter sat by him like a princess, unique for a girl of any age to join these meetings.

A dozen miles further north came Jajere. The savanna here was rough with useless-looking shrub trees dotted about in grass beaten down by passing herds. The soil was light yellow, dry and firm. Along the way were Fulani tending long-horned cattle, boys and young men walking slowly behind the dusty animals. They must have the gift of conveying calmness for the cattle never bolted at the sight or sound of the motor. The men's heads are shaved except for a tussle of hair; they wear jewelry and some have caps set on the back of the head, others wear broad-brimmed hats of woven grass. The sticks used to prod the cattle were at the ready across their backs. They are wild-looking, and, according to Ibrahim, thieves and murderers—clearly a belief reflecting a tribal prejudice.

Jajere is a large Fulani town with 515 registered voters, almost three times that when the neighboring villages are included; its concentration of settled Fulani makes it unique in the area.

Returning to Allaguerno in the afternoon a celebration was in process, a small durbar with local men and horses in full regalia to greet Musa Hindi, the candidate. When his Land Rover came into view, the horsemen let loose the strident warriors' yell and villagers shouted "Salama!" People had come in from the outlying hamlets for the rally and were dressed for it, looking their best. The candidate was attended by the supporters in an accompanying lorry. The DH and his retinue were assembled to greet him, a clear sign of establishment support. Musa Hindi, the DH and the village head took seats on chairs in the center of a crescent-shaped, respectful crowd. The Land Rover drew up before them to serve as a podium with brilliantly caparisoned horses and their riders as a backdrop. The tall, well-fleshed animals on parade with their riders were the finest horses I'd seen in Bornu. Next to them was a bullock soon to be presented to the candidate and two kids for the DH. It seemed to be an entirely Fulani crowd.

From the Land Rover Musa Hindi spoke in measured tones about the good the NPC has done, and, after a reference to Islam and tradition, descended to resume his seat among the dignitaries.

The master of ceremonies, a professional party worker, then mounted the Land Rover. Like a cheerleader, he called for rousing shouts of the party slogan, but for all his effort there was only a feeble response from the elders who possibly deemed a shout out undignified. He made a confessional appeal: as a youth he admitted he had been a member of NEPU, the Ibo-dominated party. When he discovered that his fellow party members were "godless, lawless rowdies," he turned to the party of tradition, the party of religion. "Look at the other parties, composed of town toughs and pagans! Look now at the NPC symbol, the hoe [holding one up]. You use it every day. There is your strength, there is your livelihood. You knew how to farm even before the Europeans came. Vote for this! It is familiar to you." Then he held up the symbols of the other parties. The star of NEPU: "Stars are far away. Can you touch them? What have they to do with you?" The palm tree of the AG: "someone else gains his money from the product of this tree. The people who support this have nothing to do with you." He repeated the appeal to support the party of tradition and religion, and, after more slogan-shouting joined only by the children, their elders unmoved by political enthusiasm, there came a short, unpolished speech by the local party president. The meeting was done.

Before the crowd broke up Musa Hindi, invited me to remain to see "dancers from afar." Before the dancing he and the local leaders distributed prizes such as new rigas awarded for work on behalf of the party. Then there was an instructive demonstration: a girl came up wearing a kerchief with a star, the NEPU symbol; she replaced this with a kerchief decorated with the image of a hoe, and, to applause, set fire to the offending kerchief. Three local political organizers sat humbly at the feet of the candidate while his aides covered them with handsome new cloth. The gift was a tribute to their loyalty to the party, shouted to the crowd by the praise singer. A woman received cloth to reward her work as women's organizer. Each of the musicians stepped forward to accept publicly a currency note from the now bored-looking candidate.

Following this, a sizable number of apparently unemployed young men and weary looking prostitutes began a slow dance to the beat of a drum. The young men were tough and ruthless looking; they and the women made a display of their cigarettes, smoking as they moved. In the crowd I saw two men, clearly separate from the villagers as they wore green and white robes, obviously uniforms. Bukar told me they were the party police, whose purpose is "to keep order at the dances and meetings." Toward the end, the graceful movements of the traditional dance were modified, motions become sharp and harsh and often obscene. At six it was all over in a twinkling, time for prayers. This harsh enactment of a traditional dance was nothing like the moving performances at BaraError! Bookmark not defined..

I was to stay in a small meeting hut, but I chose the more spacious school instead. The welcoming headmaster was a former middle school boy, Baba Shuwa. Sarke cooked for me in the women's section of a compound where the three wives watched with fascination as he set out the cot and laid the table.

In the evening the presiding officers came to the school for the briefing. The DH's musicians stood outside his gate in full moonlight at nine to sing his praises to the beat of a double-headed drum.

Further north. December 9

Our morning departure was delayed while the DH presented Musa Hindi with two kid goats. The candidate asked me to send him the slides I took of him when they are developed. The DH, Mai in Fulani, looks the part of a chief with his handsome Fulani turban. He showed me his horses, splendid animals, beautifully groomed.

To Kalene over the bush road. The day was hazy, almost like a sea day, but dust instead of moisture. It was deserted country save for an occasional village. At Ngelzarma with 570 voters, the villagers, expecting the candidate, were assembled, and gave us a rousing welcome. This time, not to be associated with the campaign, we retired to the polling station *rumfa* for the briefing.

These northern villages appear quiet and remote, apparently little or no influence from the main road forty miles south. It is mostly grazing country, but there were some scales for weighing groundnuts still in place, indicating cultivation in what looked like unpromising soil. Bukar tells me that a farmer may make as little as £10 a year.

At Kayere (Kaiuri on the map), with 560 voters, I tried to buck up the two lads serving as polling officers who had been browbeaten by Mali Azi. Then Bindigi, 291 voters, so named, I was told, because when the villagers repelled Fulani warriors years ago the latter yelled something that sounded like "Bindigi."

Bornu Kigi, 300 voters, is the most northern village for me to cover, over a hundred miles from Gabai in the hills. The presiding officer was a nervous young teacher from the Jajere primary school.

This was the last of our visits to the polling stations and the last meeting with the polling officers. We will visit these places again briefly to pick up the sealed ballot boxes and the reporting forms after the election.

Back in Jajere, Bukar and Ibrahim listened to the 7 p.m. news in the lawan's compound and reported that Zik had given a fiery political blast. (Nnandi Azikwe, veteran advocate for Nigerian independence, leader of the NEPU party with a base of support in the Eastern Region.) They quoted a key statistic he provided to show the backwardness of the North—only 137 GCE passes in 1957 in the whole of the Northern Region. (Bukar expects to receive his at the end of term.) A Kanuri

DANCING FOR THE CANDIDATE

THROUGH URBAN POTISKUM, DECEMBER 10

The next morning we headed south on a sandy track south to Jajere. At first it was chilly enough to need both a sweater and the Land Rover's window closed, but around 8:45, the heat began its climb. Musa Hindi passed us heading north with at least ten of his supporters, some clinging to the sides of the Land Rover like those seated on the rail of a sailboat in a stiff gale. Continuing south to Potiskum the track was worse than any we had experienced in this northern section; the groundnut lorries had churned it into deep fine sand and the center ridge scraped the bottom of our vehicle. A hazard in these unmaintained tracks is a stump hidden in the sand; the bottom of our Land Rover was almost torn out by one in this stretch. Much of the country was deserted. The few settlements along the route posed a striking contrast to the well-kept Kanuri and Fulani ones we had just visited. They appeared to be fragments of communities, and the people, probably of mixed ethnicity, have none of the dignity of their neighbors a few miles north.

Potiskum, the eastern edge of Bornu, is a junction between the main east-west road and the paved road leading south. The shoulders of its main street are lined with small shops in scrappy buildings run by Ibo and Yoruba traders with dirt parking spaces for cars and lorries. The political posters of all three parties were on display, a contrast with the one-party dominance in the Kanuri and Fulani areas. Here the cyclists pedal faster, there are more idlers, toughs, and prostitutes, giving the place a frontier appearance. When I took a walk, people, surprised by the sight of a European on foot, shouted cheerful greetings, "*samma faturi*" or "*smma*." Enormous lorries roared past, carrying groundnuts west and gasoline and oil east to Maiduguri and Fort Lamy. In this town all three political parties compete, creating potential conflict and chicanery. Potiskum was just outside my constituency; but the other villages along the main road are smaller though similar in nature to Potiskum with mixed ethnicity and entrepreneurial activity.

We headed back to Damaturu on the tarred main road which, like all modern highways, allows higher speeds and thus scenes so interesting on the bush tracks—people on foot or seated by the road, herders—pass by too quickly to observe. We stopped at Damagum where Mali Azi had several packages for me, including newspapers that I was surprised to realize I didn't want to bother with, so absorbed with the present was I—not eager to absorb news of the wider world from the *Times*. We returned to Gujba for the night to await the election.

The eve of the election, a day of rest. December 11

Friday, the eve of the election. For us AROs it was a "day of rest," that I needed because of the stiff cold I was fighting. Mr. McLeod returned in the afternoon, also having completed the tour of his polling stations. It was his plan to bring in the boxes on Saturday night after the polls closed; I have far longer distances to travel and need the daytime, so will pick up the day after the voting. McLeod, nervous, jumps from one subject to another in a scary manner though he has interesting facts and observations.

Voting day, pick up day. December 12, 13

Voting day. Gujba Polling station was quiet, the voters lined up when it opened. Nearby in "Gujba hamlets" there was good-natured pushing and shoving to get into the ballot booth; the *lawan* ordered voters into a sitting position to reestablish a line. With Yakopo driving a long Land Rover we rocked along on the main road to Damagum. We saw NA police, but there and elsewhere voting proceeded in an orderly manner. On an empty stretch we spotted two men seated beside the road. They were a DH and an NA policeman who told us that their car had run out of petrol; they left it with the driver and set out on foot to search for the nearest fuel. We turned back with them and soon found the car and driver, leaving a four-gallon supply.

We picked up the ballot boxes the next day—we were to pick up those in the north section where we had just been; others were assigned to pick up from the polling stations south of the main road. We changed to a lorry and headed to Ngelzarma, each bump shivering the kidneys. Then Allaguerno, Jajere and Kaiuri, and on to Borno Kigi at the very north, familiar places now. We arrived back in Gujba at five p.m. to a warm welcome from fellow AROs. I was exhausted after the 150 mile round-trip (as the crow flies, longer counting the diversions); almost all of the travel had been on bush tracks, giving an intense experience of the Bornu plain. The ballot boxes were intact, there had been no tampering.

I was told there would be a dance "in your honor" at night. After dark a group of village women gathered hoping to hear the radio; three of them prostrated themselves at my feet to greet me. I gave them peppermints, evoking a wry look from Ibrahim. Before retiring, a neighbor woman threw herself in front of the doorway and barely let me through. She surely was there to offer herself. What a disturbance the *baturi* brought to these lives! They will talk of it for months.

I am moved by the trust I have found everywhere; it is has been a joy to be among these people. Translation is not needed when it comes to sharing a mood or something humorous. I have felt whole villages respond with laughter and with interest though no one understood the words.

What remained was to deliver the ballot boxes to the constituency headquarters. There we opened them in the presence of the Returning Officer and the other AROs, the votes counted and the results recorded. After what felt like a two-week whirlwind of activity, I returned to the house in Maiduguri and was at the school on Monday.

As after the plebiscite, in response to David Williams, I sent in an account of the election in Bornu for *West Africa*.

West Africa January 2 1960

It was widely believed that the result of the Northern Cameroons plebiscite showed deep discontent with the ruling party of Northern Nigeria, the Northern People's Congress (NPC). Yet in the federal general election, which followed only a few weeks after, the plebiscite's voting pattern was not reproduced even in the trust territory itself, while in the whole of Bornu province, which contains part of the Northern Cameroons, the NPC emerged victorious except in one constituency. The only substantial slices in its huge majorities in the province were taken by NEPU in Potiskum and by the Action Group in Bama (Dikwa Central). Even Maiduguri, which saw a good deal of [the Action Group's] Awolowo and his helicopter, produced only a feeble opposition vote.

The NPC, however, has an irritant to its pride—the victory of the Action Group candidate in Gwoza—which is in trust territory; the hill peoples there maintained the opposition to the NPC...

For the rest of the province in rural areas NPC candidates were returned over opposition that scarcely ever numbered one tenth of the votes cast and usually one twentieth. If the farmers and herdsmen of Bornu, of whatever tribe, were dissatisfied with the government, very few of them felt free to express it in the general election polling booth.

In comparison the opposition's activities were negligible in most rural areas, and often covert. The dedicated group of NEPU supporters could do little to challenge the glamour and prestige of their opponents. The Action Group, though "the most hated party," had only the faintest support, as the election results showed.

No one pretends that meetings like [Musa Hindi's] influenced votes. It is probable that the vote would have been no different if there had been none of this activity. The keyword to use in explaining the people's vote is obedience. They were not to discard an obedience to the directives of the traditional authority, fundamental to their religion and ethics, because of this selection. It will take some years and the penetration of the often destructive forces of the 20th century before the countryside's conservativism is shaken. It is a moot point just how much these people trusted the scrupulously maintained secrecy of their ballot. In any case, they see no pressing economic or political need to change their rulers, and all the observations of commentators based in a background of the contentious politics of a western democracy will not budge them yet.

§

From the perspective of the Fune-Gujba constituency the election was an impressive administrative achievement. Over 20,000 people in an area of about 4600 mi.² had been registered, the voting places were convenient, on the day there was safety and order, the vote was private, ballots were collected and counted promptly.

Although the Northern Region was officially self-governing, like that of the plebiscite this election was a next-to-last act of colonial governance before independence. It was organized and run by the largely expatriate Provincial Administration which secured the cooperation and assistance of thousands of Africans to make it succeed.

I experienced in those 13 days the savanna, the hills, the commercial strips and the different peoples who endowed them. The greeting at Biusane, the long evening of dances at Bara, small boys in the palm groves, the gardens and orchards of Gulani and the vistas of other villages on nearby hills—these were among the unique experiences of people and places in never-to-be-repeated circumstances.

In the Nigeria Federation the Northern Region had an overwhelming advantage in population and in elected representatives. This was resented by those in southern Nigeria who had led the way to independence, and it didn't take many years before assassinations and coups and a civil war unsettled the framework. I must have been thinking of such when I commented in my article that respect and obedience in the countryside would last until "the penetration of the often destructive forces of the 20th century." Change that to "the 21st century" and the Boko Haram with assault weapons and cell phones.

Chapter Five

Creating a Map in the Mind

Over Christmas and New Year's I drove the Opel south to Lagos on the coast and east to Enugu, the capital of the Eastern Region. This was motoring almost on a continental scale, glimpses of a third of the vast country, modernizing cities and activist politics. Then back to remote Bornu and the Provincials Secondary School. The bickering in the staff room kept on: I looked in vain for a positive spirit from my colleagues, but, finding none, I found I had settled in to the GRA better than in the first months. It was the height of the dry season, chilly at night, dry heat by day. Back at school in Maiduguri in late January I recorded a tender resolution of the distress of one of the younger boys.

At school little Waziri Gwoza came into the staff room looking sick and worried. Said he wanted to go home to Gwoza to get some native medicine for the snakebite he had in December. Malam Abdakahiri assured him gently that European medicine was better. Eventually he burst into a fit of crying before the headmaster; who, after consultation with Dr. Lander, decided to send him off to Gwoza. When the boy heard this he began to eat again and now looks as cheerful and bright as he usually does. "When these boys get into this sort of mood there is nothing to do. If they make up their mind that they are going to die they usually do," was the headmaster's comment.

Section I, with the youngest students [equivalent to US fourth grade] had been bursting to ask questions about America. At the appointed hour the first question was: "Do they have wash men in America?"

Some days later there was an unexpected (and unique) incident that I termed "the chair business:" The chairs had not been returned from an intramural athletics competition. The day after the event we had to spend the first part of the morning sorting out class chairs. I took the younger boys to look at the Section V classroom to see if the older boys had taken their chairs, and, it turned out, they had. My sense of justice did not receive a welcome in Section V, however. They reacted as if their authority had been challenged, how, I could not fathom. When I confronted them the next day they were sullen; no one would say a word or respond to my questions—I was met with silence. I had reached a situation of non-cooperation; from the staff room I gathered that everyone out here sooner or later experiences something like this. Past friendliness and favor seemed forgotten. Here for the first time I experienced something below the surface, something I did not understand.

There was no other instance in my classes of such resistance. As I think back on it decades later, it likely had to do with my place as an outsider telling them what to do. When I arrived initially, one of the boys had asked me "how long are you going to stay with us? Only a year or two?" (Expatriates come on limited terms with their skills and advice.)

A couple of days later I had supper in the Catering Rest House with one of the Yoruba teachers in the school, Bako, a kind and pleasant fellow. We were joined by our second African colleague, Malam Waziri, another southerner, who ceremoniously inquired about my health. A European colleague dropped in to complain about the poor attendance at prep, the evening supervised study, another example of the laxness of administration that so bothered me. He remained for nearly an hour going over in detail (intelligently too) the negativity in the staff room. He was particularly hard this time on our colleague LL, whose opinions and unvarying cynicism he, like the rest of us, finds irritating. LL's barbs recently have been directed towards me. Preposterously he bases his comments on his study of John Foster Dulles. He accuses me of brinkmanship with my criticisms of the school not knowing what I am doing. I fly in and out like Dulles without knowing the details of a situation, etc. He criticizes even my practice of going away weekends as being an example of my diffuseness! In the staff room he barely speaks to me. I overhear points he makes to the room at large: anti-Americanism is the chief of these.

Achilles

After hours there came to be a new pleasure, a ride on my own horse. For a trifling sum I bought a broken-in stallion whom I came to call Achilles. The elderly Mohammadu, came on as horse "boy" to care for him. I began to regularly ride out beyond the city limits for a taste of the bush, returning through the darkness.

Sociability in the GRA.

Last evening I played a game of petonk before dinner with my neighbors, the Warrens, whose other guests were Vic Dugdale of the Police and two French policemen from Fort Lamy. We stood in a circle and tossed little metal balls towards a wooden bowl in the center, attempting to land them as close as possible. It was a gentle way of mixing. Vic Dugdale, the federal policeman here, is dark and handsome, a gentle, fair-seeming sort of fellow, no bluster at all. The French are young, trim hair slicked down. They offered little conversation, but joined in the game with phrases such as *"c'est dramatique"* or *"du calme, du calme."* The chief, a square, large-bellied short man dressed in a pair of loose outdoor pajamas played the game silently. At drinks he and Dugdale discussed smugglers, certain Syrian merchants, etc. When asked about recent political developments in Chad, Algeria, or the other French colonies, he calmly delivered the Gaulllist, Ve. Republique tough line, without a hint of the complexities arising from the burgeoning independence movements.

That night the moon was sighted and saluted by shotguns in the town. The Ramadan fast has begun. The students will be fasting from sunrise to sundown, meaning listless attention particularly in the afternoon classes.

Early on the following Sunday I canceled a planned one-day trip to Gwoza. However, at 9 a.m. Bukar, the garden boy, came in and chatted to me cheerfully in Hausa. Sarke told me that he had bought items for me to bring to his mother in Gwoza. This was a good excuse to resume my original plan; it surely would be preferable to spend the day on the road rather than stay in somnolence here. I picked up Bukar Zoru and Adawa Garoua at the school to interpret and set off with young Bukar and the things he had bought.

We arrived in Gwoza about noon on this sunny, breezy day. Bukar Zoru and Adawa walked through the market with the air of a superior (and amused) race. Jagoe, the touring officer, asked me to his house. He was detained, so I was entertained by his attractive wife.

I dropped in on Dixie Deans. His job has just about ceased with the cancellation of the road project. He has been suffering from combined malaria and flu and looked pale and weak. He said he was off the beer.

Spoke of Williamson: "he's down here every morning at 7:15, every evening at 5:30, driving me mad. He is so lonely that when I'm gone he sits out in front of his house and drinks and thinks about everyone who has done him a hard turn and gets pissed for two days running." So that is what was underneath the bluster of my old porch-mate at the Ali Roz house.

Returned via Bama. That town is spacious—even more inviting than ever. Mr. Lawrence met on the bridge looked dead tired, had a great swelling on his head. He told me that a relief was coming, said he had accomplished two things in this country, "got rid of" some NA official whose name I didn't catch and "Kalia Mangano" (the Permanent Secretary of Dikwa Emirate).

On the the road back I enjoyed being on the sand ridge in the fine, yellow light.

Reception for the new Resident

The building, floodlit, looked stylish. The crowd all knew each other (or, if not, knew what each other did), making for a tepid sense of occasion. There is nothing of youth in these parties. The new Resident, N. C. McClintock, is a distinguished-looking, Foreign Service type; he made a graceful speech bidding farewell to R.B.B. Eustace, the retiring Resident who stayed at the back of the crowd, drinking it up, and at the end came to the stoop of the Residency to say farewell to the crowd amid a burst of applause.

The staff room: REU never tells the headmaster what he says behind his back. He says to him "you're inefficient, but likable." Altogether a curious game.

Fort Lamy for a weekend

Saturday: left for Fort Lamy in Chad directly after classes ended at 11:30. The day hot and dry, with the harmattan still blowing. I took the road a bit too fast and gave the car several sharp jolts. Lightly loaded, it slipped about the raised portion and several times abruptly swerved to a diagonal. Stopped after Dikwa for a drink of squash. Otherwise, no lunch, enjoyed the dryness of the heat. The country opens up a few miles north of Dikwa and becomes as flat as a calm sea, a few birds soaring.

At Fitakal, Cameroon, at the immigration control compound, a massive black man was asleep in a sparely furnished room/office with a table, a chair, a mirror and the cot where he lay. The building was wooden, with blinds that open out for air. He had difficulty arousing himself and called for a colleague. The two wore old American uniforms, marked with the emblem of the new Cameroon Republic. He processed my passport readily and asked me to do some shopping for him at the pharmacy at Fort Lamy (suppositories for his child). He changed his mind when he remembered that the shops would be shut at four (they weren't). Then *Le Douanier* sat before a great meal of chicken and Heinekens and said only one word to me, "allez."

The road through this small slice of Cameroon was broad, scraped by big graders, a contrast to the rough Nigerian roads. Few people on the shoulders—they seem to be dark Shuwa, and a few Fulani.

The 60 miles on this wide road passed quickly to Fort Francean, the entry to Chad. Some patches of water, darker vegetation in the direction of the lake. The flat, intense land throws one's thoughts back into oneself. At Fort Francean, one of the massive French administrative buildings is of Moorish design as at Mora, visited on the trek from Banki.

Fort Lamy exceeded expectations. Despite the 110 miles on the hard dirt roads that afternoon, I drove about at once, enlivened by the contrast with British Africa. There were shops, outdoor cafés; the Europeans seemed unafraid of the sun, riding about on bicycles, walking, etc. I sensed a pulse about the place, style, gaiety. Houses looked as if they been designed for the tropics, some with breezeways making shaded spaces for cars, living quarters with wide windows, terraces; there were brightly colored flowers on some of the grounds, lavish municipal buildings and public parks. This evening the air is cool and dry as that of Provence.

Here was colonization importing the national style of the Imperial power. Northern Nigeria seems more than ever the product of an empire on a shoestring. The British came to trade, its administration provided stability, the PWD communications, infrastructure, but no establishments as lavish and thoroughgoing as those in Fort Lamy. It is a city built from scratch in a near desert beside the ever-changing contours of the lake. I find the GRA and the commercial strip of Maiduguri is disappearing in the gracious ease of Fort Lamy.

At the Hotel du Parc I took the rooms of a German import-export fellow who was leaving on Air France at 9:15. We had several late afternoon drinks and more at the airport (near a table where the Air France crew was downing wine with the meal). I stayed on for a dinner of lobster, Champignons a la Greque, haricotes vertes, Neapolitan, raisin cheese. My *vin ordinaire* was unworthy of such a feast.

The Air Hotel restaurant and bar were done up like an Alsatian inn. What pleased most was the vivacity of the diners, the well-dressed women, a cosmopolitan sense of occasion. It felt a welcome respite from "European" Nigeria.

For the first time in months I took the luxury of lying in bed. Thoughts quick and free. I was lightheaded, felt a surging confidence I had not known for months. Had breakfast in the smart bar at the airport (where people were drinking beer at 9 a.m.). The French seem to be themselves in their colonies, vices and virtues. I enjoyed being with them and drove about the town with a peace of mind that surprised me.

Out for a walk later and was offered a ride by a man in a 2 CV (Citroen *deux chevaux*) equipped with poofs on its canvas seats. M. Henri Leone works at the airport. We had a grenadine and soda with his roommate, just out of bed, *L'Express* and *Le Monde* lying about amid classic bachelor disorder. Henri said he liked Maiduguri because it was so green. They rushed off to their Sunday engagements, left me at the hotel.

Thus thoroughly relaxed I had lunch at the restaurant accompanied by the pop music of North America and France. I turned to it for comfort, an example of how humans can circumvent aloneness.

Left at 2:30. Very sorry to leave. Apprehensive as on the days when I had to return to boarding school or to the Army. The road seemed broader and finer than before. At the border town of Gamboru talked with a lovely young schoolteacher, a southerner placed in this remote place to teach primary school.

Drove slowly from the border on, the sky a greasy wash, the wind steady as though from the sea. This flat land becomes splendor in the golden evening light, I felt ready to weep as the sun lowered and the gold of the landscape faded—or to pray like the Muslims, head touching the earth in tribute, such was my response to the glory of that landscape in the mast of the sun. I wondered if there no better future for this beautiful land but a coarse commercial culture—given the way things were going, that seems its future.

Driving into the night I felt the sensual delight of darkness. Shuwa women headed for the next day's market in black clothes darker than themselves, only the calabashes of milk and butter picked out by the car lights.

Back to the School and the GRA

The heat increases during the day. After breakfast I was so dry that I had to go for a "Coke" at Ali Mongano's store. The students become weaker and weaker as the Ramadan fast continues.

I take Achilles to the south past the Shuwa villages. He is sturdy and obedient, though not as lively as I had wanted. However, a walk after a long trot is one of the peaceful moments of the day. I wait until the sun is down before returning.

Thursday: Two classes. Section III on "Britain's advantage in the industrial revolution," Section VI on the carrying over of English law to the colonies, a complex topic that had no relevance to these students who live in a traditional society under Islamic law, though the imported English law does apply to the expatriates and the "strangers" in the commercial areas. This is one of the topics in the curriculum that encourages indifference as it is so foreign, I was not an inspired teacher. Also, the boys become weaker still. If they could look green they would.

I find the teaching part of the day passes very quickly. After class with the youngest boys I barely remember what I have taught. I have caught some of the somnolence of the fasting boys perhaps, for the mornings seem in retrospect to be lackluster affairs. Some classes are extremely slow and a great effort—sometimes I long for a chair as a physical necessity. The technique, which seems to be accepted here, of having the class read out loud from the text is easy on the teacher but dull. There are more lively days than this; the boys are more alert in the morning, and the classroom work forces me to speak up.

Lunch today at Miss Kitchener's of the women's secondary school. Also present, Malam Dikwa and Mr. Drayton and Miss Messenger. Two and half hours of conversation, some of it "education," some of it small talk. Margaret Kitchener is a vivacious and lovable young woman—what a gulf separates her African gregariousness from the pushes and pulls that make up our non-African staff room.

A short ride this evening along the Dumbara Road to a large Shuwa village which I had not visited before. Achilles better since not having been ridden in the morning.

A weekend visit to Marte on Lake Chad

Drove northeast on the now familiar Dikwa Road. The temperature was hot, somewhat alleviated by a strong wind from the north. Turned off at Dikwa to head north to Marte. This road, built on sand, was smooth and not at all the hazard I had anticipated from reports. [Marte is about 70 miles from Maiduguri.]

Villages in this area are built on sand ridges or domes to avoid flooding when Lake Chad expands in the wet season. On the way I passed several of the artesian wells—termed boreholes by the engineers—drilled to provide a steady supply of water for the nomads' livestock. There were herds of cattle drinking at some of them; sometimes sheep and goats, each kept separate from the others by miracles of control performed by the boys in charge. My car would often startle them and leave a scene of stampeding animals behind the car, to be reorganized by the boys' commands.

The country became flatter and perceptibly drier with a few small trees. The yellow of the dried-up grasses is the predominant color.

In the villages no one stirred at the car's approach; there were a few old men seated in the shade and children playing, but most remained in the huts. During this Ramadan fast there is no farm work and no other incentive to be out and about.

At Marte a group of schoolboys in their white uniforms surrounded the car, carefully pronouncing "good afternoon." They were a bright group—brighter than any similar group gathered around in other towns. Or possibly I am prejudiced because Marte had produced several of the best students in the school. To show off their English the children chanted, "this is a window, this is a door," and so on.

The rest house was a dilapidated thatch building. Next to it was a trailer and beside it tarpaulins with soil sample cores in orderly rows. As I approached, a small red face with a broken front tooth peered out of the front door. Bob Pullen introduced himself from the sweltering heat of the trailer, announcing that he was in charge of the soil survey being conducted here. Just "out," he said, arrived in January only weeks ago, making me feel like an old timer. A graduate of Birmingham University and heralding from South Yorkshire, which explained his pleasant accent, he sympathized with my interest in seeing the country.

Visited the DH in his house. He, a long-faced, long-toothed man, greeted me cheerfully. He sat on a mat in a large bare room accompanied by two sons and the usual host of flies. My interpreter was Malam Bukar, the primary school teacher. Once the DH seated me on a small folding chair, we exchanged pleasantries for about a quarter of an hour. We then went to pay our respects to the village Mai, or lawan, whose fine house lay across the square, surrounded by a circular mud wall dotted with little turrets. His "gate" included a large wooden door. He encouraged us to climb a tower above it for a view of miles around. I thought I could see the edge of Lake Chad, but the next morning's expedition proved that it was much farther. With the fresh breeze, the long views from the tower lent an air of splendor to the land.

I had been told that the Mai had a drum from human skin in his compound, but though he mentioned that a European had made a list of these things "after the late Mai's death," he did not offer to show me drum.

The town is built on a hill; its twisting little streets give it an intricate character; the square with the houses of the DH and the lawan is at the pinnacle of the village. The mud brick walls throughout are dark brown, the sand of the paths nearly white. The sky too was so light a blue it often appeared white.

Marte became virtually black and white in the harsh midday light.

Dined in the trailer with Bob Pullen, hot and stifling with "Victor Sylvester and His Band" on the radio. After to the DH's gate for a promised dance. The moon was full in a perfectly clear sky so the dancers were visible without pressure lamps. The DH came out rather reluctantly and sat in his deep chair, first wrapping a handkerchief around his mouth so not to inhale the dust. There were three men with large drums, and two pipers who did not manage to play in unison. One stood out as particularly good, he played his instrument with a strong tremolo that was unexpected and modern in this music.

The children came first, boys leaping about in their long gowns, quite uninhibited; the girls shuffling along in a circle, their line ending with a child of about six.

With the children leaping about and the thumping of the powerful music underneath the full moon a lively spectacle was had. But it became clear that no adults were going to join in; the event never congealed. This was a show put on for the white men only. To the DH's obvious relief at about 10:30 I decided to retire, and with Bob Pullen walked back to the rest house followed by the raucous roar of the pipers. I was momentarily embarrassed by the whole ceremony, so obviously performed just for our benefit.

The lawan of Kiovoura, a village near Lake Chad about 20 miles distant, is the father of my student, Ashok JamisError! Bookmark not defined.a. His *Wakilie* arrived to escort me to the village. He brought a slender bush horse who was more stimulated by my weight than my animal back in Maiduguri. We bounded along over the black soil directly into a steady wind keeping us fresh and cool. Flocks of birds flew before us, most noticeably large crown birds in small groups. After a long flat plain we reached a stretch of woodland, then another plain, then on to a well-forested sand ridge which we followed until reaching the first of three nearby villages that border Lake Chad.

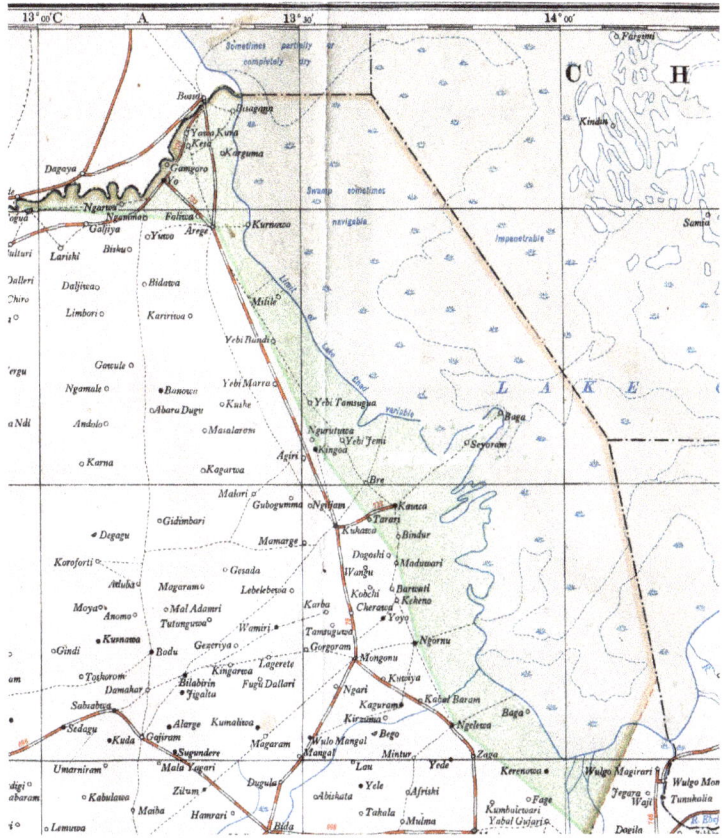

LAKE CHAD WHERE THE BORDERS OF NIGERIA, CAMEROON AND CHAD MEET.
THE EXTENT OF THE LAKE AS IT WAS MAPPED IN 1952.

Anesawa with its large, round-roofed huts, flat on the dry plain looked like how I imagine a Mongol encampment. Ashek's brother, on a lively young horse, escorted me to where the lake fisherman were based. Although the village had seemed dry, beyond the grass was tall and water came up to the knees of the horses.

On a hillock we found a group of women bringing fish to lay them out to dry. A group of men and boys sorted the fish and put them into a trench. The fish, small, dirty brown in color; flopped about pathetically in the muddy water.

Beyond I could see grass far out into the lake—a genuine "lake" of open water was nowhere in sight.

Near the fishing place a herd of cattle grazed, moving along slowly through the grass. They were followed and preceded by a flock of pure white birds, cow birds according to my escort. At intervals the herder would fire a gun to frighten them off—just why I could not discover.

It was time to turn back. The day was by now hot, although there was still a strong breeze. I did not have the raging thirst the sun and wind would normally produce because of the half glass of salt water I had drunk at breakfast. Though parched, I did not need constant liquid as I had on the plebiscite. It was a French colonial old-timer's trick to drink a glass of heavily salted water first thing in the morning to keep the thirst away for several hours.

The saddle now became painful, sitting on this trim little horse was like riding on a shaking ridge pole. Both the little horse and I were glad when Marte, slightly elevated above the plain, came into view. After eighteen miles of carrying such a burden he broke into a fast trot back to the rest house on the trailer.

There I succumbed to a gluttonous appetite for water, drinking nearly two quarts straight. After bidding farewell to the school teachers and to the DH in his hot meeting hut, I headed back to Maiduguri. The car was loaded—overloaded—with four huge bags of corn for my horse. This meant a low and cautious drive. No springs were broken, and we reached the GRA at dusk. This meant more water for me to satisfy the enormous craving this country creates.

The heat

The heat: last night the temperature must have been at body heat; the wind brings no relief. During the hot, dry days here one does not sweat. As soon as it appears on the skin, moisture evaporates in the dry heat. The temperature holds one in its grip, suspends, and when there is a break I am aware of what a strain it was. The body seems to work harder; after a time in the heat a rest becomes essential, and the blood pounds when I lie down. The dry heat can be deceptive; compared to the humidity of New York or the East Coast of the US, at first it feels not so bad, but it does not take long for its intensity to sap the body.

The last days of the Ramadan fast pass quickly. Section I scarcely remembers what was done or said in recent classes.

A trek over the Gwoza hills and a visit to the Basel Mission

Picked up Mike Lander at the hospital and headed for Bama. Intense heat—embodied in the intense light. At noon the view from the road on the sand ridge was flat and colorless.

On to Gwoza where we put up in a small rest house at the bottom of a garden. Beer at Dixie's, without Dixie, and more at the Jagoes with a nurse from the Swiss mission who had walked across the hills that day.

After this, and feeling mellow from the bitter-tasting Star beer, Mike and I went to Dr. Chandler at the Basel Mission. A highly nervous man, he served us dinner in his small round mud hut. We were late and obviously had had too much beer and were thus in a secular state. The conversation was limited—I don't remember a word of it. I did all I could to allay his nervousness, being so relaxed myself.

A sleepless might. The stars clear overhead—the wind hot and dry, a universal stillness and a dominant mist.

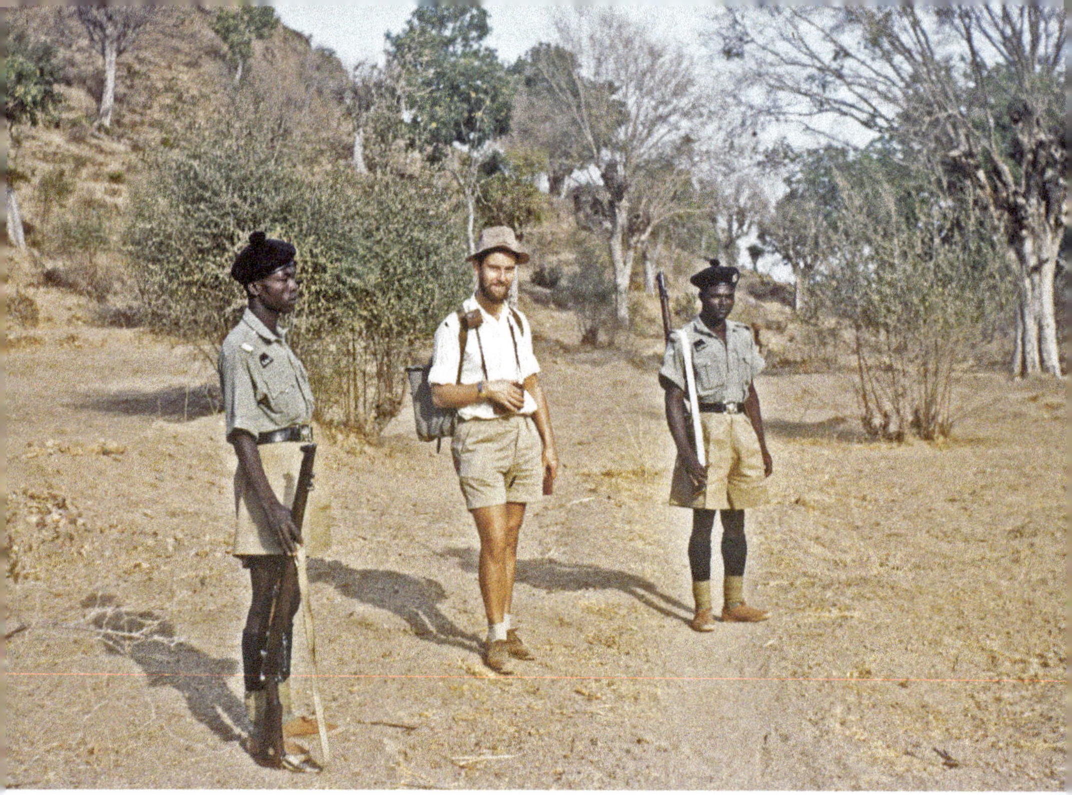

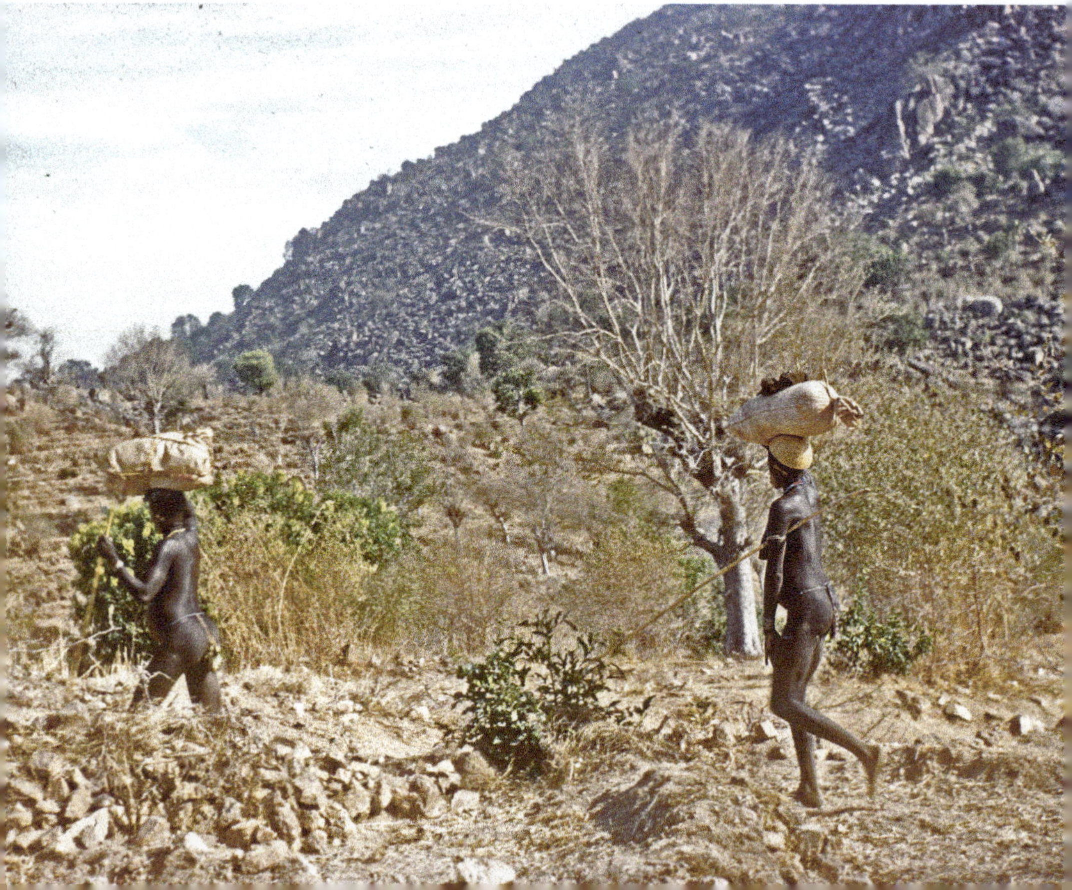

Regulations require armed escort for those walking into the hills; ours was a pair of policemen who arrived promptly to get us on our way by 7 a.m. We climbed up to and over the Gulduf Pass, the altitude and heat causing a pounding of the blood and near nausea, but once we reached the Pass, my system returned to normal.

The hill people seemed idle as on a Sunday morning. There was an Arcadian atmosphere: adults seated in the shade, children yodeling from the hillsides, the high-pitched screams of greeting from women passing on their way to market. All are naked—plump young girls, bashful grandmothers, tough, or possibly debauched, men, exhausted by drink. From one point of view, a comical, outlandish scene, but everyday life for these people. Large black rocks are scattered about, a mountainous land that would be wet with flowing streams in the rainy season, now hard and dry.

On the other side of the pass there was a dry riverbed to follow. One of the policemen pointed out a white woman sitting beneath a tree. She was the wife of the engineer at the Basel mission recounting Bible stories to a group of naked men. When we came up, the group recited the Lord's Prayer in their language. The Mission engineer, an apple-cheeked young fellow wearing a sun helmet set back on his head, showed us to the main mission house.

Mike and I stayed in the sitting room and drank squash and water continuously for at least an hour. We even brought out our pastries and ate them. It took a while for our hosts to get used to the stray creatures which had suddenly shown up, but, after a bit they, and we, relaxed and had a pleasant visit.

Fromy, the engineer, took us around the mission buildings he had designed. He had taught the hill people to cut stone which resulted in houses of handsome dark stone, sturdy and cool within. On the porch his son played with the hill children.

With the temperature at 103 we set out at 2:30 on foot over the pass back to the village of Gwoza. I noticed Mike's face was flush, and he said mine was likewise. That was the only effect of the extreme heat. At one point on the path as we rested on a rock we were passed by four young women coming from market, loaded calabashes on their heads. They were followed by a man in tatters who paused to show us his manly organ and laughingly thrust his torso back and forth to illustrate what he was going to do with the girls at home. We queried whether drink would take away the performance.

Back in Gwoza on the porch of the guest house high on the hill where I had been on my first visit, we talked with Dixie (looking puffy), and Alan Williamson (unchanged). As we took in the panoramic view, Dixie again recounted the Gwoza field day that Major Holmes had set up which ended in an orgy with the participants opening up £100 of Becks beer in a melee on the playing field—my second hearing, first for Mike.

The motor trip back was grueling. At night the bumps in the road are hard to anticipate, and I feared for the car with the pounding it took. In one village we took a wrong turn and careened off the road, bursting a pipe and nearly ending up in the ditch.

At dinner with Mike's wife, Margaret, we went over with delight the varied adventures of the two days.

The new moon was seen at 1:30 a.m., signaling the end of Ramadan and when I arrived at the school the boys were seated at their ease and enjoying the prospect of food.

Reflections on A Sunday

I am reminded by newspapers and letters that a new Africa is emerging. But the perspective from quiet Maiduguri is a narrow one on this "great movement of history." We're seeing masses of the world's peoples acquiring in a few days and months what has taken years to evolve in other countries. Most of the new polities have not done well by their newly acquired inheritance, either in understanding it or using it. Here in this corner we are spared the violence as in the Congo and Algeria.

The belief in a formal education—is it not preposterous? I think so—perhaps it can make bureaucrats—but what else? The emphasis here is on formal educational qualification, overdone in my view.

If the job is to impart a tool to deal with the rapid changes that are coming with political independence and the secular forces of the modern world, then acquiring English is useful and the pallid textbooks simply a means to that end. Here we are imparting a secular education to a society dominated by one of the world's great religions, with its own system of learning and morality. What I teach about the British cabinet system or the movement to end the slave trade is only a means to teach English. I wish the texts spoke more directly to the experience of the students.

I hear talk among the boys—"are the teachers afraid of the results of the school certificate?" Apparently they expect that if the results are poor the teaching staff is entirely to blame. They have a way of sitting back and assuming the attitude of someone who won't raise a finger to help himself. They demand the teacher "organize" the material for them. In this school there is a need for review, to set new goals—but it won't come under the present set up. Not only is the teaching material thin, the learning experience among the students is shallow and literal. At moments like this I see no future in secular modernity for these Northerners. I am here to give help, but I often sense that teaching is not genuinely wanted and that it is not being accepted.

With these low, gloomy thoughts I returned to have a quick lunch at two and fell exhausted onto my bed. Why this extraordinary fatigue? I think it comes from the heat, and partly, the dispiriting work. My gloomy thoughts gather like a thunder cloud or a flood. They have a power which I have not yet learned to counter.

At five I went out on Achilles. As he has been eating too much corn, he bites and stamps angrily while being saddled. He shied away from a dog on this ride leaving me clinging to his neck. Visited the new site of the school with Steve Allen, a lonely, quiet man who lives up there. I dread the time when the "staff housing" is completed—eight little houses all in a row, the staff living on top of each other, the staff room atmosphere expanded to 24 hours with cheek by jowl proximity. I take back my aspersions on the garden city style of the GRA.

Evening somber with gray dust and windy, Achilles plunging and bucking on the return.

Perhaps my history teaching has been confused. The suggestion is that I should give more notes, that is, summarize what the students should know. Evidently I have misjudged the boys' ability to comprehend. What they want, and presumably what they must have, is a dull series of notes telling them exactly what is what. One bitter colleague spends whole periods in such dictation. It seems that my method of learning from the text with a discussion has confused them. The prospect of changing to this even duller method is not attractive. Does dictating notes achieve anything beyond getting the boys through the school certificate?

Seems to me the school turns out boys only superficially touched with the modern world—one that is Western European in prospective. They will move into plush jobs with nothing but (perhaps) a reasonable command of English and the desire for fancy things.

An overcast morning. The clouds are dark and look hopefully full of water. Sleep is impossible—to lie in the bed is like being in a closed attic.

Yesterday cool. Gave Section VI notes—to their great pleasure. Now they know just what to think about the Prime Minister. With Section II it is an ordeal, the minutes tick by as they read about Mungo Park and his travels reaching the Niger. (This to boys whose forebears for generations knew about the Niger and didn't need to have it "discovered.")

A long Easter weekend

Car loaded and on the road just after 8 a.m. At Bama Mr. Lawrence seemed as though he had "come through" after a long bout of fatigue. Gave me a letter for the prefect at Maroua. The day mildly overcast and not hot. Carried on south past Gwoza to deserted hills.

Malayali market full of life. A few seedy Fulani traders; henna-dyed pagans unselfconsciously wandered through, taking no notice of the white man.

Stopped at Gulak to see Vaughn, the American anthropologist working among the hill Mamghi who lives in a mud-brick house with his wife and two children. The kids played with native children outside, drawing. Mr. and Mrs. very cheerful. He and his wife have had a good time on the Ford Foundation grant—the family not as isolated as I thought.

The land opened up before Mubi. A great plain, at least two streams and in the distance purple hills on both sides; the wind fresh and the clouds beginning to take shape.

At the end of the day watched the sunset as the magnificent hills to the north faded from view. Subtle long sleep refreshed by the cool air.

My body had craved that relief.

Mubi is south of Gwoza close to the mountains and the border with French Cameroons. The rest house faces east to the sun. The hills are hazy in the distance towards Adamawa. All night a strong wind—like the sea wind—through the tree in front of the porch. Now it comes in gusts. At dawn the sun, rising over the mountain, seemed to draw the winds with it.

The hills are now brown and black. The rocks in front of the house are made of lava. Young Dika Musulawa tells me that a peak to the east is inhabited by demons. "People who wish to become expert at something go there and spend a week on the mountain."

The peaks rise up evenly as far as the eye can see. Directly below the rest house is a deep ravine. There are hill people everywhere. It is an animated scene, none of the lonely splendor of the American mountains.

When I arrived, a storm had just passed through, and the peaks seemed to float on the white light ringing the horizon.

Storm clouds are large; peering into them I can see this deep darkness, "darkness visible." Last night there were rumblings to the west and occasional flashes of lightning. This sets up a mighty expectation of rain, but it is not fulfilled.

Feeling refreshed, started out from Mubi at eight. Through hills, quite high some of them, formed from the same black rock as the Gwoza hills. The car climbed upward, the air fresh and cool, and for the first time that I can remember since the *harmattan*, sparkling and clear. The native villages, mostly a collection of family compounds, have great dignity in the setting of these hills. I sensed a long established, unacknowledged grandeur.

Rocky black soil stretches out on either side of the road, more rocks than dirt. Short bushes with green leaves, perhaps freshened by the rain; the green has the brightness I have missed in the dry season.

The Cameroon border is controlled by a *douanier* who was absent on what I later learned was an amorous errand. I had to wait for him to let me through, finally he arrived in the company of a pair of evolved mission-educated boys. When the officer appeared, I was surprised to find him brisk and neat with a short beard that extended from ear-to-ear.

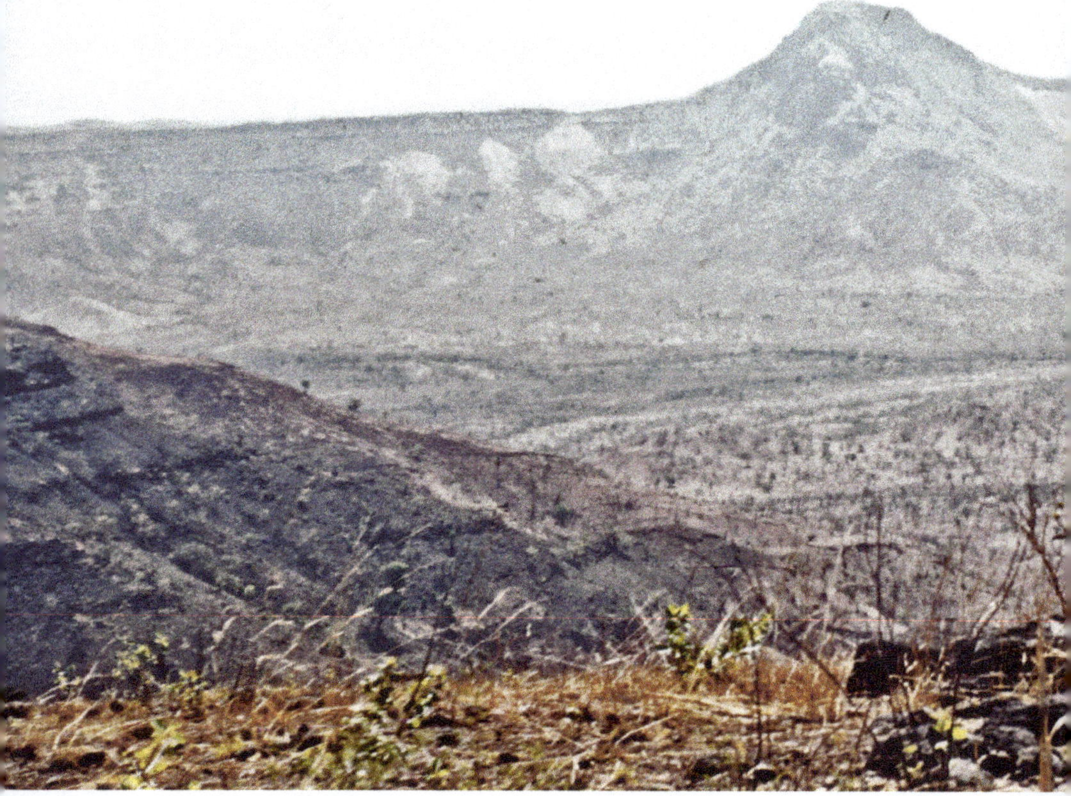

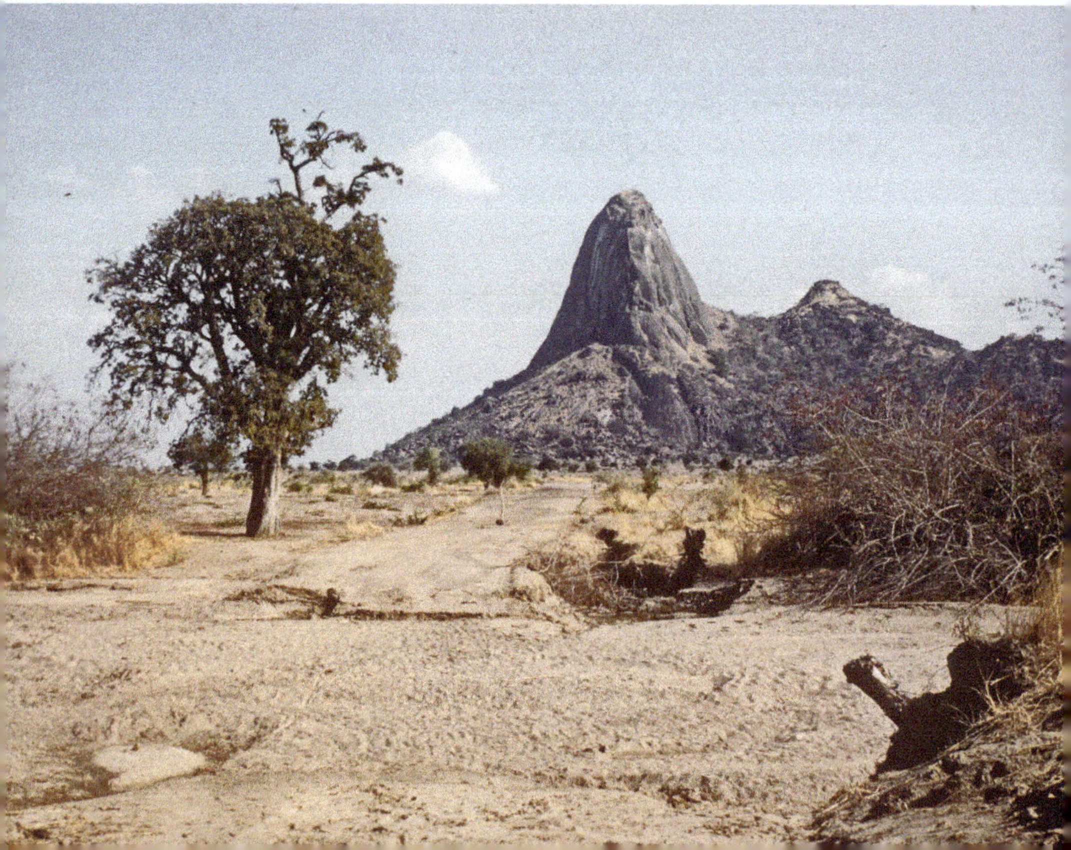

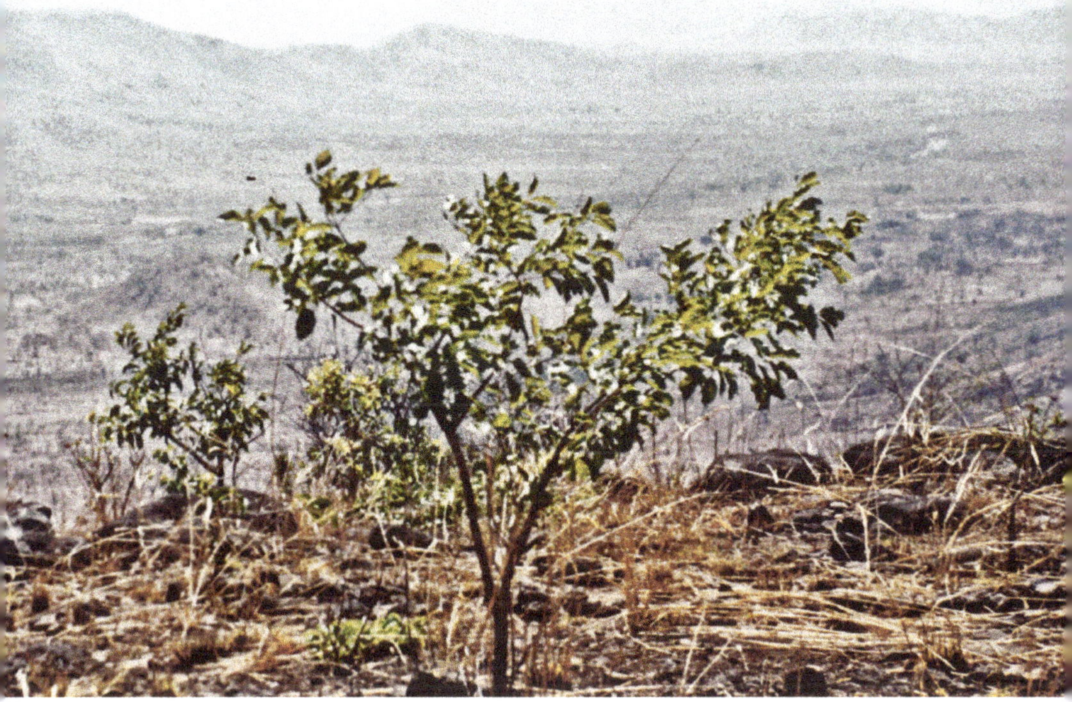

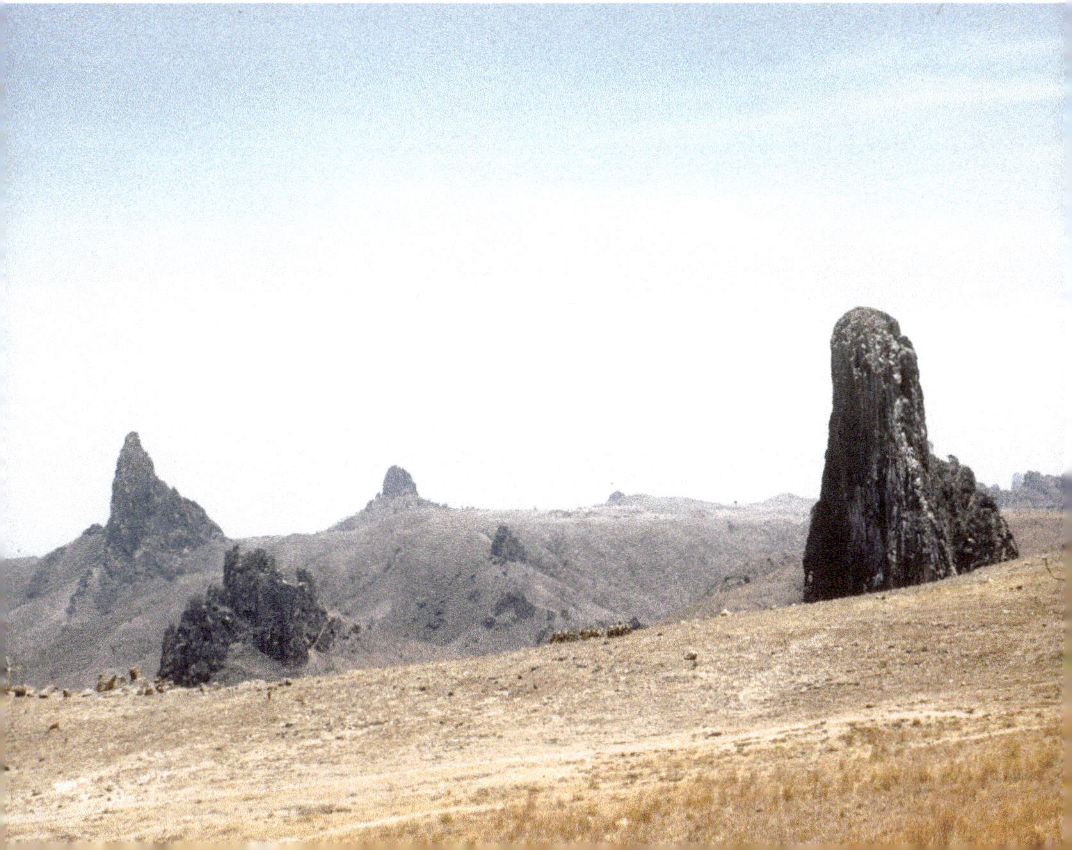

Threaded up a curving road onto a plateau now, driving north again along a high ridge. Deserted country save for an occasional village, usually atop a hill. The country to the east unexpectedly an expanse of rolling grassland. Some small huts on the side of the mountain were intended for the wandering Fulani.

Rumsiki displayed a mysterious spectacle. Great cores of rock rose out of the hills like stalagmites, sometimes several hundred feet high. They overlook deep rocky valleys. To the north in the distance smaller volcanic peaks dotted the plateau.

Rumsiki village is neatly divided into quarters. The round huts are made of firmly-packed mud, each group surrounded by a tall stone wall. A guide took me through, a small boy whose French was quite good. We visited a wedding: women of the quarter were seated under a tree near the bride's compound, chanting a song, led by one of them. My guide urged me to go into the bridal compound. No one seemed to notice or care what the white man did (in contrast to the Gwoza people who would have laughed and shrieked). I entered the compound and visited the hut of the bride, a girl of about eleven, who cheerfully accepted my shilling and retired into the darkness where her companions, grandmother and a sister, cared for her.

At the car two young women waited among a larger group. One knocked together a pair of balls on a string and looked at me cheerfully. The other offered me, at a large price, one of her pubic decorations. No thanks.

I moved on, driving through the striking landscape of volcanic remains and descending to the lower plain and to Mokolo. There I put up in the Hotel de Passage, Le Flamboyant. My room is neat, round, roofed with grass, containing a bed, table and chair, with a space for a splendid bucket shower.

I had a tasty French lunch while the proprietor and his wife talked to an energetic priest with a long gray beard in civilian clothes wearing a sun helmet. They successfully urged that he take wine as it was Easter Saturday.

I napped in the early p.m., then walked about the crumbling town. Some flame trees against the spindly green. The government buildings laid out with no particular pomp, the quarters not at all luxurious. In the village, a curious mixture of hill people in ragged clothes and a few heavy and corrupt-looking Fulani.

There was time to drive out to the hills before dark. On an intricately terraced hillside I climbed up to a group of huts on an outcropping. An old woman scratched about the sandy terrace, moving pebbles and leaves in preparation for planting. Men sat on rocks higher up, silhouettes against the sky. I watched a mother with her baby above me. She sat on a ledge as the baby pushed and pulled at her delightedly. Two sisters took care of her for a few moments—letting her climb about.

As I started to descend two young girls waved me to come up and visit. I stood below their ledge and spoke to them—to my amazement one spoke good French, taught at the nearby mission.

Returned to Le Flamboyant to find music and French children playing about. Had a drink with Pierre Mounier, a French businessman from Maiduguri and his wife. He queried: "How has your opinions of Africans changed? When I first came out here I expected to consider the black man as my equal. But they have a long way to go before they can reach our standards. The best Ibo clerk is not up to an average American or European. But perhaps we should not judge, expect them to do more than they can do. We should accept them at their own level…" And so on, an often-heard observation, negative, promoting the "us-them" dichotomy often voiced by my colleagues and others in this late colonial epoch.

To bed early. The night alternated between strong winds and a depression in the atmosphere. One lightning bolt must have shot miles across the sky for I could hear its thunder for many seconds.

Easter Sunday

Up at 5:30 a.m. on a fresh, damp-feeling morning. Deep purple clouds overhead.

The day soon became sultry and the cloud cover remained, pulling the splendor from the mountains. I remembered the views leading from Mubi the day before such as I wished for today. The dwellings in the villages of this massif are made of an ancient red earth. Without the sun to give brilliance this appeared a battered, desperate landscape. The naked figures (sometimes wrapped in a cheap blanket from the waist up) stand out in dignity within this ancient setting.

Passed *Centre Royale,* a made-up village, with beehive huts of rocks and mud reflecting a quaint notion by the authorities to "fit in" with local architecture.

Before reaching Maroua, there is a vast plain with some Fulani village and on the steep mountain sides seemingly well maintained small animist settlements.

Put up at the Complement whose reception area was a large conical hut set up within like an Alsatian *auberge.* The bedrooms are a cluster of small huts of which Hut #6 contained a double bed with a V-shaped mattress, a table, operatic chairs, and grime.

At this hour mechanics and engineers of the station are drinking in the restaurant-café. Outside were parked a couple of Citroën 2 CVs— why are none of these light and agile vehicles used in Nigeria and so many here?

Two crown birds, absurdly dignified, walked in the Complement compound, also an antelope and its offspring. Outside is the center of the African town.

Maroua at first disappointed. It seemed dry, dirty and small; I had my expectations based on Fort Lamy. The nondescript administration buildings are part of the native town, centered at one end, the commercial section at the other. There is dirt, smell, and litter to outdo any other place I've been.

Took a short promenade by auto in the direction of Mindai, another of these great volcanic cores, this one rising several hundred feet from the tableland. Here the road was unexpectedly wet; soon it will be unusable.

Parties at the Complement last until nearly midnight. What a pleasure to be near people who wish to stay up late. Even the music, floating shapelessly and pleasantly around the diners, has relaxed me. *Vive!*

The English provide for their comforts; the French for their pleasures (c.f. these small hotels with dining and music) and which do I prefer!

I slept fitfully in my lumpy V-shaped bed at the Complement. By morning I was sleeping across its breadth where the top of that V was not so pronounced.

The freshness of night carries over into only a few minutes of the day. The Complement looked damp and seedy by 7 a.m., and a moist atmosphere descended by 7:30. Some of the drinkers from the night before were in states of either slapdash hilarity through hangover pain or in somber conversation over coffee. By 7:50, for a couple of them at least, the day began anew with glasses of wine at the bar.

The music resumed at breakfast on the patio. Africa streamed past *en route* to the great Monday market. Strangely non-persistent vendors circulated among the breakfast guests. A prefect or sous-prefect, in a tan sun helmet dealt with one young Fulani vendor by telling him that "I am not an American, understand?" *Madame la patronne* passed back and forth keeping her temper on edge with "*les boys*." Dyed hair, shapeless dress that had once been a sack-style, she speaks with her mouth full of food.

Delivered Mr. Lawrence's note to the house of the *chef de region*. The chef himself was not present, but a sous-prefect was taking breakfast in the Residence. The building rested on a pinnacle high above the town—a difficult place to get to in the rains. The *sous prefet* is a young man in his mid-30s. He trembled slightly as he bit his cigarette. Told of his interest in the animist people, and that he had recently served in Bamileke in the south, where "to be an administrative officer was no joke." He had a grave view of the recent disturbances there which he said are increasingly black against white. "As in all of Africa, independence comes much too quickly—"yet, you cannot stop them."

Unfortunately, the museum and craft shop were closed. The road to Mora as was as broad and well cared for as I remembered from the trek during the plebiscite.

Mora looked different from my car than it had from the Land Rover of the cotton factory owner. Stopped at a small shop run, incredibly enough, by a French woman, and had a beer early in the day. It had a delicious effect, and it would not have taken much prompting to go on—though if I had continued, it would have meant a nap under a tree before returning to Nigeria.

The owner of the shop was a middle-aged Frenchwoman who, amid the clutter of parcels and boxes and tinned goods, fiercely supervised her "boy" as he packed a picnic lunch for a dark eyed young European woman and a young man with a furrowed face. A Fulani woman of about 35 sat with them; when the owner was out of the room she threw small pieces of paper at the man with quick gestures as though she had great affection for him. There was about her a quiet dignity and a wisdom and considerable female attractiveness. I shan't forget the expression in her large eyes as they looked about the shop.

Beyond Mora stopped at the customs house where one of my friends from that previous visit was on duty. As I arrived an unshaven Lebanese mechanic from Maroua was passing through; later a tall black man from Chad came with a load of hides and skins heading to Maiduguri. I noticed two men with rifles on the back of the truck.

Deserted road to the turn off on a sand track to Bama, the worst miles of the journey. The car went pounding along over the treacherous hidden bumps like a ship at sea. Anxious to "save" it, I winced at every shock.

In Bama Mr. Lawrence offered me lunch in his office. We talked of India, Nigeria, his district here, etc. He seems to have triumphed in this tour, come through his trial of fatigue with spirit.

In a cheerful state of mind after this lunch, I headed back to Maiduguri. Gave Dave, a pleasant young fellow, a ride. At the house I needed a brace of whiskey to pull my spirits up to anywhere near a sticking place.

Tuesday: the staff room unusually cheerful. Students quite listless—VI had four boys absent, asleep in their beds. I am not at all sure of the effectiveness of my teaching, but this somnolence makes it harder. There is always the nagging worry about their opinion of me.

Thursday: the birthday of the Queen of England celebrated throughout the Federation of Nigeria. For the last time? This holiday gave me a chance to catch up a bit—my conscience has been pricking me about the state of preparations for examinations, etc. My boredom with the seven subjects makes them pass from the mind like a poorly remembered dream. In the a.m. went through the mechanical process of marking the common entrance papers; the mistakes in English make me feel hopeless about the rise in standards that this country is supposed to be experiencing.

Staff room thoughts about the students are generalized and pessimistic. The boys emerge as individuals again when one meets them at library hour or at evening prep.

At prep there are countless excuses. "I was boiling water in the kitchen for my throat; the nurse says for me to drink half water." "I was talking with my brother and did not hear the bell." And on and on, always with the most engaging smile.

Here's another prediction of the future of this land and people to be added to the collection. This one from DO Pembleton a few weeks ago: "It will be like the situation in Britain after the Romans left."

The two communities—black and white, talking about each other, sizing each other up.

Rode Achilles slowly out along the Dunbara Road. A white thundercloud, surrounded by a deep blue purple sky to the east. The rain is somewhere near Maiduguri but has not arrived to wash away the stickiness.

It was pitch dark when I rode Achilles home—the moon rises later in the evening now. Mohammadu was just about to go to Dr. Lander to tell him that surely I had been thrown.

Dramatics in the Senior Primary School: short Kanuri plays, containing a surprising amount of scatology (there was one about a man who passes stool three times near his father-in-law's house). They were roughly done, without polish, but entertaining.

THE HEAT RISES

Yesterday, a high temperature and humidity, comparable to Washington, though there the discomfort would have been increased by the heat absorbed by the tarred streets. Unexpectedly, I find I can bear up quite well, even in the boiling classrooms.

At the school, the usual listless prep, some absentees quite brazenly gone to the town.

Malam Waziri of the Senior Primary School was due to arrive at 8 a.m. to rehearse its dramatic society. The boys had brought pressure lamps to the the football field and lit them. When he arrived after 8:30, the younger ones crowded around him, and a few of them began beating on a drum and a kerosene can in festive greeting. The play began with an Ibo song he had learned at teacher training, and he soon had nearly 100 boys leaping around him, following the steps of the dance closely and making their own zestful variations. No children anywhere can be as gracefully expressive as these little African boys. Whatever their life must be in the Senior Primary School—and it is probably rather bleak (I think of the little figures asleep all over the football field on many nights)—this dancing reminds them of their carefree village life. I remembered the little children in Marte the evening of the dance there.

The play they were rehearsing was Waziri's own version of *The Merchant of Venice*. It was a severely truncated story: Antonio and Bassanio made the loan, and the trial scene came next without Portia's mercy speech. The boys stumbled over the lines, not aided by M. Waziri's blocking, which insisted that every scene should take place seated. However, the performance was plausible and could be improved with practice—which encouraged me to think of possibilities with the older boys.

Malam Waziri understands the temperament of these boys better than we Europeans. He does not get rattled by the disorder and confusion and does not try to order it back into line again (which causes so many whites to become shrill and high pitched when trying to order a group of Africans).

I watched the football match in the afternoon with Ithacan Idrisa, the NA councilor for education and social services. Told me how he felt about education in English—"the English held us back with all this talk about the vernacular. When I went to Bauchi [Education Training College], they would not let us do anything but Hausa—there was three years lost. Now after this independence, you will see there will be a great change in this country. We will gather ideas from all the other countries of the world to help us. Look at Pakistan, how well she has advanced since her independence. During the 60 years of British rule they kept us down in order to keep law and order. They did not educate our intelligent ones." "But I have heard of direct rule among the Europeans in times past—of how the kings were cruel. Even, at one time there were people who were more powerful than kings... When I was in England I saw the long hall between the House of Lords and the House of Commons with all the pictures of history and some of the things that were done to the kings… We will convince the people to better themselves."

When I asked him how he was going to move the mass of the common people: "Previously, they had not been given a chance. I am not so sure about the time after independence—perhaps some of the poisoned darts of the European civil servants, with their repeated, 'they can't run it without us, etc.,' may have penetrated."

I was cheered to meet this man who obviously did care. Here is another dimension that one does not see from the school.

Monday. Remained indoors yesterday a.m., pale sunlight, but a ferocious humidity caused my body, even under the fan, to go damp with sweat. Read *Mani*, Patrick Leigh-Fervor's book about a part of the southern Peloponnese. All of a sudden recovered the ability and desire to read. I devour books rapidly as of old. Also books on the lands to visit over my leave, I wonder if perhaps I have become used enough to this country to allow myself the time to read of it. The historical and descriptive books I read before my arrival I fail to remember—now that I have had some experience of the country these facts have considerably more meaning.

There remains so much to be done. In contrast to the gloom of a month ago and the time preceding I find I am looking forward to a return. I must do something about languages. And then collect stories, customs, etc., also I look forward to drama work with the boys. After all this wobble, have I found feet here at last?

Tuesday: The sky to the east had turned a menacing blue-black. In Maiduguri the sweat poured from my skin as though I had wet it with a shower. This house, always hot and close, became intolerable. Went to Mbouta with Abba Bashir from VI Form as interpreter. He minded the heat more than I. A true town boy, nothing I could do would excite him about the artesian wells or the plan to settle the nomads by providing all-season water. His face wore an expression of boredom and pain; despite his intelligence, he is diffident with me. I missed Bukar Zoru's ease and interest and verbal flair. Abba wears a sullen expression—or is it reserved? Somewhat weary, and calculating? Yet there is this intelligence, which he uses quite steadily in class.

Monday. A storm threatened Maiduguri but did not give us the relief of rain. The wind currents began to move, however, bringing us air that smelled fresh and lean, washed by some nearby water. This meant a sound sleep.

Section I knew exactly what they should about cavemen, Lake Dwellers and Hadrian's Wall. When I talked about Roman baths, Baba Malam Abba, the dark, bright eyed little boy at the back raised his hand and said "Whippoorwill"—I had imitated the sound of water flowing—it seems that he thought I was speaking about birds.

Horseback riding becomes an increased pleasure since Mike Barber advised me to make the Achilles do what I wish. Gone are the unhappy times of him getting his own way and biting. He is full of strength and spirit.

Tuesday means six classes in a row after breakfast. High humidity—southerly, clammy, damp atmosphere. The flask of squash assumes a great deal of importance in the breaks between classes.

One class seems to have got the meaning of "irrelevance." Baba Shehu stood up in the midst of a discussion on Old Ghana and asked me when I was going on vacation. He was hooted down by cries of "irrelevant." It all became uproarious.

A storm in the direction of Gwoza. Low mutterings of thunder. Young Bukar and Mohammadu assured me, with the definiteness the local people have about the weather, that there would be no rain in Maiduguri.

I rode into the stream out by the water supply. Achilles became excited by the wind and exuberantly plunged and cantered, no doubt looking handsome with the wind catching his mane.

The sky facing us had mountains of deep purple on the horizon fading to a light blue; occasionally a silver edge of cloud appeared. Behind me the sun was blocked by a thick cloud which radiated a deep pall about the edges.

As I headed back the view to the west was surmounted by a great cloud, whitish streaks from it seemed to be falling to the south, forming a great curtain over the setting sun.

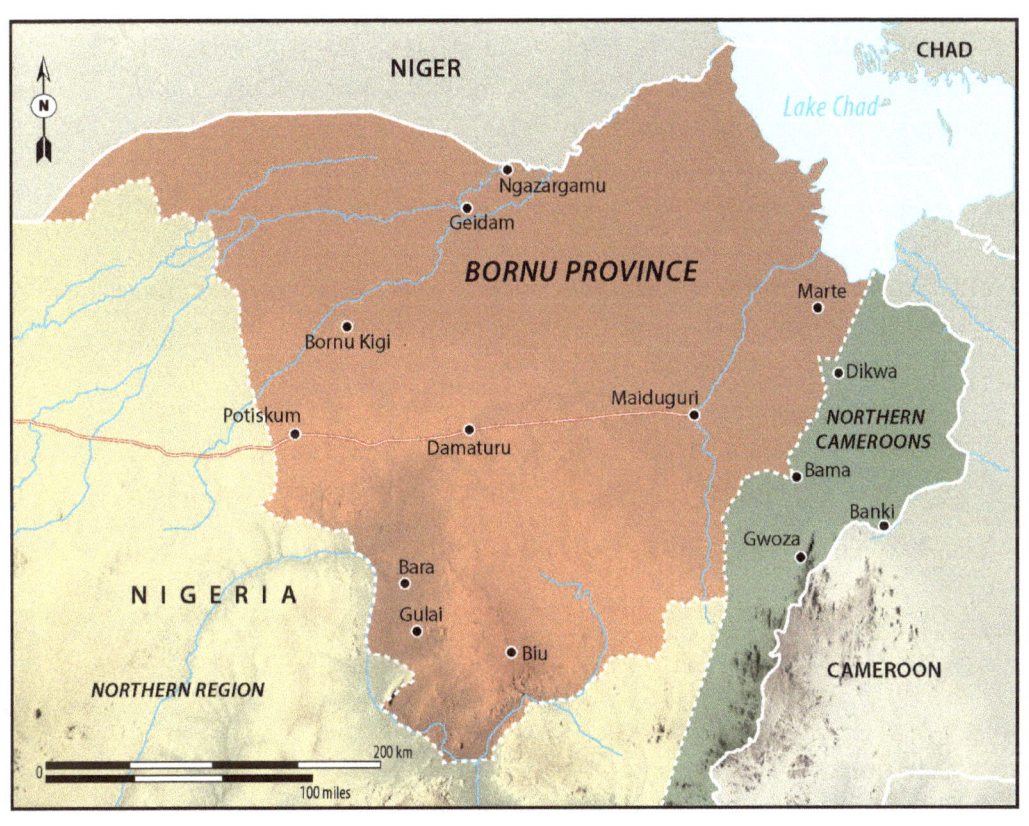

Note Ngazergamu by border with Niger reached from Geidam by bush tracks.

An official visit

The visit of the Resident and the Waziri [the senior advisor to the Shehu, in effect the prime minister of the province] along with the Council came to the school yesterday, which I did not see. This official visit provoked the usual infuriating comments in the staff room. The head was critical of the resident: "He came without notice, he seems to 'flannel' the Africans—I'm not sure whether he is insincere or he does it because he thinks of himself as the Mr. McClintock of Bornu." He implies darker motives: "he's got a wife and two small children to look after, so naturally he is anxious to please his masters. He flannels away, not addressing words to the Europeans who have the task of drumming some sense into these people," he says, accusing him of thinking of job security, deeply suspicious of anyone who "flannels" the Africans. They assume the time will come to accept or reject those who "flannel" and those who don't. No one of the Europeans on staff except Margaret Lander, seems to think that the resident might be interested in doing his job well; for any of us, this should involve being responsive to the people who hire us to perform a service.

LL gave a supercilious chuckle when he heard that Zanna Laisu referred to "dirts" in the classroom. "A councilor, ha! Much to say, these people can govern!"

My ride last night was less idyllic. Not far from the police barracks, at the third touch of the spurs, Achilles reared up and dropped me on my back behind him. He went off at magnificent speed, kicking his heels behind him. I caught him only after a chase through the bush.

The Provincial Secondary School Historical Society Expedition, April and May 1960

An approach I used to stimulate interest in history among the older boys was to encourage the formation of a history club, more grandly entitled the Provincial Secondary School Historical Society. Recruitment was helped by the promise of a field trip to a remote spot at the very north of the province, close to the Niger border and the Sahara. We were to visit the ruins of Ngazargamu, the ancient capital of the kingdom of Bornu, beyond the northernmost point of the constituency in the Federal Election where I had seen camel caravans. There is no reference to Ngazargamu in the curriculum and neither I nor the boys had access to the concise description available half a century later with the click of a mouse to Wikipedia:

Ngazargamu was the capital of the Bornu Empire from ca. 1460 to 1809. Situated 150 km west of Lake Chad in western Bornu (now within Yobe State)], the impressive remains of the former capital city are still visible. The surrounding wall is 6.6 km long and in parts it is still up to 5 m high. The town was built by Mai Ali Gaji (1455–1487) after the final defeat of the Dawudid branch of the Sefuwa ruling dynasty.

The city was then an important center for trade and learning, at its height home to around 20,000 inhabitants.

In 1809, after several years of indecisive warfare, Ngazargamu was besieged and destroyed by Malam Zaki jihad, in the Fulani jihad.

The ruins are 20 miles north of Geidam, a trading center, with no designated roads or tracks. The NA provided two lorries on the back of which the boys could stand or sit on benches, either of which required stamina for a trip of almost 170 miles, about half on rough bush track. Sarke and I sat with Ali, the driver, in the high cab of the lead vehicle, giving us an expansive view of the country. The fifteen older schoolboys who enthusiastically joined our expedition brought mats and bedrolls to sleep in the open. We were headed to parts of the province most had never seen.

The first leg was along the paved road to Potiskum, 144 miles; and from there 126 miles north on sand and clay to Geidam, a market town and District headquarters. It is camel country with traders coming from the Sahara. I looked forward to meeting the distinguished DH whom I was told had been honored by the Queen.

As it was the end of the dry season, it would be hot, and, though there had been some rain, the terrain could still be negotiated by the lorries.

Geidam, the nearest market town to Ngazargamu, is at the junction of roads at the center left. At the top is the border with Niger. The river carried water from Lake Chad.

The lorry that was due to leave at one finally got off at two, delayed by the boys coming from their dormitories. It could be possible to be enraged at this sort of thing, but here if one has a school masterly sense of precision one would go wild with frustration nearly all the time—as my colleagues do.

I enjoyed sitting high in the cab of the Thomas Traveler to better see the land beside the road without having to dodge oncoming traffic in my car on that familiar stretch of highway. We also traveled at a slow speed, as Ali, our excellent driver, never exceeded the legal limit of 35 mph.

Rain had fallen past Beini Sheikh—a heavy one. The sides of the road, although prepared with deep trenches, already are deeply eroded. Planting of maize in the fields.

At the highway stand at Damaturu, as I bought seventeen bottles of "Lucky Orange" for the boys and the drivers at Mrs. Mlamowa's bar, I noticed aphrodisiacs for sale outside the door.

Night was falling as we headed north from Potiskum along the bumpy and wet road to Geidam.

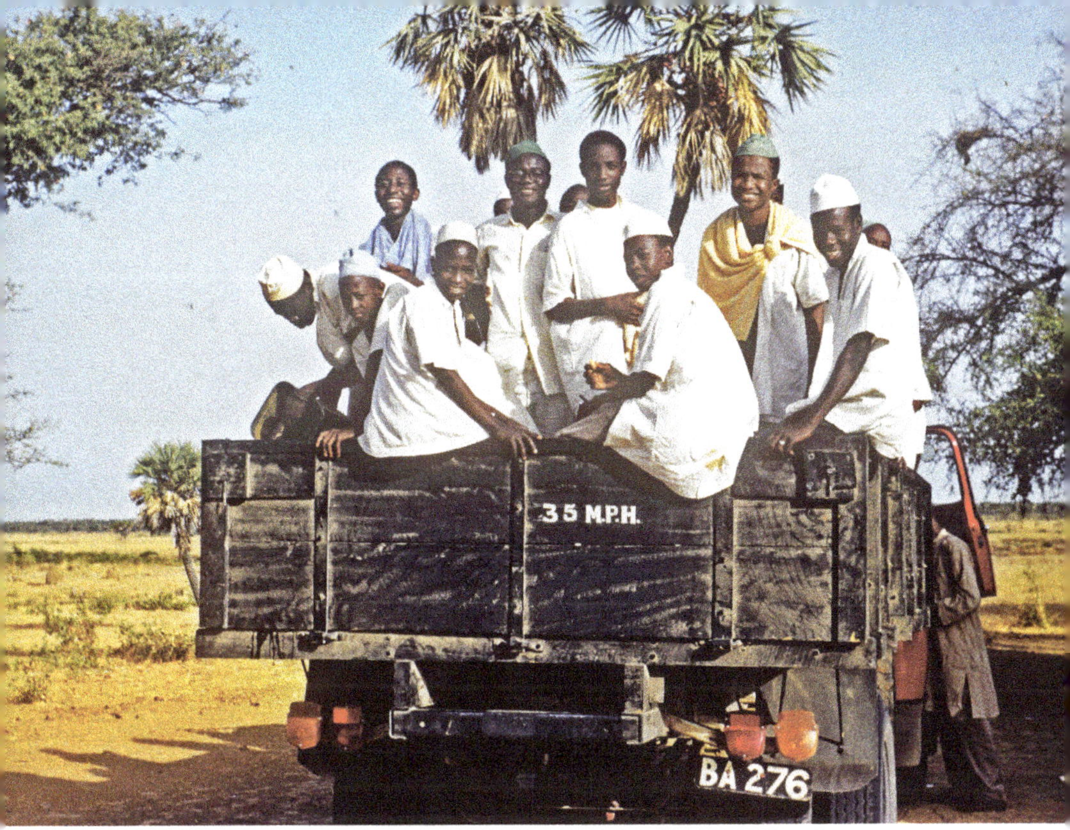
35 M.P.H.
BA 276

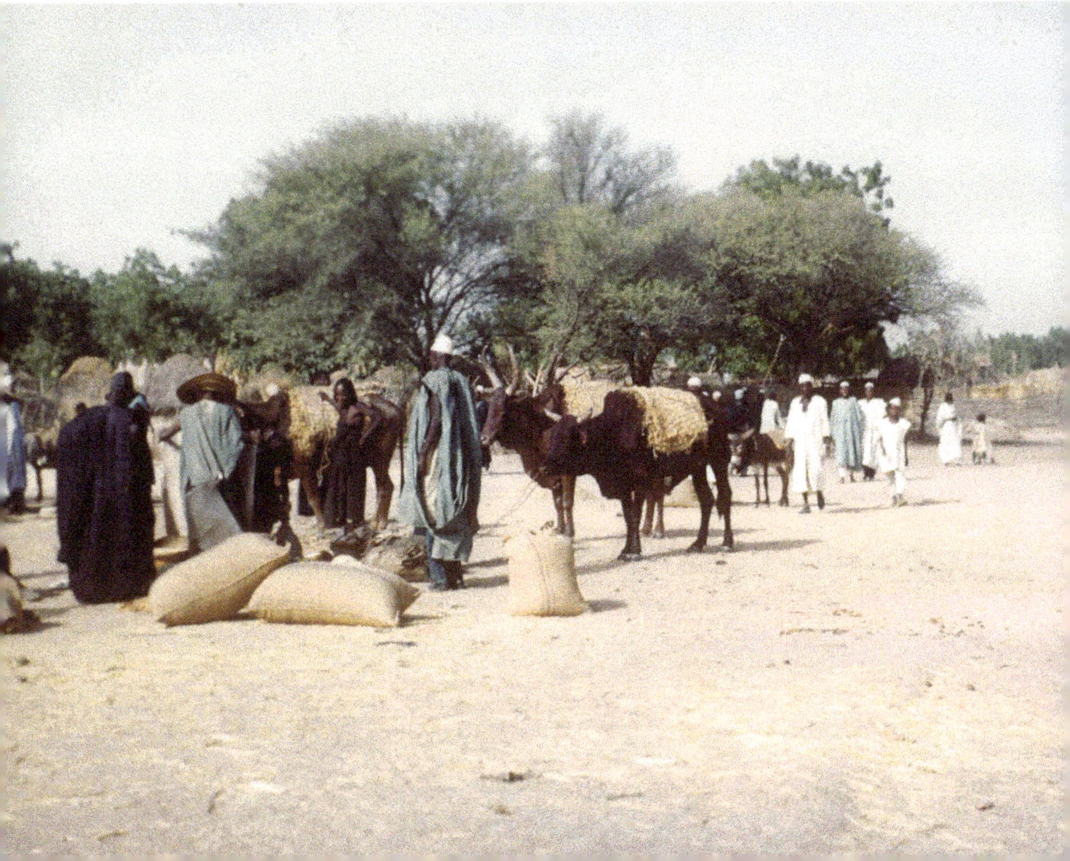

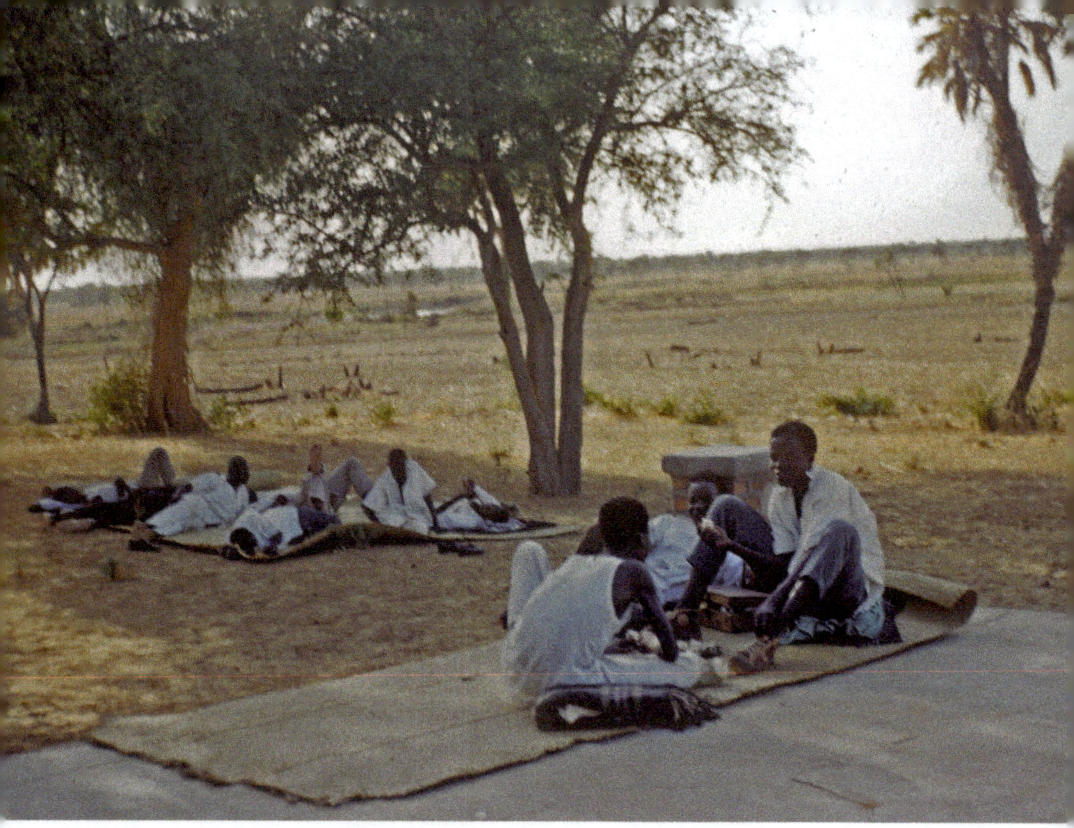

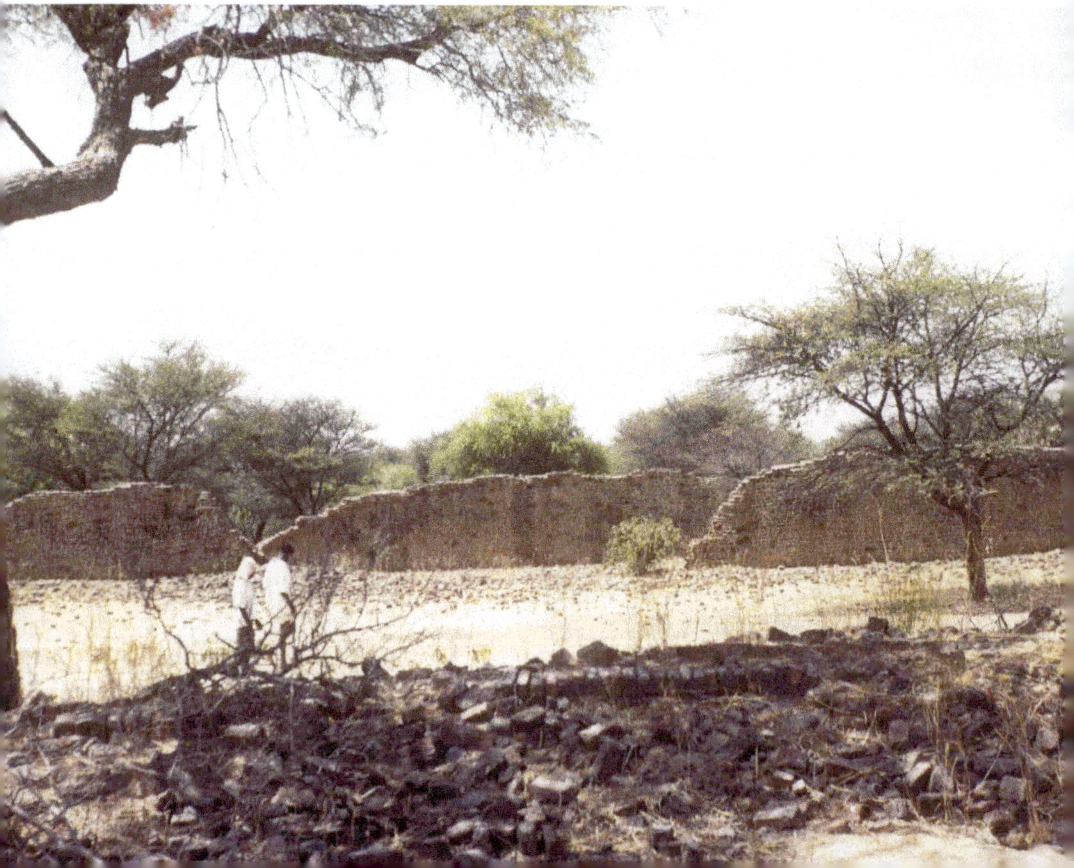

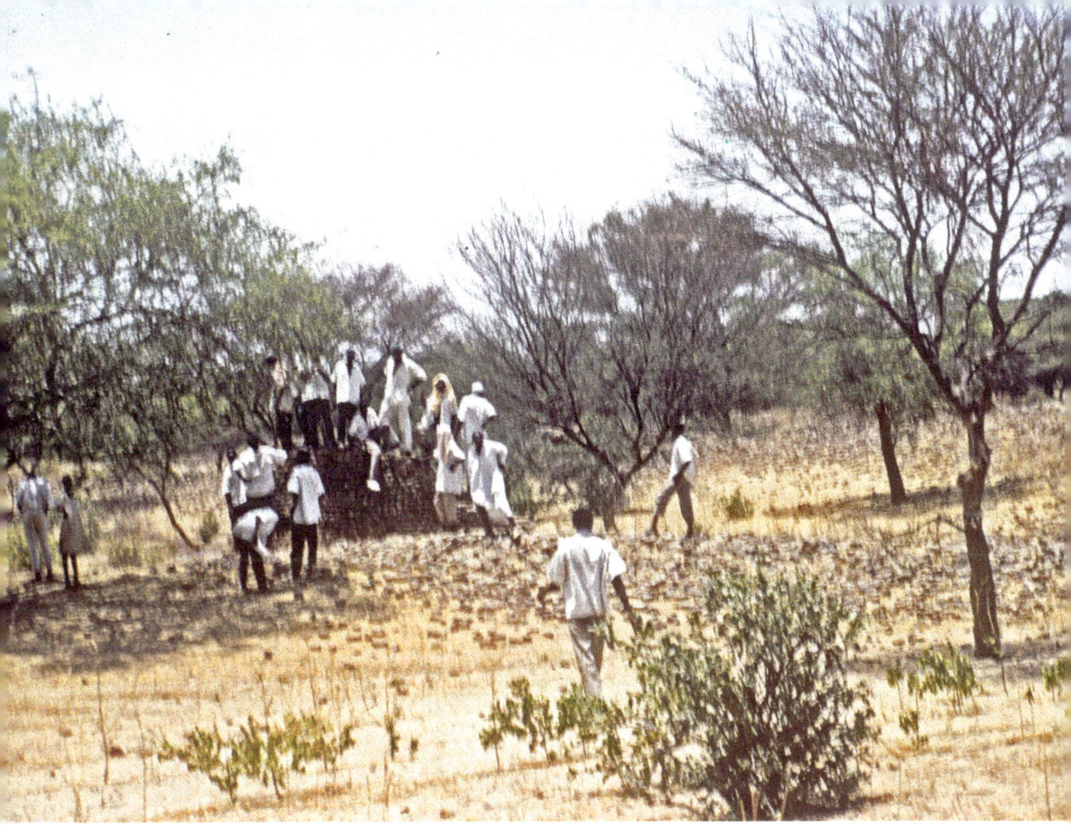

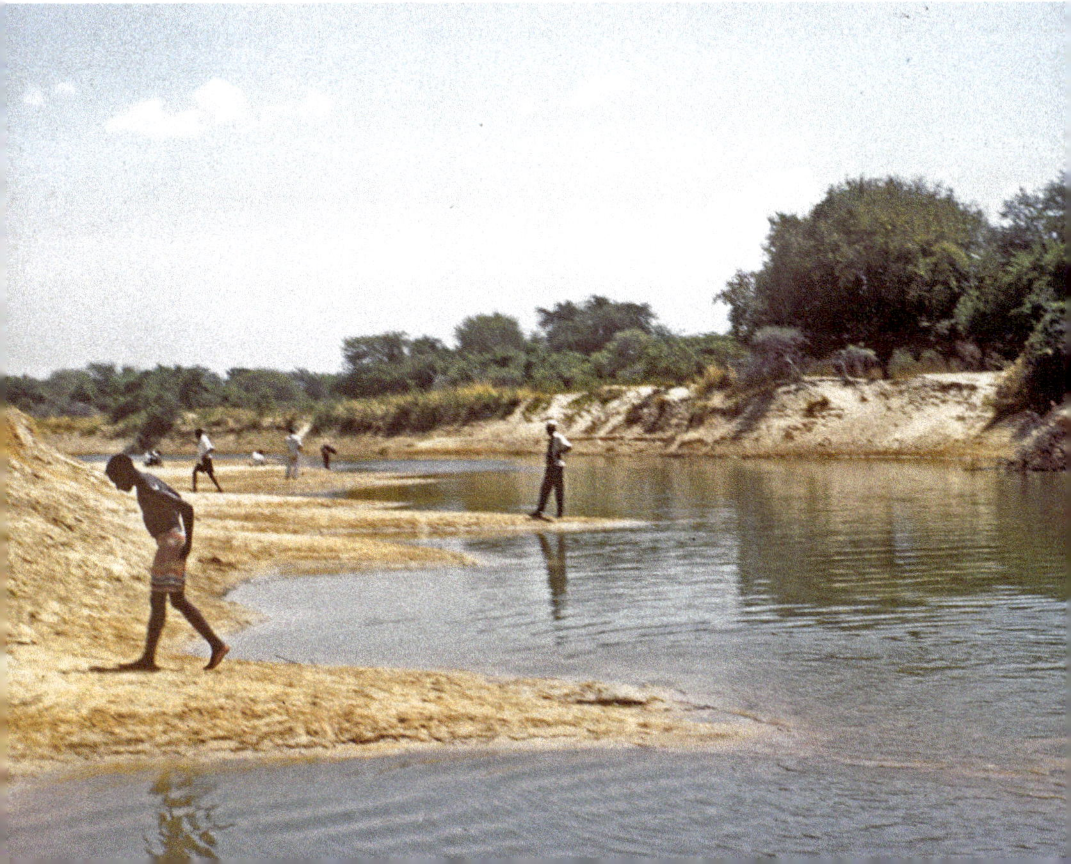

The road seemed endless. I asked Ali rather shamefacedly several times whether it was the right one. In the seemingly total dark, the only light was from the headlamps, making this sand strangely white. Rays from the new moon were obscured by the dust of the *harmattan*. The lorry shuttered and bucked on a bad sand stretch accompanied by cries of annoyance from the boys.

Arrived Geidam about 8:30 p.m. and found the DH away, watching explosions being set off to deter bird predators. We had some difficulty over rest houses, finally settling on one, though imperfectly perceived in the dark. The guard from a neighboring house, a bearded man with a cane, came to welcome and invite me to the "bank manager's house." Once the boys went off to town for their evening meal, I followed him.

Near the white light of a Tilley lamp I heard English inquiring after the *batturi*. Close to the light I saw a mustached face, sporting racy long black hair, a European in a dressing gown and pajamas. In his mosquito-proofed house, I found watercolor prints of Scotland placed liberally on the walls, a rug on the floor, chairs with matted armrests like 1940s airport waiting rooms.

My host, Mr. Milton, served a cold bottle of Star beer, surely one of the best drinks I ever had. He thought I was the "bird man," responsible for the explosions, but seemed glad of company. He is the BWA [Bank of West Africa] manager, one of the two Europeans living in Geidam.

During our chat, a lorry appeared in a neighboring field. Ali summoned me to come with him to pay my respects to the returning DH. Yemini Mustapha, M.B.E [Most Excellent Order of the British Empire] had a chair waiting beside him in front of the mud and brick wall that surrounded his house. We conversed in English—from time to time assisted by Bako Balewa crouching at our feet. About us in dark patches sat the elders, occasionally called upon by the DH—some sent for errands, another to fetch *serkin barake*, the keeper of the rest houses. In the darkness I could sense a dignified and warm presence. He spoke of "my friends," the banker whom I had just met and the Cohens. [Ronald Cohen had lived in Geidam with his wife Diane not long before while doing fieldwork for his Anthropology PhD.] He told me that the Cohens had named their child Selima which gave him much pleasure.

[I later learned that Ronald Cohen with a PhD from the University of Wisconsin had a distinguished career with appointments in several universities. In 1967 he published *The Kanuri of Bornu*.]

I soon returned to the rest house whose door was locked, but Sarke had set out a pressure lamp which spread its white light. I put my bed beneath a tree; the boys slept on mats on the terrace. Animated chatter in Kanuri continued loudly for some time.

I slept soundly until the very early morning when I awoke with thoughts moving quickly, as though I had not slept at all, the boys too were stirring in this moment of dawn. I enjoyed my tea in the delightful early freshness. At seven the boys in their kaftans went to greet the DH. They kneeled and repeated a prayer with him, looking swell. On the *dendal* there were other sights, the NA police squad Land Rover—a testament to Geidam's size—and primary school boys doing disciplined PT.

The face which I had not seen when we spoke last night, was grave and elderly. Malam Yermina proudly showed me the most recent letter he had received from Ronald Cohen, now at the University of Toronto.

Back to the rest house for the boys to change out of kaftans and to have breakfast at the nearby Ibo hotel. The jolly innkeeper pointed with pride to photos on his wall of the founders of the Nigerian independence movement including the Ibo nationalist, Nmandi Azikwe or Zik—not a figure honored by Northerners who have an edgy relationship with the Ibo.

To reach the ruins we headed north, beginning a grueling search to find a way through the bush. Ali turned the steering wheel frantically, looking for patches of grass in the sand for traction. Each hillock became a crisis. We were stuck several times; the boys jumped down to place sections of corrugated iron sheets beneath the tires which flew up alarmingly behind the lorry after they provided the necessary traction to pull us out of the sand. The iron became flecked with specks of rubber from the tires. It was a challenge of strength and skill for the drivers to continuously manipulate the steering wheels. They had to make fearsome choices approaching the hillocks. In our lorry Ali was not helped by contrary directions shouted from the back by our uncertain guide. For the boys it was an adventure, and they jumped off delightedly every time we got stuck.

The sand is held in place by a few scattered thorn trees and sparse grass. As noon approached, the heat became intense, over 105, maybe 110. The dire moment came when the effect of the salt cocktail wore off, and my thirst began to rage. However, the boys were cheerful and even energetic in the sun.

Stopped at Digeltara market, about 30 miles from Geidam on the Damasak road. In the market there were about a score of camels and 100 horses, a busy and prosperous place. The heat was so intense I wondered how people could carry on trade.

The lawan of the village, a young, rather shy man, received me in the shade by his gate. Delightfully cool, I sat in his chair facing his house to watch the bustling market through a doorway framed by two of the attending elders.

At noon we headed across even more barren country, the last five miles to Ngazargamu. At the site we found a grid of built-up sand ridges—yards apart with burnt bricks scattered about; beneath were the ruins of what the locals told us had been an outer wall. Within were the outline of squares showing what would have been buildings, much depleted now by erosion.

The boys were excited by the ruins, particularly impressed by the burnt bricks. This was the Shehu's palace—we could see the outline of the walls in places. It must have been 300 yards square.

From the ruins a group of us walked towards the river on a tricky passage over the outer wall and across barren land with only cattle traces. Suddenly the vegetation changed to grouped palm trees and, in their midst, the remains of brick walls. As we walked carefully through the bricks we came upon a doorway which had survived and two or three walls about seven feet in height. There was a far larger number of bricks on this site amid tall palm trees and clumps of palm shrubs. The boys called the hillocks dust heaps, meaning that they were formed from collapsed structures. This was a ruins of once large and imposing buildings, still powerful even in ruin. We spied nearby cattle grazing by a river (the Yaho which flows gently to the west from Lake Chad) and suddenly history and archaeology vanished from my and the boys' thoughts as we ran into the water. It was dirty, but not sluggish, and cooler than the air. At the deepest it was four and half feet, at the edges two and half or three feet, fine for playing and bouncing in or just sitting. The boys played a long game of tag which I sometimes joined.

After this burst of energy, I lay in the blissful coolness of the water, hoping that my body would absorb enough moisture to allay the thirst I knew would become acute in the afternoon.

When we left the river, the weakness that the heat normally induced overtook me. We walked slowly through the ruins again, but my thoughts were fixed on the cool water that was in my flask in the lorry. Some villagers had brought water to the lorries from the river for the boys. We sat for a time, and left by 2:00, expecting that the return journey would take as long as had the morning one. I gave in to my thirst and drank all the cool water in the large flask, knowing as I did so that later I would have to drink the water of the lawan of Digeltara. Thirst becomes the most powerful need I have ever felt—exceeding any hunger or lust I have known. The mind sparkles with thoughts of tall cold glasses in luxury hotels by the sea, the sea itself, all cool drinks that I have known. One becomes a glutton; there is no stopping the desire for liquid.

Ali had become experienced now in driving in semi desert, coasting and crashing through the sand, zigzagging like an attacking destroyer at sea. We skirted the "wall" of Ngazargamu again, and, after some indecision about the route by our guides, reached the market town of Deilawa.

At the lawan's invitation, I sat in the guest room of his house and drank deeply of his water, served in a bowl, colored slightly by the corn that is put in it "for gentlemen." With great courtesy the lawan presented me with four chickens to bring home.

The return went swiftly. Ali had learned the route—there were no more indecisive consultations and Ali could reduce pressure on the accelerator. I spent the rest of the journey with open mouth to keep my teeth from chattering, hoping that the lorry would not get stuck in the sand. This it never did, in answer to the equally intense hopes of the boys attempting to sit or stand in the open body of the lurching vehicle.

Arrived to Geidam towards five. Drank a bottle of beer and a pot full of tea. Visited by Mr. Milton, out for a walk with his walking stick and accompanied by two dogs. I continued taking my tea in a deep sweat making me look ill, perhaps, but satisfying after the dryness of the day.

Before dark Malam Selima arrived to visit, driven in a blue "Bel Air" Chevy, his presence endowing the car with a dignity I did not know it had. I was concerned that the 8 p.m. hour I had proposed for him to speak to the boys would be inconvenient. Seated on chairs on the rest house terrace, we settled it that he would instead arrange for some of the old men of the town to come speak with boys. The gathering was to be at the rest house, rather than at the DH's gate.

I visited Mr. Milton for a beer at dusk. The other European resident of Geidam was present, George, the manager of the Levantis store, a young Cypriot with a slim beard. We sat in Milton's suffocating living room while the out-of-doors was becoming beautifully dry and cool.

The old men were late for the gathering. Ali explained that it is the custom for the older men to go to bed immediately after prayers, and even though the DH had detailed six of them to come to us, they had all gone to sleep. Ali had to wake them and only two would come. I was apprehensive that we had embarrassed them, but they seemed pleased to be there. They gathered their robes about them and sat on the mat, only their bald heads visible, like two great bowls. The boys sat facing them on their mats.

The men recounted, not in any great detail but in a soft duet, the history of Geidam, claiming they did not know about anything else. Geidam was founded after the end of the warlord Rabeh's time and coincident with the coming of the Europeans. It was settled by people from nearby who came on the river by canoe. Others came later in canoes such as the Europeans made. They took bricks from the ruins of Birni and Ngazergemu to build the town of Geidam.

In those days a man was rich who possessed a donkey—this the men repeated several times. Trade was chiefly west to Damasak, Ngurru, and sometimes as far as Kano. There they stayed with other Kanuris because they did not know Hausa.

Very early, when they were still young men, the first European DO came with soldiers—they gave his name, but I did not catch it. The second European DO who came was carried in by bearers, as were, also, his dogs.

The boys asked questions about the old city we had seen during the day. The men replied that they knew nothing at all except what concerned their own town. Maladu Gari broke in to explain in English that "because these men are so old they tell of nothing but what they saw with their own eyes. Their religion tells them to only tell truth, and they are so old they know that their days are near, so they must be careful only to speak about what they have seen."

The old men remained resistant to questions about myths, about the sea. They answered questions with the repeated observation that a man was rich in the old days if he possessed a donkey. While the boys felt some frustration at this repetition, they were generally pleased by the little old men. One of them was almost blind, and the other he referred to as his son—this scarcely seemed probable. For their time, I gave them a dish full of kola nuts that seemed to please them, and Ali drove them home in style on the front seat of the lorry.

The chatter from the boys on the terrace was somewhat subdued that night, and I slept peacefully until the moment the dawn awakened us in its delightful coolness.

Sunday. After my breakfast at seven, most of the boys went into town for their chop of *gari*. Two of them joined me to walk slowly to the river where we found a couple of men trying to smoke a squirrel out of a hole. The river winds beneath an attractive bluff near the bush rest house. The cliff must be 100 feet high and is inhabited by 200 or so birds with orange bellies and deep red wings. They live in the holes in the cliff and seem to float in and out and noisily fly in disorganized squadrons above the river.

There are gardens on this side of the river and fish in the water. Fishermen, with fine nets and large wicker baskets scour the stream. On the grasslands beyond the river, there is a line of palms.

The three of us sat by the edge of the river, kneeling to feel the full coolness of the air as it crossed the water and watched a small, green island alive with birds—a moment of pure deliciousness that Africa affords from time to time, so welcome after the incessant struggle of most days.

We made a farewell visit to Malam Selima. As we were seated by his gate, he asked me whether I would like to see a "Sudanese ass" within. I assented quickly and was passed through the guest gate into the complex. Each passage seemed to lead to another. In the courtyard just inside the entrance there was a cement wall. Several servants worked about it, pulling up water from a well and carrying pots in several directions. We saw about eight different horses, including two albinos and a small "malana" horse. The Sudanese ass was tall with a long tail and long ears. M. Selima told me, through Bukar, that this ass could travel to Maiduguri in a single day, faster than any horse. Nearby were three great rams, one white, one with deep coarse hair like wool, and a high-spirited black one with long horns who tried to butt us from his tether. Everywhere were grooms and lackeys seeing to these animals, cleaning their stalls. M. Selima looked on with a slight smile as we inspected his stable, standing erect in his rich blue gown with a tight collar about his neck, rings holding a stone on his fingers. While Malam Selima's household compound included ample area for his animals, cared for and nutured, even the poor take great care of their animals, keeping them next to their huts at night if they don't have compound walls to keep them within. Such a contrast to the distance we "Europeans" keep from our animals.

Outside the gate, before our departure, he brought out a pair of native shoes and a cap for me to give to Dr. Cohen in New York during my leave. He said he looked forward to a durbar for Princess Margaret in October. [I delivered the shoes and the cap to Ronald Cohen that summer.]

When I bade farewell I assured him I would return.

The trip back went smoothly although by midday the sun had beat into the back of the lorry enough to down the spirits of the boys. At Laterwa we took a break beneath a great tree, according to the locals a venerable one and the biggest for miles around. The shade was cool and refreshing.

The road from Laterwa to Damaturu was bumpy and the sky overcast, a largely deserted country. At Damaturu I sat in the private room of Mrs. Mlamowa's to drink soda water and write notes in this book. In a moment of almost suffocating humidity before a storm, young Imam Abdul came in to eat a meal, lively and enthusiastic in contrast to his sleepiness in class. He produced cubes of sugar from a briefcase and put about eight into a glass of water, stirred it up thoroughly and drinking it as he spread a whole piece of bread with margarine from a tin also extracted from his briefcase. When he finished, he said, "we Negroes eat more than Europeans—I expect you have noticed that."

We overheard three drunk Ibos in the large room talking English about God and prayers, most of it incomprehensible, all in a curious intonation, the sentence starting high, "just I want to say..." and ascending from there.

The boys, who originally had wished to stay in Damaturu for an hour, called me from my comfortable chair. It threatened rain. We saw clouds dropping columns of rain only a few yards from the road. We had to move. At Maiduguri Airport a fierce sandstorm came from the direction of the town. We arrived at the roundabout amid driving rain. The members of the Historical Society vanished the moment the lorry reached the school. The rain stopped soon after—none in the GRA where the atmosphere became heavy and dense. As I looked into the green wall of trees surrounding this house, I missed Geidam and the splendor of Bornu.

On this expedition:

Makinta Chibook	Malu Gari
Baba Makaaldam	Mustaphah Samu
Imman Abdul Salam	Uwawa Gasbua
Hyelni Bassey	Bukar Zoru
Wutowa Mbaorga	Mamulawa Mamadi
Nuktthar Alkali	Mustapha Dangus
Kyari Mante	Babba Hamuwa Gwoza

Monday: Assigned to an interdepartmental Board of Survey of the "CRPB" government store with a solid man who looks like a US Army sergeant, Richards, a well-sinker. He looked at his car identical with mine and said, "I get a pound a night sleeping in that thing—I've done 2000 miles this last tour." Blackwell, the chief clerk in the Principal Engineer's office, also a member of the "board," a bright Ibo, neatly dressed in whites, has a tendency to cock his head and wear a half smile while he listens. In the hot shed we counted every item from pipe fittings to toilets, aided by a nervous storekeeper who lost his head at the slightest discrepancy we pointed out. The YS (Yard Superintendent) told me of his recent posting—"Kaduna was lovely—by 3 o'clock in the afternoon you were done and miles away in your head—I figure on another ten years on the coast, not here, there is going to be too much confusion, but go where the salaries are… You spend your whole time out here wishing—wishing that the rains would come, for the rains to stop, or that your leave would come."

"We are not changing."

Tuesday: an introduction to a party at the Residency. Such is the state of society here that I was pleased inordinately by the social "prestige" of being invited. The initial invitation bore the phrase, "we are changing" (meaning to formal dress), but a following note read, "we are not changing."

I prepared for a stiff evening. The resident, N. C. McClintock greeted me at the door—tall, immaculately dressed in a double-breasted suit. His wife, in a long dress, was seated comfortably on the settee on the terrace. She must have been a very pretty blonde-haired young woman—and she retains some of those looks, with an appealing softness and gentleness. The resident's poise is carefully cultivated—he seems, in fact, to be playing a role continuously—as a diplomat must. I do not find this objectionable, chiefly because his position, after all, is a role to play. (Remember the disparaging comments of my colleagues about how the resident was playing up to ("flanneling") his "Masters," i.e., the Africans.) [See a notice of his fascinating memoir of service in Bornu in the References section.]

The other guests were a touring magistrate, a tall New Zealander, affable with a torrent of pleasant small talk and warm feelings. And, to my surprise, as I had expected only European guests from the GRA, the Waziri of Bornu [Shettima Kassim] and Zanna Laisu. My first real contact with the Waziri—a rough, intellectually impressive man, though reserved—some of his remarks in the adapted style of English small talk.

The tone of the evening required matters of political or administrative importance to the emirate to receive merely a glance. Not surprisingly, given my lowly status, in my conversation with the Waziri he was not more than politely forthcoming even about his recent visit to the US. I felt Kanuri pride, concern for the emirate above all things. Just being in his presence I understood the admiration often expressed about his ability.

Zanna Laisu, the NA councilor, was also a guest, a rolling man, ham-fisted and uncouth, hitting the table to make a point. But once his initial suspicion of the white man passed, he became affable and even matey. He told me that his grandfather, a famous imam of Marte, did not cause the village to rise in the air when Rabeh came, but by a powerful prayer, made Marte invisible to the attacking army. When I called him "Malam Zanna" he corrected me and told me that "Zanna" was a title, he was turbaned by the Shehu: "a malam can be any fool."

The Resident led conversation in measured tones and cadences. His wife talked to the judge about their children.

Slept well on the cool night following this unusual evening.

Wednesday: examinations. LL met me at 6:35 with an outburst in response to my comments about how casually the boys were facing the prospect of exams. "They can never, ever run anything for themselves. They just can't do it. And the *expenses*... we aren't giving Africa freedom, we're only giving it to a bunch of hoodlums and Teddy boy politicians. That's it in a nutshell, isn't it?"

The boredom of preparing the history examinations was suffocating. It is a particularly dull subject in this curriculum, and there is no way of varying it because of the rigidity of the school certificate requirements. So much of this educational system seems dull, stereotyped and irrelevant to the problems the boys will face. Above all, it does not begin to teach them to think for themselves. The language problem should be the first to tackle, then this ineffectual syllabus should be revised!

Hot, sticky afternoon and evening. Rode past the rifle range. To bed at 9:15.

Friday: history examinations. I have a pile of scripts here, in the car and in the staff room. Correcting them is a trial—three or four papers are readable—I wish at times that I had someone to share the humorous disorder. After a certain number, the whole experience blurs, lost in a maze of the disorganization and confusion in the students' papers, I don't know whether I am marking fairly or not.

The rain at last

In the early afternoon rumbles of thunder wake me from my nap. Great passages of wind at intervals seemed to push the house from either side. On the porch I see the clouds overhead, no particular shape, but a mass of light and dark. As intermittent drops of rain fall, enough to make the earth smell wet, darkness descends prematurely. Mohammadu arrives to attend the horse, upsetting my sense of time; it was as dark at 3:30 as it usually is at 6:30.

After I pull down the sashes the rain begins to fall steadily, outside is now cool and my muscles recover their normal suppleness. The experience of a normal temperature seems novel, reminding me just how difficult and oppressive the previous heat had been. The rainfall makes a delicious sound, enjoyable for its own sake, equally the contrasting dry interior of the house. At last! Here is a great event in nature after weeks of fulminations. I did not realize how powerful my longing for this change of season was. Just to sit on the porch watching and listening to the rain is luxury.

I was glad to look forward to sharing the rain with someone, for I had been invited to the Landers for a drink. We sat out on their porch with white wine from a Fort Lamy demijohn, Margaret blossoming with her pregnancy, Mike weary-looking in a strange mood altogether. I sympathize, he is badly overworked, and his work calls for a skill and concentration that must be enormously taxing.

Monday. With the rain, the weather has mercifully turned. Yesterday morning was clear—brilliant—with the leaves freshly green in the light, a sweet-smelling breeze playing through them by the porch where I have my tea. The sky is light where for months it has been dark; I see clouds on the horizon. In the evening a great mass of purple color to the southeast over Gwoza, at intervals a sharp lightning bolt heads towards the earth. Over the GRA, a strip of irregularly shaped heavy clouds—dark along the bottom, a dazzling white and pink on the top. This reminded of Baroque ceiling clouds; there should have been a Michelangelo to reveal a giant beneath them holding them above the GRA houses.

Sunday p.m.: to and from Mbuta for a load of corn. The road badly bunged up since my last trip. The evening's rain had done its work—some puddles on top of the fringes. The heavy lorries plow great ruts into the earth, so the car must circulate about the edges of what was once the road. In a few weeks or less the route will be impassible.

The market was smaller than last time. My companions, Tijani Baluna and Ashekh Marte, were more enthusiastic about the journey than Abba Bashir, had been. Ashekh, being a Shuwa, had more to say about the customs of the people. These "black Shuwa" were settled farmers. They had once been the slaves of the nomads who still hold slaves though most have been set free. The "black Shuwas" had been captured in raids on villages in far off places like the Mandara Hills. [Gwoza and south in Cameroon.] They were pagans who had by now intermarried and become Shuwa, though deemed of a lesser order than the light-skinned aristocrats like Ashekh himself.

In the market a man sold old pieces of paper and powder to be used against witches, the first indication I had that witchcraft was prevalent among these people.

Three Bornoje Fulani youths were in the market. With long braided hair and prominent, almost buck, teeth they wore cowhide shirts, each with a goat skin bag slung over a shoulder. These Bornoje Fulani are considered fierce and wild. Ashekh and Tijani asserted that "they live in the bush all the time, and are very dangerous." These youths were indeed wild-looking; carrying themselves differently than the Shuwa, Fulani or other nomads of the north. In this little market they looked like mountain people on a spree. They were unconcerned by the camera and posed naturally. Then they ran off, evidently pursuing a new idea.

The troughs by the wellheads were full of water, but there were only a few horses and cows drinking. I watched as the dignified old lawan stepped up to the spigot with his retainers and turned it on as though to demonstrate that water could still come. But with the rains the herds can now drink from pools in the bush and no longer need the precious borehole water.

Stormy night but with only a pattering of rain. Violent winds overhead and a muffled sky. The morning cool, restoring the skin and muscles. A deep refreshing sleep.

Monday. More correction of exams, confronting the gibberish of sections I through V. The usual staff room chatter—LL seems to hold me responsible for the great blunder made by the CIA pilot over Russia. He is delighted that the USA should have embarrassed itself just before the Geneva summit conference. [A US reconnaissance flight was shot down over the USSR, the "U2 incident," that threatened, but did not suspend, the first summit conference between the US and the USSR in the Cold War.]

DM concludes with the others that our effort to push the boys through school certificates is a waste of time.

These afternoons I have just enough energy to ride Achilles for a bit. Visited the new school site and the dreadful cramped little house into which Steve Allen has moved. The sky looked beautiful over the bush, but soon the open spaces will be crowded in by another ill-sorted group of buildings for the TTC [Teacher Training Course].

The difficulties of going over exam papers with the boys include hurt feelings and resentment. I marked one paper 58, but reduced it to 52 because of its "total" impression. This prompted an anguished response by Gorgiri Lawan which embarrassed me. They now think that the papers were unfairly marked; it does not occur to them that they may have done badly, and a fail is merited.

A LIVELY APPROACH TO EDUCATION

Visited the Craft School to inquire about my car. Roy Gristwood took me around. The place was full of activity, ditches being dug, trees being watered, etc. These boys, contrary to most northerners, have the satisfaction and pride of building a place themselves. Roy is a man who is proud of his work, a forthright person with no trickery or neurotic turnings in him. He has vigor and drive to spare. His effort with the Craft School encourages me to think that it can be done. The doubts I have that my criticism of our school is unjustified fade when I witness this contrast.

Thursday. Letter from Dad last night, in which he speaks of being unable, at first try, to finance his new venture. If this fails, a great deal will go with it, not only a large sum of money, but a last effort to turn the factory around. I can't help feeling that he has let himself get too tired, and his judgment has suffered. The letter brings back all the gloom of the Connecticut house.

Read *L'Education Sentimentale* (in translation). The interesting interweaving of observation and comment makes me restlessly search for novels on such a level. I seem to have returned to being able to give myself up to someone else's sense of form and experience after a long stay in books of comment and analysis. I am tired of the persistent over-emphasis of this era on politics.

Yesterday—chatter, the usual in the staff room—putting my nerves at a higher pitch than I realized. The essays from VI are so bad I am depressed by them, and loath to push on with the work. It is ridiculous to teach these lads the intricacies of UK parliamentary democracy. Only the highly educated can understand it even there. To mold a new nation something more easily grasped is essential.

P.M.: Brisk ride out past the old firing range and the Shuwa village.

At Yerwa Senior Primary School a dramatic evening. The football field done up handsomely with lights. Little plays on old themes; the boys possess a freedom and agility of movement that tempts me to try to work with them—why have I sat around so long? The disparaging comments of the two colleagues seated to my right did not take the pleasure out of the evening. Comparisons with work in an English school at the same level are pointless.

Sunday. Last night's rain has set the birds to singing. There is a pleasant odor of damp after a fresh night, but the humidity even at this hour promises an uncomfortable day.

Yesterday concluded my marking, with results depressing to the extreme. It seems that my time has been wasted, not only are the staff and the principal of the school unpleasant, but the very work itself came to naught. There were a few moments in the morning as I summed the averages that I felt close to cracking, a sharp desperate feeling that came up suddenly. The humidity was high, and the electricity had failed so that the fan did not turn.

A DINNER PARTY FOR MY TOP STUDENTS

I invited three students from Section VI for dinner at the house which turned out to be a delight, Bukar Zoru, Kyari Marte, and Paul Koongafa. Their presence in my house combats the endless stream of abuse of the schoolboys by my colleagues in the staff room, and the undoubted inability of most of them to cope with the dull education that is offered. Here I had the cream of the crop.

The lads were polite and forthcoming in conversation, not at all tongue-tied by the strangeness of a European dinner party. The ounces of gin I had before dinner helped me lead things off, and I think they had a good time. Kyari asked me, "When you return home, will people think you are a hero?" I assume he was thinking of the wider world's image of Africa as a dangerous place.

The boys considered the sauce peculiar: "this is what our people drink when they are sick." They lingered a long time over the rather tough little chicken. There was no embarrassment when I gave them instructions for using utensils in the European manner.

After dinner, a plate full of sweets, from which they took a good handful. I showed the slides of the federal election, and some of Morocco. Their comments were reserved but appreciative. Kyari made some points—usually on the subject of the differences between European customs and Kanuri manners, provoking a conspiratorial sort of giggle. But few boys of that age anywhere could have carried themselves in such a poised manner. There were no difficult awkward silences, they had already embodied the legendary Kanuri dignity. Simply unprecedented at this time in history.

Monday. A hot afternoon. Although I was tired, sleep was impossible. Flies. At three I drove along the Bama road slowly to the end of the tarmac, storm clouds increasing to the southeast. The land on the ridge has become as dry as it could without turning to dust. The thorn trees beyond hold the sand in place; there is almost no trace of the grass that held the surface not many months ago. Recent rain has swept the surface, turning it a caramel color and packing it down. There were some fields already planted, evidenced by rows of disturbed sand. A few farmers and children were out, dropping seeds into little holes rather than bending to do so.

A pattern: on return from a ride with Achilles just before dark. Have squash and gin sitting on the steps of the porch while I watch the darkness come to the neem trees and the smooth, flat driveway disappear. I put the armchair onto the porch, Starke brings the lamp and another gin and squash. I read a book and enjoy the luxury of groundnuts.

The greatest satisfaction of my nine months here has been contact with a people who are in a basic, all-enveloping relationship to their land, though I know there are lands with more physical variety and religions with more intricacy (with temples, perhaps—I am thinking of that beautiful film, *Father Panchali*). I cannot say, on such short acquaintance, what qualities of spirit I like about these people. The prevailing European attitude seems to be that they are inefficient, revealing a misplaced sense of values. They are what they are, rooted to the land, different in outlook and drive, but living with a profound apprehension of their physical surroundings. I know what they look like; I do not know their moral qualities, except one: their helpfulness to each other and to strangers. I would have been revived by contact with any people who lived so close to the basic pattern of life; but I am happy that I found them on the broad, sandy plain of Bornu.

Thursday. Staff room is snappy. Two colleagues engage in a conversation so hateful that it almost prompted an outburst from me. About someone: "He knew the right way to get along in this country, fill your car full of black faces... Used to go with them to Kaduna every week for a film, etc. etc." Both are beyond the point where they could imagine that someone would do that sort of thing for pleasure or interest or because he enjoyed the company. In conversations like this these men become monsters, dehumanized, motivated by selfishness, meanness and jealousy. They are not always so, in fairness, but their attitude yesterday assumed a horrible grandeur—possibly because they were exaggerating to antagonize me. On looking back, I think the relentless bitterness and unkindness of my fellow teachers served to encourage me not to return to the school the following year. Their poor attitudes towards the country they were serving and the pupils they were teaching felt simply inaccusable to me.

Last views, Potiskum and Kano
Hotel del Mar, Tripoli

Saturday: left Maiduguri at one after a hectic time paying bills, storing the loads, and saying farewell to Sarke and Bukar and Mohammadu, to friends, Barber and Peter Crews. EWG averted his eyes when I shook his hand—nothing was said but goodbye.

Then it was all over. My strong cold and my exhaustion gave me little room for enthusiasm or reflection. My passengers were Yakuba Potiskum, Azi Ali Biu, and Viyoru Farouk—none used to talking freely in English. The road was like an oven; the blasts of heat nearly burned my arm.

At the Potiskum rest house a cool breeze and a fine, yellow light. The rains had come in strongly there, and the neem and other trees were a bright green. I went to bed immediately—only prevented from falling asleep by what I hope are my last Nigerian flies.

Don Eldring in the lounge for dinner—his quiet, thoughtful talk about the agriculture work in his two divisions was interesting.

Malam Suleiman came by to invite me to a party. When I arrived later, I found him seated outside his compound on a mat with two friends. He introduced a large man in Western dress as "cousin," a fellow with a broad, perceptive and intelligent face. Alhaji Ibrahim, an NA contractor, a gentle-looking Hausa sat on a two-seater sofa with his "outside girl," a Fulani who kept herself wrapped up in a blanket with only eyes showing, watching me intensely. From time to time she emerged from the cover and accepted a cigarette, and I could see her beautiful round bosom, slender brown arms, and smooth shoulder—"brown" does not do justice to the beautiful color. Her eyebrows were arched high; her face was perfectly proportioned. She smiled when teased by Malam Suleiman on being shy with a white man.

Above us were the stars in a perfect night sky without a moon. Malam Suleiman talked eagerly of friendship, of the Europeans he had known. We had several bottles of Becks, and then he threw on a green gown and a slightly cockeyed hat; "my uniform," he said, and we went over (without Alhaji) to the Progressive Bar nearby.

There a group of children were pounding on calabashes and pulling on a violin to make a local version of rock 'n roll. A group of Hausa girls sat facing the male drinkers. One of the latter was in a pair of close cut riding britches, a little pillbox hat with a plume on his head. The usual go-between, dressed as a woman, whom I had seen on a previous visit, was absent. The dancing was less wild this time with the child band. Malam S. prompted several announcements by the house announcer, and spent the rest of the time arranging women for his guest.

Suddenly the Progressive Bar emptied out into the streets, the dark streets of Potiskum, and the noise ceased.

Pushed on to Kano. Saw the small villages of Hausa land set close to each other, the markets full of people in the white kaftans of the Hausa. This gives an impression of greater sameness, and there is a lighter feeling than among the Kanuri.

The day was brilliant, not as hot as the previous. I stopped for a drink of water from Syrians at Bornu Kurdu. The grass is beginning to grow again outside Kano.

Into Kano, a dry, dusty GRA with no character; the *sabn gari* a maze of streets and turnings. The Central Hotel provided me with a tiny room in what looked like an old barracks block. I needed the rest and remained inside until after dinner.

Visited the Niger Club in the *sabon gari*—very quiet on a Sunday night. I immediately noticed the hostile, self-centered attitude of the Southerners in Kano. Talked to a big Hausa girl in a white dress who had drunk a good deal of stout. She was introduced to me as someone who was "married" to a white man. She told me of her "boss" who had taken care of her for the past seven years, and she had "protected him when he was slashed by people in Benin. I played with him and served him." He left two weeks ago from Lagos, never to return to Nigeria. "He arranged for some people to come to the dock to keep me from throwing myself in the water—I do shake and I do cry! Oh boss! He say if I need cash to write him." She showed me a photo of boss, a man with a kindly look about him. He had been an ECN engineer.

In Kano: The indifferent Ibos who work in the hotel—how insolent they can be and get away with it, all because of the color issue and independence. This is a new phenomenon for me. I have left the warm world of the tribe, where everyone knows everyone and recognizes each other's place in the culture and, to a certain extent, all help each other. Kano presents the dog-eat-dog world of the disinherited.

Monday: bicycled about Kano, even to the airport where I was dealt with by a humorous police inspector re: my visa.

Tuesday: letters, business of various sorts. A smallish man came to my door at 9:30 a.m.—Bob Murphy, an anthropologist from the University of California, here to work on the Tuaregs. In shorts, a comfortable looking shirt made of towel material. He seems poised, talk being no effort for him. He wasn't pressed for time, and took me about the old city in his minibus.

We saw the Emir of Kano seated in front of his palace with courtiers in white and red domino behind him and petitioners seated on the ground before him. We could see the turban of the Emir above the waiting petitioners. There was neither movement nor noise, an entirely static scene whose grandeur had, for the first time for me in Northern Nigeria, a repellent all too visible authoritarianism. There is nothing comparable in Bornu where the NA may be oppressive, but the old Shehu's court would never require such subservience.

I reflect that it is the contact with the antique life of the soil and the land in Bornu that is the experience I most value from my nine months stay, a reflection generated by my contrasting experience of this city.

Climbed the mosque tower to see Kano spread out in extraordinary disorder around us. Pan roofs on the fringes, but within the city mud houses and walls. The sites around the post office and the central office are a shambles; this semi-European section, established with the arrival of the white man, is shabby and uninspired.

Seen off at airport by Bob Murphy. Alhajis, the title given to those who had successfully completed their Hajj to Mecca, were expected from Mecca on various planes. Dozens of Hausa people crowded public rooms and restaurants at the airport, an anonymous mass of people with none of the individuality of the Kanuri of Bornu. The Alhajis arrived and were surrounded by their followers and sycophants. Our formalities were delayed by the prayers of a richly dressed great man and his followers, all kneeling in the immigration hall.

A smooth flight, wedged in the middle between Mr. Baldy, a Norfolk PWD engineer, and a dental surgeon from the US who had been serving in the Northern Region.

Before dawn reached Tripoli, a cool day in the sea breeze. I slept until noon at the Hotel del Mare. Walked for the rest of the day in the clean and unexpectedly tidy town. It is an oil boomtown, dollars being passed in the bars, and prospectors in their Land Rovers coming and going.

The amphitheater at Leptis Magna
(Britannica.com)

The view from Leptis magna

Drove to Leptis Magna in a rented VW to see the Roman ruins, some partly submerged in the sea. Sat for a long time on the very top of the Roman Theater and watched the sea in the clear light. Felt my brain come back into focus. How gentle and civilized the Mediterranean seems after the rough land I had just left. The Romans created grandeur for their comforts, seen in these impressive remains. It is organized and consistent in style, inviting contemplation of the life it once contained.

Nigeria keeps in my thoughts and in my dreams rather as the Army did, although not so overpoweringly. Now I ask myself what do I think? How do I sum up? And, as always, what to do next? Those preoccupations almost make me forget the luxury of this cool sea air and the fragrant courts of the hotel. But I owe all the inner clarity to the outer brilliance of the sea and the air here.

After Nigerian independence, Bornu in the northeastern corner with no natural resources became vulnerable. As the decades passed, Lake Chad reduced in size to 5% of what it had been in 1960, desertification moved south, population growth strained the urban areas, agriculture declined, a small minority of males and almost no females were educated. Vast numbers of the unemployed who could not support families became easy recruits by the terrorists. The deliberate killings, kidnappings, and arson of the Boko Haram exacerbated these conditions. The horror of the fate of its land and people defy description.

I did not return for a second school year as I had planned. I chose not to carry on with hostile colleagues and a lackluster curriculum, a bitter retreat from a land and a people that I found so richly meaningful.

In the twilight of the order that then prevailed in Bornu I was able to enjoy bush touring, land and skyscapes of drama and beauty, to observe traditional societies on the eve of their dissolution in the melee of modernity. There came to be a map of the places and people of Bornu in my mind. I want the reader to know what this moment in world history was like in a special part of Africa.

Epilogue

I left with a map of Bornu in my head. A happy possession from my stay was a vivid sense of place. I had come to know Bornu Province from Lake Chad down the Cameroon border, south to the hills at the edge of the Bornu plain, along the main road with its scrappy towns, Kanuri villages, and the tracks to reach them. It was thanks to the unexpected assignment to the elections that this sense of place had time to blossom. I quickly learned to enjoy the bush and it varied shelters. From my participation in the plebiscite I gained a uniquely intimate experience of village life, from the federal election I came to know the sweeping views of the savanna and the still green hills and villages where children had never seen a white man. From those experiences my passion to see more of this dramatic country was born—traveling in almost weekly overnights to villages like Marte near Lake Chad, Gwoza, the hill villages south of the great plain, the History Club field trip to the ruins from the centuries long Bornu Empire, I

I have radiant memories from these places: riding through the Banki dried up riverbed in the late afternoon light; women sorting fish by Lake Chad; the view from the Gwoza rest house of the pond below, cattle grazing, a woman come to bathe; the long evening of dances at Bara; the plantings on the Gulani hillside; the two old men whose bald heads gleamed in the light of the lamp as they told of the founding of Geidam.

And there were wild juxtapositions such as the Kumshe durbar set off by my tiny entourage, the village head from "French" who had just returned from a castle in Geneva studying *Rearmament Morale*; playing on the lawan of Mbaga's mat with the Swiss model train; the ancient Par in Gwoza ceremoniously serving the pagan beer, stirred with his long fingernails; stopping for a loan figure in the dusk, M. Cuypere, the Belgian journalist traveling Africa on the cheap with the monkey skin bag is baggage.

With the exception of the Banki lawan, the welcome I received from the village elders was forthcoming, in the southern hills celebratory. The primary school teachers used the occasion of a visit to get the charges to speak English, "good morning, sir," followed by peals of laughter. If I walked in a village troupes of wide-eyed small boys followed. The competent Sarke made it all possible, loads packed in the car, nothing omitted, camp bed and table set up a matter of minutes, squash in the glass, pressure lamp lit, a hot meal in the serving dish. He unfailingly put his years of experience to make me seem like an old timer.

By working within I glimpsed the British colonial system as it had evolved, a fascinating live history lesson. Also, my assignments involved responsibility, the tonic I sought.

Bornu is a long way from Ghana and the coastal cities of Nigeria where independence movements were then flourishing. "Independence means freedom for the Native Authorities (NAs)," one of the visiting scholars reported from a confidential talk with the Resident. District Officer Lawrence in Bama lamented that there was no qualified civil service to replace the expatriates. He spoke freely about the corruption in the NA over which he had "indirect rule." Using a grand historical parable, DO Pembleton predicted "it will be like the situation in Britain after the Romans left." My fellow teachers were routinely apocalyptic. The British were leaving peacefully, without the conflicts in French Africa and the Congo. They may have believed there were leaving "too early" and dark times lay ahead, but there could be no turning back.

"Remember, in the bush, as far as the village head is concerned, you are the DO" was the advice from Pembleton as I left for plebiscite duty. He meant in terms of giving orders, but in almost all my encounters the elders and village heads treated this neophyte with a respect that had been built up by district officers over the decades—as my student, Bukar Zoru commented.

In remote Bornu the anticipation of independence was matter-of-fact; if there were echoes of Wordsworth's "a joy it was to be alive," in anticipation of independence I did not hear it. The NA cut loose from restraint became pervasively corrupt, ultimately prompting the movement which became Boko Haram decades later.

The school was a disappointment. With the impatience of youth I looked to enthusiasm, a sense of purpose among teachers and students, but instead immediately found low morale. A craft school nearby gave a practical education without the often- disheartening struggle of having to master the art of writing essays. Our History Club expedition enlivened the year. As my notes indicate, I did expect to return, though I was wary of the continued staff room backbiting. When I returned to the city I remembered what M. Cuypere pronounced at breakfast: "I see you have your books, but you must lack the spiritual refreshment that comes in Europe with its concerts, the theater, congresses—it is a sacrifice to come out here." Yes, for a career of decades, but what Basil Davidson promised came to be: "You'll have an experience to carry with you for all your life, fascinating and deeply attractive people at a critical turning point in their history."

Half a century later all the people and places on my Bornu map have been ravaged by the Boko Haram, the latest intrusion of a modern world. In the late 19th century what remained of the Bornu empire was put under British suzerainty by agreement with other colonial powers, opening the land and people to western European influence. The territory had no minerals or other resources to benefit the colonial power. Early in the 20th century Bornu, as part of Northern Nigeria Federation, was joined with the coastal colonies to form the Federation of Nigeria. Like the rest of predominantly Muslim Northern Nigeria, the traditional Muslim political and judicial structure remained, while British authority was exercised through indirect rule. This western influence eliminated most raiding. In the 1950s the colonial power stimulated infrastructure improvement in Bornu—roads, airport, artesian wells; Kanuri farmers profitably developed an export crops, groundnuts, whose oil is used in industrial processes. Western goods appeared in the markets, there were elections, a parliamentary government, and Western education. In the 21st century influences from beyond the borders facilitated the rise of an insurrection that used weapons and digital devices developed in the despised western world to eliminate western education and secularism.

Preserved in notes and photographs, this is a view through a visitor's eye of a land on the cusp of great change, the full dimensions of which would unfold over decades. Let these words and pictures evoke what was.

The greatest satisfaction of my nine months has been my contact with a people who are in a basic, all-enveloping relationship to their land. In other places, there are lands with more physical variety, there are religions with more intricacy... I cannot say, on such short acquaintance, what qualities of spirit I most like about these people. The prevailing European attitude seems to be that they are inefficient, revealing a misplaced sense of values. I say they are what they are, rooted to the land, different in outlook and drive, but living with a profound apprehension of their physical surroundings. I know what they look like; I do not know their moral qualities, except one—their helpfulness to each other and to strangers. I would have been revived by contact with any people who lived so close to the basic pattern of life; but I am happy that I found them on the broad, sandy plain of Bornu.

References

The preceding narrative is based on the journals I kept during my time in West Africa in 1959-60. I have included here the published material I have read on the Boko Haram. Not included are what must be thousands of media reports to be found on Google Search using the names of the villages and towns that I once had visited. The news items found in such searches report abductions, assassinations, arson, flight, relocation to refugee camps, bombings and more.. I include other items of historical interest that enrich understanding of the past history of the area and the book of essays I edited published in 1962.

The Boko Haram insurgency

Virginia Connolli, *Boko Haram: Nigeria's Islamist Conspiracy* (London: Hurst & Co., 2015).

Leslie Roberts, "Nigeria's Invisible Crisis: Hunger amplifies infectious diseases for millions fleeing the violence of Boko Haram" Photography by Andrew Estabo, (Associated Press. *Science*, April 6, 2017, 356 (6333), 18-23.)

Mike Smith, *Boko Haram, Inside Nigeria's Unholy War*. (London: I.B. Tauris. 2015) Kindle Edition.

Other

Barth, Heinrich Barth, *The History of Bornu* Kindle ebook, from 1857 London publication.)

Cohen, Ronald, *The Kanuri of Bornu*. (New York: Holt, Rinehart and Winston, Inc. 1967.)

Professor Cohen and his wife did field work in Bornu. As in the account about the trip the History Club took to Geidam in the far northwest of what was then Bornu Province, they had a special friendship with the DH there who gave me a cap to deliver to Cohen on my return to the US.

Cooper, Malcolm, *The Northern Cameroons Plebiscite 1960-61. A Memoir with Photo Archive*. Mandaras Publishing. Electronic publication, London 2010. http://www.mandaras.info/MandarasPublishing/CameroonsPlebisciteMemoir-Cooper2010.pdf.

Jansen, Jan C and Jurgen C. Osterhamme, *Decolonization, a short history*. Princeton University Press, 2017, Kindle edition.

Comments on the above by Krishan Kamar, in review article, "Farewell to trumpets." *Times Literary Supplement*, 7 September 2017:

Empire is being reassessed as is decolonization – a pallid term as Jansen and Jurgen confess in their short history, although they agree with Dietmar Rosamond that it is "perhaps the most important historical process of the 20th century." When the United Nations was formed in 1945, there were 51 members, not very much more than the 32 states had founded the League of Nations in 1919; now UN membership is made up of 193 formally sovereign nation states. Most of these are the result of decolonization, though their territories were mostly formed by the old colonial powers, not by the new nationalist leaders, and there have been remarkably few changes in orders since independence (40% of the length of all international borders in the world today, Jansen and Jurgen point out, were originally drawn by Britain and France). If we live in a world of nation states today, that is largely because of decolonization ... they helpfully draw our attention to aspects of it that are not usually stressed or sometimes even noticed. For instance, unlike most accounts that focus on nationalist and anti-colonial movements in the colonies, Jansen and Jurgen show how thinking policy in the Metropole's to a great extent shaped the emergence of anti-colonialism and the final outcome in the form of independent states. They pay particular attention to "late colonialism," the energetic efforts by the Metropolitan states in the 1930s and 40s to modernize their empires and put them on a more rational and efficient footing. This involves such things as the "native physician" of the colonial civil service, constitutional reform that gave native populations a significant degree of political participation, increased technical education, and a variety of new schemes to improve industry and agriculture. One result of the new attention to the colonies, not necessarily intended or welcomed by policymakers, was the rise of new native elites the confidence and education to confront their European rulers with new demands, usually couched in terms of European values of equality and freedom and European practices of citizenship. Not for the first or last time Europe gave its opponents the weapons with which to assail it.

Judd, Peter H., *African Independence: the exploding emergence of the new African nations.* Edited and with an introduction by Peter Judd. (New York: Dell Publishing Co, 1962).

I include this volume I put it together two years after returning from Nigeria. It includes an article by Charles Bennett, the historian and visitor to Maiduguri whom I accompanied on a visit to Bama and a discussion with DO Lawrence in 1959. Basil Davidson who was so encouraging at the start of my journey also contributed an article, as did the Lagos attorney and participant in the indepence movement, H. O. Davies whom I met at when he was at Harvard and again in Lagos. This was a mass market paperback said to have sold 70,000 copies, evidence of the interest of the US public in the newly independent African countries in the early 1960s.

Articles and authors:
Congo Destinies, Basil Davidson
African Culture Themes, Ezekiel Mphahjlele
Commonwealth West Africa, David Williams
A Personal View of Nigerian Independence, Tai Solarin
French Speaking Tropical Africa, Pierre Stibbe
The Local and Constitutional Problems of Independence, H. O. Davies
Africa and the United Nations, Alex Quasion-Sackey
Race and Central Africa, George Bennett
United States foreign policy toward the newly independent states, Henry L. Bretton

Kirk-Greene, A.H. M., *Maiduguri and the Capitals of Bornu*. (Noala, Zaria, 1958.)

Lugard, Frederick, *The Dual Mandate in Tropical Africa*. London, 1922. (Kindle ebook c. 2016)

McClintock N. C., *Kingdoms in the Sand and the Sun: An African Path to Independence*. (London: Radcliffe Press, 1992.)

N. C. McClintock became Resident of Bornu Province in 1959; my journal reports a reception at the Residency in Maiduguri in 1959 and a party there a few weeks later. This memoir describes his service in Northern Nigeria including years as DO Dikwa, Mr. Lawrence's predecessor. The majestic, tall Shuwa Arab whom he brought as his messenger to the Bama District headquarters still served as the DO's Messenger on my visits. McClintock points out the lawlessness in Dikwa Emirate, and relates how he managed to replace a corrupt emir. (It could be that local resentment of this action had prompted the destruction of the the primary school in Kumshe that I learned about on my visit.) He recounts a search over days and nights for a murderer amid the "pagans" of Gwoza. He conveys his admiration for the Waziri of Bornu with whom he worked closely for a two-year period after Nigerian independence. In relation to the immediate aftermath of indepence his view accords with many colonial officers with a viiew that "we left too soon.

Perham, Margery, *West African Passage: A Journey through Nigeria, Chad, and the Cameroons, 1931-1932*; Edited and with an introduction by Anthony H. M. Kirk-Greene. (London and Salen, NH: Peter Owen. 1983.)

As a young don at Oxford Marjory Perham undertook an extensive tour of Nigeria and Cameroon in which she interviewed colonial and native officials, spent days in offices making notes on public records. She wrote letters to friends to serve, as she noted, as a travel diary. These lively and observant letters are as delightful in references to human character and place as they are informative of practices in "native administration" in those years.

_____, *African Apprenticeship, An autobiographical journey in southern Africa, 1929* (New York, The Afrikaner Publishing Company, division of Holmes and Meir, Publishers, 1964.)

_____, *Lugard. Volume 2: The Years of Authority 1898-1945*. London: Collins. 1960.

_____, *The Colonial Reckoning*. (London: Collins, 1961.)

Based on BBC Reith Lectures, this classic by the eminent scholar reflects on the achievements and the finale of European colonial governance and the transition to independence of former colonial territories.

Shaw, Flora [Lady Lugard]. "Bornu" in *A Tropical Dependency: An Outline of the Ancient History of the Western Soudan, With an Account of the Modern Settlement of Northern Nigeria*. (London: Nisbet, 1905).

Taub, Ben, "The Emergency. Around Lake Chad the world's most complex humanitarian disaster is unfolding." *The New Yorker*, December 4, 2017. Kindle Edition.

Acknowledgments

A debt I can never repay is to the attentive and capable Sarke who took over my household and provided care and feeding in the bush and on the many expeditions to Bornu villages. With him I acknowledge young Bukar Gwoza and Mohammadu who tended Achilles. I remember Mike and Margaret Lander for their company and friendship, and I thank the dozens of Africans and Europeans mentioned in this narrative with advice, good humor, sharing knowledge. I salute my students, particularly Bukar Zaoru. A half century has passed with violent changes. I never saw them again, but they live for me in these pages. Similarly here I celebrate the dedicated colonial officers I met and worked with: John Lawrence, Peter Crews, John Pembleton.

I acknowledge too the good fortune plus advice that brought me to Bornu and the experience of its land and people at a propitious time.

My contemporary and friend, the historian, David Chandler read early pages of wielding his blue ballpoint to improve sentences and paragraphs. I had useful comments from friends who read an early draft: Tom Johnson, Sandy Walcott, Maggie Chandler, Griselda Warr, and Margaret Beels. Stephanie Smith, scrupulous editor sharpened the writing and supported necessary cuts and clarifications. Her warmth and enthusiasm as well as skill made completion of the manuscript a satisfying joint project. Wendy Walker and Tom LaFarge guided me to Tod Thilleman of Spuyten Duyvil Press who skillfully laid out text and images.

About the Author

Peter Haring Judd graduated from Harvard College AB cum laude in 1954; he served two years in the US Army as an enlisted man in Staff Communications at the Pentagon. In 1959-60 he served as Education Officer in the Northern Region of Nigeria, assigned to the Provincial Secondary School, Maiduguri. In 1962 he published *African Independence: the exploding emergence of the new African nations*, a mass-market paperback that sold tens of thousands of copies. (New York: Dell Publishing Co, 1962), For a list of contributors see References supra.

He earned a PhD from the Department of Political Science at Columbia University in 1970, with a dissertation, "British Perspectives on the United States, 1840-1860."

He was with the Corporate and Environmental Planning Department at Northeast Utilities in Connecticut for 20 years, with numerous writing assignments and latterly planning a system wide energy conservation initiative. In 1983 he was appointed Assistant Commissioner, Energy Conservation Division in the Department of Housing Preservation and Development (HPD) New York City. He retired from city service in 1991. His book *The Hatch and Brood of Time: Five Phelps Families in the New World, 1730 1880* (Boston: Newbury Street Press, 1999) received the year 2000 award for family history from the Connecticut Society of Genealogists and, the Donald Lines Jacobus Award, the leading award in the fiedl from the American Society of Genealogists. His *More Lasting than Brass: A Thread of Family from Revolutionary New York to Industrial Connecticut* (Boston: Northeastern University Press, 2004) received the Grand Prize in genealogy from the Connecticut Society. In 2008 he published a three-volume account of the direct paternal and maternal ancestries of his four grandparents, *Four American Ancestries: White, Griggs, Cowles, Judd…and related families*. In 2008 he published a two-volume compilation of family letters, *Affection: 80 Years of Family Letters, 1850s 1930s, Haring, White, Griggs Judd Families* of New York and Waterbury Connecticut which received the Connecticut Society's Literary Awards prize in family history in that year. In March 2008 the Association of Professional Genealogists Quarterly published his article, "Adding muscle and sinew: spicing up a family narrative." In

2012 he published *The Akeing Heart, Passionate Attachments and Their Aftermath: Sylvia Townsend Warner, Valentine Ackland and Elizabeth Wade White*. A revised edition, *The Akeing Heart: Letters between Sylvia Townsend Warner, Valentine Ackland and Elizabeth Wade White*, was published in 2018 by Handheld Press, UK. With Tod Thilleman as designer he is presently preparing a revision of *Affection: Ninety Years of Family Letters, 1850s-1930*: in an edition to include a paperback and ebook.

He is a professional actor and performed regularly in New York smaller theaters. He lives in Manhattan's Upper West Side and over the years has actively supported a number of the city's musical and theater companies.

www.peterhjudd.com

www.ingramcontent.com/pod-product-compliance
Lightning Source LLC
Chambersburg PA
CBHW041312110526
44591CB00022B/2887